Japan's Foreign Relations

Also of Interest

Japan and the New Ocean Regime, Robert L. Friedheim, George O. Totten III, Haruhiro Fukui, Tsuneo Akaha, Masayuki Takeyama, Mamoru Koga, and Hiroyuki Nakahara

The Modernizers: Overseas Students, Foreign Employees, and Meiji Japan, edited by Ardath W. Burks

†*Japan: A Postindustrial Power*, Second, Updated Edition, Ardath W. Burks

†*Japan's Economy: Coping with Change in the International Environment*, edited by Daniel I. Okimoto

†*The Hidden Sun: Women of Modern Japan*, Dorothy Robins-Mowry

The Japanese Diet and the U.S. Congress, edited by Francis R. Valeo and Charles E. Morrison

The Fragile Entente: The 1978 Japan-China Peace Treaty in a Global Context, Robert E. Bedeski

The United States and Japan in the Western Pacific: Micronesia and Papua New Guinea, Grant K. Goodman and Felix Moos

Japan and the United States: Economic and Political Adversaries, edited by Leon Hollerman

How Japan Innovates: Comparison with the U.S. in the Case of Oxygen Steelmaking, Leonard H. Lynn

†*The Security of Korea: U.S. and Japanese Perspectives on the 1980s*, edited by Franklin B. Weinstein and Fuji Kamiya

The Sogo Shosha: Japan's Multinational Trading Companies, Alexander Young

†Available in hardcover and paperback.

Westview Special Studies on East Asia

Japan's Foreign Relations:
A Global Search for Economic Security
edited by Robert S. Ozaki and Walter Arnold

After World War II, Japan reemerged in the arena of international relations as an almost exclusively economic power without military might or territorial ambitions. Within some thirty years it transformed itself from a semideveloped state to a technological superpower with an economy that today is the second largest in the free world, next only to the United States, accounting for over 10 percent of total global production. The management of a rapidly growing industrial state with little domestic supply of resources necessarily requires great skill in the difficult task of maintaining sufficient access to overseas markets to sustain internal economic activity. Not surprisingly, then, Japan's foreign relations from World War II to the present have been heavily conditioned by economic considerations.

This collection of original articles investigates how the economic growth of Japan has affected the pattern of its foreign relations and where and to what extent economic principles have had to be compromised for political, legal, cultural, or ideological reasons. The contributors, experts on Japan's economy, politics, and foreign relations, analyze the state of Japan's foreign relations with North America, the EC, Oceania, the Soviet Union, COMECON, China, ASEAN, the Middle East, Latin America, Africa, Korea, and Taiwan, focusing on developments in the last seven years and predicting likely trends in the 1980s.

Dr. Robert S. Ozaki is a professor of economics at California State University, Hayward. His publications include *The Control of Imports and Foreign Capital in Japan* (1972), *The Japanese* (1978), and *Amerikajin to Nihonjin* (Americans and Japanese) (1980). He has served on the advisory editorial board of the *Journal of Asian Studies* and as a Fulbright-Hays lecturer in Japan. **Walter Arnold** is an assistant professor of political science at Miami University. He has published articles and reviews in *Canadian Review of Studies in Nationalism, Der Betriebsoekonom,* and the *Annals of the American Academy of Political and Social Science.*

for

Japan's Foreign Relations: A Global Search for Economic Security

edited by Robert S. Ozaki and Walter Arnold

Westview Press / Boulder and London

Westview Special Studies on East Asia

Copyright © 1985 by Westview Press, Inc.

Published in 1985 in the United States of America by Westview Press, Inc., 5500 Central Avenue, Boulder, Colorado 80301; Frederick A. Praeger, Publisher

Library of Congress Cataloging in Publication Data
Main entry under title:
Japan's foreign relations.
  (Westview special studies on East Asia)
  Papers presented at the 35th Annual Meeting of the Association for Asian Studies, held March 25, 1983, in San Francisco.
  Includes Index.
  1. Japan—Foreign economic relations—Congresses.
2. Japan—Foreign relations—1945- —Congresses.
I. Ozaki, Robert S.   II. Arnold, Walter, 1946–
III. Association for Asian Studies. Meeting (35th : 1983 : San Francisco, Calif.)   IV. Series.
HF1601.J376   1985   337.52   84-13069
ISBN 0-86531-778-X
ISBN 0-86531-779-8 (pbk.)

Printed and bound in the United States of America

10   9   8   7   6   5   4   3   2   1

Contents

Tables

Preface

The objective of this volume is to investigate how the economic growth of Japan has affected the pattern of its foreign relations and to examine where, and to what extent, the principles of economic complementarity have had to be compromised for political, legal, cultural, or ideological reasons. The central theme of the book is that the trends and issues in Japan's foreign relations have been overshadowed by the adjustment problems in the process of integration of its domestic economy with the world market.

After World War II Japan reemerged in the arena of international relations as an almost exclusively economic power without military might or territorial ambitions. Its economy grew at a phenomenal rate from the mid-1950s until the oil crisis of 1973. Even after the oil crisis its overall economic performance was much better than that of the other industrial nations in the West. In the short span of some thirty years Japan transformed itself from a semideveloped state to a technological superpower, a rare event in the annals of world economic history. Today it is the second-largest economy in the free world, next only to the United States, accounting for over 10 percent of total global production.

Japan's economic expansion is striking because the country is small and mountainous, without industrial resources. The management of a rapidly growing industrial state with few domestic resources is a difficult and precarious art, requiring the cultivating and maintaining of sufficient access to overseas markets to sustain the dynamics of internal economic activity. To pay for imports of vital industrial materials Japan must export enough of its manufactured products: "Export or expire" has been its fate, dictated by the structural properties of its economy.

The Introduction, by Robert Ozaki, reviews Japan's postwar economic growth and the geopolitical circumstances affecting its foreign relations and economic security. The twelve chapters are organized into three parts: Part 1, Advanced Industrial Countries; Part 2, Socialist Countries; and Part 3, Developing Countries. Each chapter surveys Japan's foreign relations with a specific country or group of countries.

In Chapter 1 Frank Langdon discusses the evolution of Japan's relations with the United States in the context of the close political, economic, and military ties between the two nations since World War II. In recent years relations have been strained by the persistence of a large bilateral trade imbalance in Japan's favor and the rapid influx of Japanese-manufactured exports into the U.S. market while the United States plays the role of a supplier of primary goods to Japan. Langdon's chapter also includes a survey of Japan's relations with Canada, which have been less strained because of the absence of a conspicuous trade imbalance, the small size of the Canadian market, and the basic complementarity between Japanese manufactures and Canadian natural resources.

Both Western Europe and Japan are highly industrialized and resource poor. The European Community (EC) constitutes a large, attractive market for Japanese exports, whereas it offers few primary goods of great importance to Japan. Marlis Steinert, in Chapter 2, reviews the recent trade frictions between the two and the related issues of perception gaps and the organizational structure of the EC, which make its negotiations with Japan difficult and at times confusing.

Despite Australia's rich endowment of natural resources, relations between Australia and Japan have been less than harmonious. In Chapter 3 Alan Rix analyzes the sources of the uneasy relationship: Japan's external policy, tilted toward the United States; Japan's move away from energy-intensive industries, which, together with the global recession, has exerted a negative effect on Australian exports to Japan; communication gaps; and shifts in Australia's policy toward protection of domestic industries and resources, which affect Japan's trade with and direct investment in Australia. Rix also discusses New Zealand's frustrations with its small-nation status and inability to gain favorable terms for exports to Japan of agricultural and fishery products.

Part 2 comprises three chapters concerned with Japan's relations with the socialist countries. Relations between Japan and the Soviet Union are in poor shape and show few immediate signs of improving. Fears of a security threat from the Soviet Union are leading Japan to reassess its security relationships and engage in closer military cooperation than hitherto with the United States, as well as to consider more seriously than in the past the regional aspects of its defense. Nevertheless, J.A.A. Stockwin argues in Chapter 4 that there may also be some practical limits to their mutual hostility. These limits involve the deeply embedded tradition in Japan of an undemonstrative approach to foreign and defense policy and the opportunities that access to Japanese technological sophistication would provide for the Soviet Union in seeking to develop its easternmost provinces.

One basic principle of Japan's external policy has been to achieve economic security globally by developing export markets for its manufactures and by cultivating import markets in every corner of the world to procure primary goods that the country lacks. Chapter 5, by Joseph Goldman, is a case study of how this principle has been applied to Eastern Europe, notwithstanding its small weight in Japanese trade, the political-ideological differences between Japan and the East European countries, and the heterogeneity of East European nations in terms of their stages of development and bureaucratic machineries.

In Chapter 6 Walter Arnold surveys the vicissitudes of China-Japan relations from the early optimism and enthusiasm at the time of the opening of the Chinese economy to the subsequent disillusionment and increasing frustration for Japan as China, inexperienced in international capital-technology management and financially deprived, began unilaterally to cancel large-volume trade-investment contracts. He argues that the relations are sustained not so much by their profitability as by the Japanese government's long-term geopolitical considerations in light of China's strategic position in East Asia and the world.

Part 3 focuses on the developing countries. Chapter 7, by Willard Elsbree and Khong Hoong, deals with the ambivalent relationship between Japan and the Association of Southeast Asian Nations (ASEAN). Although Japan is troubled by the incoherence of ASEAN as a regional organization and its pressure for greater Japanese aid and preferential treatment of manufactured imports from the region, the ASEAN countries are anxious about domination of their national economies by Japanese economic power, the concentration of resource-procurement-type direct investments by the Japanese firms in the area, and the importation of pollution-prone industries from Japan as a result of the structural transformation of its economy.

William Campbell examines in Chapter 8 the origins of Japan's critical dependence on oil from the Gulf and of its unwitting involvement in Middle Eastern politics. His chapter and Chapter 9, that on Japan-Africa relations by Hideo Oda and Kazuyoshi Aoki, illustrate how relentlessly Japan has pursued its economic interest: It readily adopted a pro-Arab policy stance after the first oil crisis for the sake of securing a vital supply of oil and preferentially allocated its economic and technical aid in favor of those countries in Africa that possess exportable resources while it remained indifferent to racism in the resource-rich Republic of South Africa and to the rising expectations of many African states toward a Japanese leadership role in their developmental efforts.

Korea and Taiwan, both former colonies of Japan, offer different pictures. In Chapter 10 Edward Olsen shows that Korea-Japan relations have been heavily conditioned by the colonial legacy, geopolitical constraints, and military-strategic considerations rather than by economic rationality. He suggests that the precariousness of the relationship is due in part to Japan's tacit preference for the status quo of a divided Korea, inasmuch as either of the alternatives—unification of North and South Korea or military conflicts between the two—poses a threat to Japan's economic welfare and security interest. In contrast, Walter Arnold provides in Chapter 11 a remarkable account of how Taiwan and Japan, caught by the one-China policy of the People's Republic of China, lost their formal diplomatic connection but nevertheless have pragmatically managed to sustain growing and closer commercial ties via a network of paradiplomatic organizations.

Despite the instability of Latin American politics, Japan's economic relations with the region have expanded, although political and cultural interchanges have lagged behind. In Chapter 12 Akio Hosono discusses the nature and characteristics of the dynamic, strong complementarity between the two in conjunction with their different developmental stages, resource endowments, and needs for diversifying the geographical distribution of their external trade.

This book originated in panel no. 4, "Japanese Foreign Relations: Recent Trends and Issues," presented at the thirty-fifth annual meeting of the Association for Asian Studies, March 25, 1983, in San Francisco. The four papers presented at the meeting that discuss Japan's foreign relations with the United States, the EC, China, and ASEAN, respectively, formed the book's nucleus. Additional papers were commissioned to cover other regions of the world with which Japan has held significant economic relations.

We are deeply grateful to the authors, scattered globally, for contributing their chapters to this volume. Needless to say, without their expertise, cooperation, and patience our project would have been impossible. Our thanks are due also to the following individuals: Jean West and Dotti Pearson for their excellent secretarial services; Jennifer Bland and Perry Sekus, who served as competent research assistants; Cecilia Ozaki for her skillful editing; Deborah Lynes of Westview Press for her guidance and encouragement while the book was in the making; and Masaei Saito, the Japanese curator of the Asia Library at the University of Michigan, Ann Arbor, who provided us with generous bibliographical help. The project was partially financed by the Office of the Dean of Arts and Sciences, Miami University.

The views expressed herein are the authors' and do not necessarily represent those of the institutions with which they are associated.

Robert S. Ozaki
Berkeley, California

Walter Arnold
Oxford, Ohio

Introduction:
The Political Economy
of Japan's Foreign Relations

Robert S. Ozaki

Japan's Postwar Resurgence

In August 1945 Japan stood in ruins, having suffered a total defeat in the Pacific War. Its empire, which had once covered much of East and Southeast Asia, had collapsed. Soon the U.S. occupation authority began to introduce a series of sweeping democratization measures, such as the dissolution of *zaibatsu* (the family trusts that through the organization of holding companies had controlled most of the major industries in prewar Japan), the institution of land reform, the passage of prolabor laws, and the imposition of a new (peace) constitution, Article 9 of which explicitly prohibits the maintenance or use of armed forces as a means of solving conflicts with other nations. The U.S. occupation's central objective was to destroy the seeds of Japanese militarism for good and to let the country be reborn as a political democracy.

Initially the United States was intent on making Japan a harmless agrarian society with only small industries producing light manufactures. With the advent of the cold war and the realization that the country could hardly support itself without a substantial industrial base, the United States reversed its policy to one of facilitating Japan's recovery from the war and encouraging its redevelopment. Some $2 billion worth of economic aid was poured into the country during the occupation period, and the deconcentration of the *zaibatsu* was halted at a level much below that which had originally been planned.

The years immediately following the end of the war constituted a period of chaos, confusion, hyperinflation, and the need for massive reconstruction of the war-torn economy. Dark clouds of pessimism hung over the crowded islands. Few predicted the "economic miracle" that would transform Japan into an industrial superpower in the next thirty years.

1

Large U.S. special procurements in Japan induced by the Korean War during the early 1950s gave Japan's domestic economy its first postwar boom. Contrary to widespread predictions that a slump would follow the cessation of hostilities in Korea, the Japanese economy managed to grow rapidly after the mid-1950s. The trend of accelerated growth continued throughout the 1960s and up until the first oil crisis of 1973, the real growth rate averaging 10 percent for the period.

In 1974 the Japanese economy registered a slightly negative growth rate for the first time since the war. Yet Japan's overall economic performance since 1974 has been impressive relative to that of other industrial countries. Its economy had recovered from the oil shock by the end of 1975, started to grow at 4–5 percent per annum, and withstood the second oil shock of 1979–1980 with resilience. Under the impact of the deepening global recession its growth rate decreased to 3.8 percent in 1981 and 3.2 percent in 1982. Despite its slowdown, however, the Japanese economy has been free of stagflation (the coexistence of high inflation and high unemployment) of the sort that has been plaguing the U.S. and West European economies in recent years.

After thirty years of sustained growth Japan has become an industrial giant and a technological powerhouse, now producing 10 percent of the world's total output. As early as 1968 Japan surpassed West Germany in gross national product (GNP). It is generally believed that since 1981 Japan's industrial output has exceeded that of the Soviet Union, making it the second-largest economy in the free world, next only to the United States. The Japanese GNP is about half the U.S. GNP, and the Japanese population is approximately half the size of the U.S. population, making the Japanese per capita income today roughly comparable to that of Americans. Japan is the world's largest producer of steel, automobiles, ships, consumer electronics, and many other advanced industrial products.

Japan is a small island country—smaller than California—with mountainous terrain, a high population density, and a poor endowment of natural resources. All odds being seemingly against it, it does not strike one as the most likely candidate for rapid economic growth. Its record of transforming itself from a semideveloped economy to an industrial superpower in a matter of thirty years is unprecedented in the annals of economic history.

Factors in Growth

A nation's foreign relations assume many dimensions: political, diplomatic, military, economic, and cultural. Historically a great nation typically meant a state possessing powers in all these spheres, a hegemon capable of influencing lesser states politically as well as economically. To build strong armed forces requires a large, well-developed industrial base. Hence, a military power has almost always been also an economic power.

Japan and its foreign relations after the war show some striking contrasts to its own past and to the historical norm. Japan emerged after World War II as perhaps the first example in human history of an economic superpower that was not at the same time a military power. Economics has dominated Japan's internal politics as well as its dealings with the outside world. It has held no territorial or ideological ambitions vis-à-vis other states. Probably no nation has ever concentrated so much of its energy on the accomplishment of economic ends as postwar Japan. Having learned the futility of militarism, it turned to pacifism and redefined its goal to be accelerated economic growth to catch up with the West. Many domestic conditions were favorable to achieving this end.

An abundant internal supply of labor that is well educated, highly trained or trainable, disciplined, and diligent certainly helped the process of industrial growth. The fact that the Japanese are, by world standards, a highly homogeneous ethnic group has meant that the country could build a national consensus with relative ease and without potentially resource-draining minority problems. Thanks to the democratization measures executed by the U.S. occupation authority, Japan after World War II became a freer, more open, and more mobile society than in the prewar years, a condition conducive to economic growth. The *zaibatsu* dissolution substantially raised the degree of competitiveness within the domestic economy, freeing the talents and innovative abilities of many Japanese executives, which had previously been suppressed by the rigid, *zaibatsu*-controlled industrial structure. The group orientation of the Japanese contributed to the buildup of corporate synergy as well as to the intensification of interfirm competition. Political stability under the probusiness Liberal-Democratic party provided a unity of purpose—a continuity of policy toward growth by means of which the country could mobilize its resources without suffering from disruptions in the domestic political process.

These internal factors might have been necessary but were not sufficient to account for Japan's "economic miracle." There were other factors to be reckoned with.

Favorable Circumstances

Defense

One reason for Japan's postwar economic success is that it allocated less than 1 percent of its GNP to defense, and so could invest most of the nation's resources in the private business sector. Article 9 of the "peace" constitution is one explanation. The militant pacifism of the Japanese in reaction to the national catastrophe of the Pacific War is another. The absence of national borders connecting Japan with potentially hostile neighboring states has presumably lessened the tactical need for its national defense. But these do not provide a total picture of why Japan managed to avoid the burden of military spending. It is doubtful that for these reasons alone Japan could have escaped the burden if, say, it had been occupied by the Soviet Union after World War II.

The geopolitical circumstances surrounding postwar Japan were peculiarly suited to realization of its newly chosen policy goal and placed Japan in a position to be able to exploit them to its own advantage. After the war Japan became a close ally of the United States, and through the mutual security pact the United States agreed to absorb most of the cost of Japan's national defense. Without the protective cover of the U.S. armed forces in and around Japan, the course of its postwar defense history would have been considerably different.

Resources

Japan is an industrial country with little indigenous supply of natural resources. The country is fated to have to import resources to feed its domestic industries and to export manufactured goods to pay for the imports. Any external constraints on Japan's imports or exports automatically limit the extent to which its domestic economy can expand. In this respect the political economy of the world after the war has been significantly more favorable for a resource-poor industrial country like Japan than that before the war.

The global supply of industrial resources is heavily concentrated in the underdeveloped parts of the world, and most of today's resource-rich but less developed countries (LDCs) were colonies of the Western powers until after World War II. There was a tendency for the Western powers to preserve deposits of resources located in their colonies in lieu of uninhibitedly exploiting and exporting them. For a nation in need of resources, this implied that its territorial rights and status in terms of the existing power blocs had much bearing on how much of what resources it could acquire. Not surprisingly, gaining an access to vital resources was often a hidden, if not openly professed, motive for military maneuvers.

The situation radically changed after the war. The majority of former colonies achieved independence from the Western powers and started to export their resources autonomously in order to finance their internal economic development. A beneficiary of this trend, Japan could import resources from diverse sources throughout the world far more freely than was imaginable before the war.

Technology

Revolutionary technological developments, accelerated by World War II, were another postwar trend favoring Japan. An advanced technology became available in the production of coal, iron ore, petroleum, and other resources, substantially increasing their supplies to meet the rising world demand for them. Consequently, at least prior to the 1970s, the world did not face a severe shortage of resources.

Progress in transportation and communication technologies also benefited Japan immensely. Geographic distance, which inflated the cost of transportation, in the past constituted a significant barrier to the free flow of resources. Even if political obstacles were absent, a nation could economically import heavy and bulky mineral resources only from relatively nearby sources. The postwar reduction in the cost of transportation enabled Japan to import ever-increasing volumes of resources to fuel its domestic industrial expansion. The advancement of communication technology further facilitated Japan's intercourse with the world economy.

Japan's economic growth was spearheaded by the explosive increase in private investment in plant and equipment, and rapid capital formation in the private sector was sustained by waves of technological innovations. Japanese enterprises actively borrowed, digested, and improved technologies from the Western countries (mostly from the United States) and adapted them to their particular needs. In this sense Japan's growth may be construed as a gigantic process of catching up with the advanced West through technology absorption. The capacity to quickly absorb and effectively apply transferred technologies, rather than developing them internally, itself requires considerable talent, worthy of merit. The fact remains, however, that Japan's postwar economic performance would have been less remarkable were it not for the availability of advanced technologies from the West.

Bretton Woods

The international economic order of the free world after World War II was maintained under the political, economic, and military leadership of the United States. The economic framework of Pax Americana was formulated at the Bretton Woods conference shortly before the end of the war. The so-called Bretton Woods system was designed to achieve mutual prosperity of the free nations by encouraging free multilateral trade under U.S. hegemony. To accomplish this end, the International Monetary Fund was established, with the U.S. dollar as the system's key currency fully convertible into gold. The member nations officially pegged their currencies to the dollar, although the exchange rates might periodically be adjusted in the event of "fundamental disequilibrium," that is, persistent balance-of-payments deficits of a severe magnitude. The member nations could draw from the fund to finance short-term external imbalances. The General Agreement on Tariffs and Trade (GATT) was founded as the organ to settle trade disputes and promote free trade. The World Bank was charged with the role of providing long-term credit to the LDCs for their developmental projects.

The system worked well for a quarter century after its inception. The dollar remained stable and strong, the U.S. economy healthy and productive. There was a virtuous circle of economic growth and international trade. The free world as a whole enjoyed an upward trend of prosperity, and the volume of trade increased faster than the world's economies. It is in this setting that Japan's accelerated growth continued, with its exports expanding twice as fast as world trade.

Japanese Exports

Contrary to the popular image, Japan's growth was not "export-led." Its exports accounted for 10–13 percent of its GNP, a weight much less than those of the West European economies. This, of course, is not meant to deny the strategic importance of exports for Japan. Export in general serves three separate though interrelated functions for a nation's economy: (1) as an effective demand it stimulates the nation's economic activity, (2) it is a means of paying for imports, and (3) it may be promoted as a cushion against internal recession. As a percentage of GNP, Japanese exports can be termed small. Yet they carry a strategic implication for the nation's economy: Without exports Japan could not import resources, and then its industrial machinery would be quickly brought to a halt. Similarly, shrinkage of the domestic economy may be averted if enough can be exported to offset the deficiency of internal demand. We thus realize that to a large extent Japan's growth was made possible by the world prosperity and the system of free multilateral trade allowing for a rapid expansion of its external trade.

Japan could pursue the task of becoming an economic superpower without arms while maintaining a quiet, low-posture policy in the arena of foreign relations as long as the weight of its economy in the world remained relatively small and global prosperity persisted. The scene began to change in the late 1960s.

International Economic Disorder

History indicates that the viability of an international economic order presupposes the presence of a leader nation powerful enough to impose a common code of conduct upon other nations. In the absence of such a hegemon the system is destined to disintegrate as each nation attempts to practice its own rules, not necessarily consistent with those of others. Once-flourishing Pax Britannica collapsed with the vanishing of the British empire. Postwar Pax Americana remained intact as long as the U.S. leadership position stayed sufficiently strong.

The growth of Western Europe and Japan led to the relative decline of U.S. economic power. U.S. industries, one by one, started to lose the competitive edge they once held in the world market. After the Vietnam War stubborn stagflation and sluggish productivity plagued the U.S. economy. As early as 1958 the U.S. overall balance of payments recorded a deficit. In the mid-1960s even its trade balance began to show chronic deficits. The dollar, the foundation of the Bretton Woods system, became a surplus currency. Gold continued to flow out of the United States, and large sums of overvalued dollars piled up abroad, especially in West Germany and Japan. Speculative attacks on the dollar frequently disrupted the foreign-exchange markets. The weakened and unstable dollar was no longer capable of sustaining the fixed-exchange-rates system. In August 1971 President Richard Nixon announced the suspension of full convertibility between gold and the dollar, in essence bringing an end to the Bretton Woods system as the term was originally understood.

After a period of currency realignments the new system of flexible exchange rates was introduced in the spring of 1973. Under this system currencies freely float up or down, in theory always in the direction of correcting nations' balance-of-payments disequilibria. After a decade of practice we have learned that the flexible-rates system is no panacea for international monetary problems. Often a currency fluctuates to a degree that cannot be adequately explained by such fundamentals as the rate of inflation, productivity change, or the size of imbalance in current transactions. The most important advantage of the flexible-rates system is said to be that since it frees nations from the necessity of coping with external disequilibria, each nation can concentrate on its internal economic problems. In practice things often do not work out that way. A balance-of-payments deficit may last over a prolonged period of time. High interest rates, induced by tight U.S. monetary policy, have in recent years been increasing foreign demand for dollars to be invested in U.S. securities, resulting in dollar revaluation. This in turn causes a rise in the U.S. trade deficit and domestic unemployment. Despite its short-comings the system continues because no one can think of an alternative that a majority of experts can agree is a definite improvement.

The precarious state of the international economic order, the spread of global recession, and the rise of protectionism all added to Japan's difficulties. By the early 1970s the country reached the point at which it could no longer afford the luxury of single-mindedly concentrating on internal goals while minimizing involvement in international political affairs. East and Southeast Asian countries have been concerned with the overpresence of Japanese goods and capital in their lands and are fearful of the possibility of their becoming Japan's de facto economic colonies. Japan's relations with the United States and Western Europe have become increasingly strained as these nations, hard hit by recessions, accuse Japan of disrupting their domestic markets with aggressive export drives and of not importing enough of their manufactures. Japan's countercharges notwithstanding, the West has cultivated a fixed image of it as a free rider who takes full advantage of the free-trade system in exports but refuses to liberalize imports in order to protect domestic interests. More recently the United States has been exerting pressure on Japan to assume a greater share of defense expenditures. The oil crisis of 1973 made a mockery of Japan's principle of separating politics from economics in foreign affairs, as the Arab states demanded that it adopt an anti-Israel position as a price for obtaining oil. The oil crisis also reminded Japan of the fundamental vulnerability of its economy.

National Security

Scholarly definitions of *national security* abound. It generally means to build the international and domestic conditions suited to preserve and promote national welfare, values, and interests and to protect them from threats of all sorts, actual or potential. It is an ambiguous concept. *National values* and *interests* are variables rather than constants. Protecting political democracy and freedom has been a value in postwar Japan, but was not in Japan of the 1930s. Colonial interests were a matter of grave concern to prewar Japan, but not today. The meaning of *threat* is often subjective. The opinions on whether or not the Soviet Union is a threat to Japan differ among the Japanese themselves as well as between the United States and Japan. The effectiveness or availability of instruments to enhance national security change over time. Given the possibility of nuclear holocaust and the stronger world public opinion against war today, the use of force is a more difficult option to choose now than in the past.

For about two and a half decades after World War II national security as such was not a serious issue to Japan. It fought an abortive war, lost it, and was completely disarmed. In the spirit of the new "peace" constitution Japan no longer held the dream of territorial expansion through aggressive means. Instead, it busily occupied itself with the job of internal economic redevelopment and growth. National security needs were duly met by the U.S.-Japan mutual-security pact. There were no impending foreign threats to Japan's peaceful existence, so its diplomacy was passive and reactive rather than positive and autonomous.

As long as world prosperity lasted, Japan's policy of noninvolvement did not face serious difficulties. The nations' economies were becoming more interdependent. There was a general recognition, however, that greater interdependence was a prime mover of world prosperity.

Interdependence

Interdependence is a double-edged sword. It promotes global economic growth by allowing world resources to be more efficiently allocated among nations. At the same time, greater interdependence implies higher dependence on others, hence a higher degree of potential vulnerability. As long as the world systems are working well, interdependence is a blessing; once the systems start to falter, it may turn into a curse. Vital resources are not evenly distributed throughout the world. Sixty percent of the world oil supply is located in the Middle East. Eighty percent of the world's food is produced by five countries: the United States,

Canada, Australia, Argentina, and France. A cutoff of the oil supply by an Arab state can immediately cause a national crisis in an industrial economy situated in an opposite corner of the globe. Only a few months after an innovation takes place in one country, the product embodying that innovation may begin to flood the market of another country.

There is an element of paradox about interdependence. Although it is a consequence of free trade, its growth unavoidably generates more economic and political frictions among nations. Hard hit by foreign competition, the nations in turn call for new rules and regulations. Interdependence, a product of free trade, thus has an inherent propensity to restrict free trade.

Japan has always been resource poor. Access to strategic resources was one of its serious concerns in the prewar period even though its economy then was far less industrialized than today. It is interesting to note that from the end of the war through the 1960s, access to resources was not viewed as a major problem in Japan. Seemingly infinite supplies of oil, coal, iron ore, and other resources were readily available at low costs from overseas. The only concern was to export enough to pay for their imports. The situation began to deteriorate in the early 1970s. The Japanese had the first taste of the fragility of their economic existence in 1972 when the United States embargoed exports of soybeans to Japan, causing a conspicuous nationwide shortage of soy sauce, beancurd (tofu), and beanpaste (miso)—common items in the Japanese diet. Then came the oil shock in the fall of 1973.

Economic Power

Being a super economic power without arms creates its own problems, especially when the country lacks its own supply of strategic materials. Japan imports 99.8 percent of the oil it consumes and is 50 percent import dependent for food. Most rare and strategic metals are not available domestically.

As a last resort a military power can use or threaten to use force to dissolve international conflicts. To an unarmed economic power the same option is not possible. *Power* means a nation's ability to impose its will on others. In the context of outright hostility a wealthy nation without arms cannot use its wealth per se as an instrument of settling a conflict on its own conditions. In this sense *economic power* is a contradiction in terms.

On the other hand, a wealthy nation, even without arms, can do a lot more than a poor nation for its national security. Hostility between nations does not suddenly erupt in a vacuum. A nation can cultivate, if not command, respect, prestige, and admiration from others through means other than military might. Economic aid, technical assistance, cultural and educational exchange, and the like can be effective ways to promote international peace and understanding. A rich nation is able to utilize its wealth to finance these expensive, nonmilitary programs toward building better foreign relations.

Economic Security

In the early 1970s *economic security* became a serious national issue in Japan. There has been much discussion on what it constitutes and on how best to achieve it.

What are the options? One is to heavily rearm Japan, to make the nation an economic power *and* a military power. This alternative, however, involves many difficulties. The generally accepted interpretation in Japan of Article 9 of the peace constitution is that Japan's armed forces are strictly for defense only and that whatever arms the nation builds and maintains shall remain small. This consensus is found not only among socialists but also among the majority of the more conservative general public. Any constitutional revision to implement the rearmament option, therefore, would likely stir a major political crisis in Japan.

Japan imports voluminous amounts of resources literally from all over the world, and the cost of building and sending warships and troops to ensure safety of the sea lanes and to protect all its economic interests abroad would be staggering. Japan's major rearmament would in all probability destabilize its relations with Asian countries, jeopardizing the prospects of the Pacific Basin initiatives. It would certainly complicate and add tension to Sino-Soviet-Japanese relations. Furthermore, the smallness of the Japanese islands makes the nation particularly vulnerable to nuclear attack. In the event that it would decide to build nuclear arms for the purpose of deterrent, it would have to deploy far more nuclear warheads than, say, the Soviet Union in order to hold an effective parity. Merely finding enough land spaces to install the necessary launching sites within the Japanese isles would be an impossibility.

Japan's economic fragility stems from its critical import dependence on food, energy, and industrial resources. One solution is to increase self-sufficiency in strategic items by raising their indigenous supplies and reducing domestic demand for them. Unfortunately the basic structure of import dependence will not alter in the foreseeable future.

In the early 1960s Japan's import dependence for food was about 30 percent. It has risen to the present 50 percent as a combined effect of population increase, diminution of arable lands through urbanization and industrialization, and increase in per capita food consumption. Every piece of arable land is already intensively utilized, and the land productivity of Japanese agriculture is among the highest in the world. Only improbable breakthroughs in agricultural technology and/or the drastic fall of food consumption to a near-starvation level will bring Japan self-sufficiency in food.

With respect to energy, efforts to reduce import dependence have been made on all fronts: conservation, improving efficiency in energy use, and development of alternative sources such as nuclear, solar, geothermal, ocean current, and coal. Nonetheless, Japan's heavy dependence on oil as the main source of energy is predicted to continue through the end of this century.

At present Japan holds a one-hundred-day reserve of oil and much smaller reserves of other industrial resources. Stockpiling strategic materials for emergencies is useful and important but scarcely provides a fundamental solution to Japan's vulnerability.

Economic security can be assured only in the context of a harmonious, peaceful, and prosperous world. The breakdown of the system of free multilateral trade or international political crises that disrupt the supplies of vital resources would quickly bring about a major dislocation of the Japanese economy. The best strategy then is for Japan to do everything possible to promote the viability of the world economic and political systems.

Comprehensive Strategy

In December 1981 the influential Industrial Structure Council, an advisory body attached to the Ministry of International Trade and Industry, appointed a subcommittee of academic experts and prominent business executives to examine the question of economic security. In April 1982 the subcommittee released an interim report[1] meant to stir debate toward building a national consensus. The report emphasized the importance of a comprehensive approach encompassing economic, political, diplomatic, cultural, and educational means and, inter alia, made the following recommendations:

1. Japan should remove the remaining trade and investment barriers as much as possible, further liberalize its domestic financial institutions, and take initiatives to strengthen and broaden the GATT provisions as an instrument of promoting free world trade.

2. High technology should be the engine to boost and revitalize the now-stagnant world economy. To this end, the fruits of research and development in high technology need to be internationally shared instead of monopolized by each nation. Japan should encourage, and actively participate in, joint international high-technology research with other advanced countries.

3. Economic security is not bought by goods and money alone. While conventional economic and technical aids to the LDCs are important, no less important are cultural and educational exchange programs with all nations to promote international friendship and understanding. Japan ought to invest far more in these areas than in the past.

4. Along with such internal measures as conservation, stockpiling, and development of alternative energy sources, Japan should work hard toward a greater harmonization of North-South as well as East-West relations as a way of enhancing its long-term economic security.

5. The best way to ensure Japan's food security is through an increase in world food production. Expanding aid in agricultural technology, export credit for fertilizers, and other means of raising agricultural productivity of the less developed food-producing countries is therefore desirable.

6. A wholesome and realistic way to gain safety of maritime transportation from the standpoint of Japan's economic security is to make positive contributions to peace in areas adjacent to such strategic sites as the Hormuz and Malacca straits, the Panama and Suez canals, and the Cape of Good Hope.

7. The government should continue to play a developmental and cooperative role vis-à-vis private businesses in generating and disseminating new technologies as well as in facilitating structural transformation of the nation's industries.

Prospects

In short, what the report recommended was a comprehensive, non-military "offensive" to promote world peace and prosperity as the optimum strategy for Japan's economic security. What is not clear in the report is specifically how Japan's defense plan is to be integrated with the economic security measures. Also problematic from the Western perspective is the suggested continuation of Japan's "industrial policy," which may be construed as a violation of the principles of a free market economy.[2] Further, it is not certain that the ruling Liberal-Democratic party has sufficient political will to carry out a wholesale liberalization of the Japanese economy in light of the evident political clout possessed by the now-protected agricultural sector.

The international economic order is presently in a state of flux, yet no revolutionary development is in sight. Instead, we will likely be witnessing a series of evolutionary changes in that order, Japan unavoidably being a large part of the process. Given their long history of isolation, the Japanese are said to be of an insular mentality, better at followership than at leadership. How and to what extent the comprehensive peace offensive recommended by the subcommittee will affect Japan's external policy and foreign relations in the forthcoming years remains to be seen.

Notes

1. Ministry of International Trade and Industry, *Economic Security of Japan 1982* (Tokyo, 1982).

2. See Michael K. Young, "Economic Security: Japan Reviews Its Options," *Journal of Japanese Trade and Industry* 2, no. 1 (January/February 1983), pp. 31–33.

Part 1

Advanced Industrial Countries

1
Japan and North America

Frank Langdon

Gaining Entry to North American Markets

Japan's foreign relations since regaining independence in 1952 have been dominated by the struggle to integrate itself into world markets. Saddled with a pacifist constitution drafted by the U.S. occupation officials in 1946 and dominated by a strongly pacifist public opinion and political party opposition, Japan has relied on U.S. military protection. It has only reluctantly agreed to modest rearmament in return for entry into North American markets and for North American sponsorship in the liberal world trading system under the General Agreement on Tariffs and Trade (GATT).[1] Incorporated into the Western alliance system against the Sino-Soviet bloc during the early cold war, Japan was also long cut off from its natural and complementary trading partners on the Asian continent and reliant on more expensive raw materials from North America.

The warfare that erupted in the early 1950s over Korea pitted the United States, assisted by its allies, including Canada, against North Korea and China, backed by the Soviet Union. Americans and Canadians alike lost their lives in the effort to defend the noncommunist states, including Japan, and to maintain a strong military position for the United States and those who became its allies in East Asia. John Foster Dulles, appointed by President Harry S Truman, played the leading role in negotiating the San Francisco Peace Treaty of 1951 with Japan. The same day Japan signed the treaty in the Opera House it signed a bilateral security treaty at the Presidio of San Francisco lending military bases in Japan exclusively to the United States and ensuring protection of Japan from communist military and political pressure.

The Soviet Union refused to sign the treaty permitting the continued U.S. military presence and political influence in Japan. The People's Republic of China had not been invited to San Francisco. Instead, Dulles and U.S. senators persuaded Japanese Prime Minister Shigeru Yoshida to sign, albeit reluctantly, a peace treaty with the rival Nationalist government on the island of Taiwan to ensure that the San Francisco Peace Treaty would be ratified by the U.S. Senate. Japan was induced to join the committees coordinating the embargoes of strategic exports to communist countries; the one for China (China Coordinating Committee, or CHINCOM) was particularly restrictive. Thus, Japan came to be largely cut off for a long time from trade with China and North Korea, which had been important Japanese sources of food and minerals.[2] It was cut off also from potential sources of fuel, minerals, and forest products in Soviet Siberia. Poor relations with the USSR still restrict access there. Instead, Japan came to rely heavily upon the more distant and expensive supplies of North America.

Isolated by the occupation, Japan was slow to recover until the burden of economic aid for Japan and then the cold war stimulated the United States to look upon Japan as a potential ally rather than a defeated enemy. The emergency supplies of grain and cotton supplied by the U.S. occupation authorities helped the U.S. government to dispose of surplus stocks and paved the way for the later lucrative agricultural trade with Japan; it has become the largest market in the world for U.S. farm products. It is also the second-largest customer for Canadian wheat (China is the largest). U.S. surplus and obsolescent military aid was sent later—a precedent for the inadequate Japanese military equipment today.

When Germany was granted independence in the Western zones by the United States, Great Britain, and France, it readily agreed to rearm and introduce conscription in order to become a full North Atlantic Treaty Organization (NATO) ally. As one of the group of allies, it no longer was a threat to the others. Australia, New Zealand, and the Philippines—still fearing Japan—insisted on bilateral security treaties with the United States before agreeing to the San Francisco Peace Treaty.[3] Japan, without other allies, remained heavily dependent upon the United States, but it rejected conscription and all but the most modest defensive military role. It ruled out nuclear weapons for itself and would not let the United States bring them in under its constitutional limitations. Much of the public and the opposition parties opposed U.S. bases and the security treaty. Unlike the German or British socialists, they preferred neutrality in the cold war or even favored China and the Soviet Union.

Under the occupation the U.S. leaders insisted on opening up Western markets to Japanese exports despite attempts by Great Britain and other allies to restrict the Japanese textile and shipbuilding industries, which later became strong competitors. To increase export earnings and foreign food supply for Japan, the occupation officials authorized Japanese Antarctic whaling expeditions against Australian objections. When the West Coast industry in Canada and the United States tried to restrict Japanese offshore fishing, Dulles arranged for a separate tripartite North Pacific Fisheries Convention with Japan, Canada, and the United States. It required Japanese abstention from fishing for the chief food fish, such as salmon, halibut, and herring, in the eastern Pacific.[4] Thus, economic restrictions were kept out of the peace treaty but were permitted to some extent by the separate fisheries convention. U.S. policymakers refused to protect their home industry from Japanese canned salmon exports, which were permitted to undersell domestic U.S. producers.

Canada's commercial treaty with Japan made room for Japan in its market. During the 1954 debates in the House of Commons a U.S. official was quoted approvingly on the need to provide outlets for Japanese trade to keep Japan from being drawn into the sphere of the communist bloc. The opposition Conservative party and Canadian Commonwealth Confederation (CCF) speakers agreed on the strategic need to keep Japan on the Western side as well as on support of the commercial treaty as a means to ensure a market for Canadian resource exports to Japan, the most important point for Canada. About that time, when Japan was eagerly trying to join the signatories of GATT, both Canada and the United States took the lead in sponsoring Japan's entry to help it obtain the most-favored-nation tariff treatment by the other adherents. Great Britain, Australia, and France tried to keep Japan out and only slowly and reluctantly extended the favorable trade treatment. Canada also sponsored Japan's entry to the Colombo Plan against Indonesia's objections. Within Canada, the Canadian Manufacturers' Association and the Canadian Textile Association deplored admitting the competing Japanese textiles at lower tariffs after their battering from U.S. and British low-priced textiles.

Thus it was that the comparatively wealthy North American countries, the United States and Canada, which had suffered the least war damage, welcomed Japan into their domestic markets and world trade generally. For them the strategic and military desirability of Japan's adherence to the noncommunist side in the cold war was paramount, inclining them to accept Japanese commercial competition while gaining an important commercial outlet of their own for agricultural and resource exports to Japan. The European states, like Japan, were chiefly exporters of manufactured goods and suffered more directly from Japanese competition, which they consequently were reluctant to face. In contrast to Japan's previous warlike behavior, its government now only rearmed to the minimum degree necessary to ensure U.S. "cooperation" in opening its markets, transferring new technology, and keeping the Soviets at bay. The U.S. use of Japan as its main base in East Asia achieved its global strategic goal of containing the communist states' expansion and extended influence. Obligated only to defend its own territory, Japan will not go to the defense of its ally if attacked elsewhere.

The "miracle" of Japan's extraordinary economic achievements in the 1950s and 1960s was greatly facilitated by the uninterrupted large-scale world trade growth, the comparatively liberal world trade regime into which Canada and the United States had ushered Japan, and the new heavy and durable-goods industry backed by the bureaucrats of the Ministry of International Trade and Industry (MITI).[5] Also, by 1965 the chronic balance-of-payments deficits of Japan ceased, and it racked up trade surpluses as a result of its new competitive and high-quality consumer goods and machinery exports. Except for aircraft, U.S. manufactured exports lost their competitive edge, leaving the United States—like Canada—more an exporter of raw materials. Canada had exported raw materials to the large Japanese market that needed them both for its own domestic use and for manufacturing for export, but Canada's small population and market could not absorb enough Japanese exports to give Canada an unfavorable trade balance.

Japan's protected market with high tariffs, quotas, and barriers to foreign investment was tolerable when it was weak, but when it joined the Organization for Economic Cooperation and Development (OECD) and the International Monetary Fund (IMF) as a full member in the mid-1960s, it came under pressure to reduce the protective measures. It did so to a major extent by the early 1970s. With détente, under President Nixon, the cold war receded as the superpowers dealt directly with each other on strategic matters over the heads of their allies. Therefore, as military matters declined in importance, the two oil-price crises, inflation, unemployment, and severe recession took center stage and both Japanese protectionism and competition assumed major importance.

The competition from traditional Japanese exports like textiles, clothing, and shoes was reduced in the 1950s and 1960s by informal voluntary export restraints (VERs) whereby Japanese government or industry agreed to temporarily limit exports of items that the United States and Canada claimed damaged their industries. Japan was more likely to capitulate to the United States on such restraints than to Canada because it felt a greater obligation for the economic and defense benefits it had received. It agreed more reluctantly to similar restraints to Canada, even though that country was willing to share a larger part of its market with Japan. The advantage of the VERs was that they avoided direct bilateral restrictions by either the United States or Canada that would have violated their obligations under the GATT.

When President Nixon demanded textile restraints from Prime Minister Eisaku Sato in 1969, foreign exporters had only about 4 percent of the U.S. market, of which only half was due to Japanese textile exports, scarcely a damaging proportion.[6] By 1971 the president was ready to use the Trading with the Enemy Act to stop Japanese textile exports in his frustration at Japan's failure to comply. His insistence was due to the desire to carry out a pledge to U.S. textile producers who had supported his election campaign. Backed by his national-security assistant, Henry Kissinger, and his secretary of the treasury, John Connally, he launched an economic offensive against his allies.

On August 15, 1971, to the universal consternation of the United States' trading partners, the United States abandoned the gold-exchange standard to depreciate the dollar and levied a 10 percent surcharge on foreign imports. The damaging import sanction was lifted only two months later when Japan, Canada, and Western Europe revalued their currencies upward to turn the terms of trade in the favor of the United States. This was only the opening skirmish in the ongoing trade war that still seems to be in progress among the allies. In the face of those cataclysmic Nixon shocks the Japanese textile industry quickly capitulated to a governmental compromise that satisfied the president and ended the surcharge. It was a Pyrrhic victory, because soon afterward the Japanese producers themselves were priced out of the market both at home and abroad by cheaper textiles from the newly industrializing countries (NICs) like South Korea, Taiwan, Hongkong, and Singapore.

Another Nixon shock was administered on July 15, 1971, just before the trade sanctions. The president announced a visit to China to improve relations with the other major communist state. It was a dramatic reversal from previous policy toward China, a hostile one that the United States had imposed on Japan. Only a few months earlier the U.S. secretary of state had solemnly reassured Japan it would be fully informed of any change in China policy, yet Prime Minister Sato was told only a few minutes before the public announcement. The outcome was Sato's fall from power and a sharp but temporary wave of anti-American sentiment in Japan. Japan took an independent initiative in granting full diplomatic recognition to China, seven years before the United States did, and also repudiated its recognition of Taiwan.

Smarting from their treatment by the Nixon administration, the Canadian and Japanese cabinet ministers met in Toronto in September for regular consultations. Japanese Foreign Minister Takeo Fukuda said "Japan and Canada should form an alliance" to press for U.S. reconsideration of its surcharge.[7] This was a rare example of even a tentative inclination to join the other allies to get the United States to change its policies. Canada was inclined to criticize Japan's protectionism, but both countries were dismayed at the loss of "their special status" with the United States and increased their efforts to diversify their trade to reduce their economic dependence on the U.S. market. Canada launched a decade-long federal government campaign, "the third option," to increase trade and cultural contacts with Japan.

Protectionism Against Japan's Competitive Exports

During the period of détente with China and the Soviet Union that followed the Nixon-Kissinger initiatives, the United States also withdrew from its military involvement in the Vietnam War. It permitted its military forces to decline while the Soviet Union continued its steady buildup of nuclear missiles and air and land forces, as well as a blue-water navy not only in the NATO theater and in the Middle East, but in East Asia as well. At the same time, the USSR negotiated arms-control agreements and human-rights accords to encourage friendly economic ties with the United States and with the other NATO allies who were inclined to be increasingly independent of the United States.

Japan was dependent for 99 percent of its oil from abroad, most from the Middle East where the Organization of Petroleum Exporting Countries (OPEC) succeeded in exacting enormous oil price increases during the October War between Egypt and Israel. After an initial bout of sharp inflation and a halt in its previously very high economic growth, Japan managed to quickly absorb the full impact of the enormous oil price increases by increasing the productivity of its already highly efficient industries or by phasing out some of the more wasteful or high-energy-using industries. Canada and the United States, blessed with huge oil and gas supplies of their own, protected their consumers and less efficient industries to retain their political support by keeping domestic prices low, thus encouraging wasteful and inefficient use of energy. The result was a leaner, more efficient Japan that became even more competitive in world markets for its manufactured exports and—correspondingly— a Japan more impervious to the less competitive U.S. or Canadian manufactured exports to its own market. This led to a period of "unceasing acrimony," as it has been termed by Nobuhiko Ushiba, former ambassador to both Canada and the United States and a chief negotiator in the trade conflict in the late 1970s.[8]

The principal issues between Japan and the United States have been the protection demanded by U.S. firms in electronics—chiefly color television, steel, and automobiles together with demands by the U.S. government for greater entry into the Japanese market for telecommunications equipment and agricultural products. Canada, too, has entered the fray in defense of television, steel, and automobiles. The U.S. government negotiated orderly marketing agreements (OMAs) with Japan to limit color-television exports, and Canada imposed antidumping duties and provided tariff remission to producers within Canada, mainly Japanese and U.S. companies, in return for greater production in Canada including that for export. Although the large steel producers in central Canada, like Algoma Steel, have wanted to penetrate the West Coast market further, it is usually cheaper to buy offshore from Japan. When the Canadian company succeeded in obtaining a countervailing duty on Japanese steel exports, the furious opposition of the provincial government and steel users obtained an exemption and a return of the duties paid.

Although the U.S. government is basically in favor of free trade, it has seized on large and growing merchandise trade deficits with Japan as symbolizing damaging types of exports that are too predatory. The bilateral trade balance rose from around $1 billion to about $4 billion from 1970 to 1972, the time of the Nixon shocks. It then fell back to under $2 billion until 1976 when it jumped to $5 billion; in 1977 it hit $8 billion, and in 1978 $11 billion.[9] In 1976 Japanese color-television exports captured 40 percent of the U.S. market, a jump of 153 percent in eighteen months. In 1977 Secretary of Commerce Juanita Kreps said, "Trade deficits of this magnitude and duration are simply unacceptable to the United States, both economically and politically."[10] However, in

1979, the year of the second great oil price increase, the yen increased in value against the dollar quite sharply, making Japanese exports much more expensive in North America. The trade deficit with the United States dropped back sharply to $8 billion. In Canada the sales of Japanese cars declined by 50 percent. A rise in the yen or fall of the dollar, as at the time of the Nixon shocks, can influence the trade pattern quite considerably.

Gaining Entry to the Japanese Market

Gaining entry to Japan's market has proved to be harder than keeping Japan out of North American markets by voluntary restraints, orderly marketing, antidumping duties, countervailing duties, import surcharges, or currency manipulation. Those various types of temporary protection are intended to be exceptions or outside the freer trade arrangements enshrined in the GATT, which is strongly supported by officials of Canada, Japan, and the United States. It would be much more desirable if the North American countries could export more of their own products rather than restrict Japanese exports. They have therefore exhorted Japan to buy more from them and to remove quotas, simplify customs procedures, and modify stringent health and safety rules. These steps have proved difficult and have been taken rather slowly and with no appreciable change in the overall trading pattern. Nevertheless, high-level visits and special selling missions have been undertaken by government officials to try to improve the North American exports.

Prime Minister Pierre Trudeau went to Japan in 1976 where he signed a Framework for Economic Cooperation intended to facilitate Canadian exports. Trudeau particularly urged the purchase of high-technology items like aircraft and heavy-water nuclear power reactors, which are produced by federal crown corporations in Canada. However, even strong support by MITI, the trade ministry, was unsuccessful in swaying the Japanese Atomic Energy Commission. Japan decided to go ahead to produce its own advanced thermal reactor. Like Canada, the United States also tried to promote the sale of its manufactured exports. However, unlike Canada, the United States was successful in selling aircraft to Japan, and all but one of Japan's power reactors is of U.S. design. Secretary of Commerce Kreps visited Japan with an entourage of officials and business people to spark larger exports for the United States, but the outcome has been disappointing. Japan's increased purchases of imported manufactured goods are mainly from the lower-cost developing countries whose new industries are apt to be more competitive in the Japanese market.

The Canadian and U.S. products that are most competitive in Japan are farm products. Japan has most of its quantitative import restrictions or quotas on farm products to protect its own high-cost producers. Part of the rationale is that Japan must be able to produce some of its own food in case overseas supplies are interrupted, as U.S. and Canadian grain embargoes have given good grounds to fear. The grateful Japanese farmers are overrepresented in voting because of the large exodus of surplus farm labor to the cities, but they faithfully support the ruling conservative party that could well lose its Diet majority if it were to subject them to full foreign competition. For example, Japanese producers receive two or three times the world price for rice. North American farmers also demand favored treatment such as the railway Crow Rate in Canada that enables them to haul their grain at about one-fifth of the cost to the railways. The U.S. government imposes quotas or differential tariffs on Canadian beef when its price is too competitive with U.S. beef. The GATT has made little headway in reducing protective agricultural measures.

Nevertheless, Japan is the United States' best market for farm products and one of the best for Canada. This has not prevented the U.S. federal government from orchestrating an almost frenetic campaign to increase beef and orange exports to Japan. Success might please members of Congress from orange- and beef-producing states and perhaps deflect some of the agitation for protection by the automobile and steel industries. Even if the agricultural quotas were completely removed by Japan, its imports would probably only amount to something less than $1 billion, a small dent in the trade deficit that has received far too much misplaced attention. There has been significant overproduction of oranges and beef, in some part due to the decline of exports to the largest U.S. foreign market, Canada. An ironic aspect of the campaign is that the United States not only restricts beef but also allows Japanese mandarin oranges to be sold in only six states.[11] The excuse for their exclusion is the fear of citrus canker. Canada would like to sell beef and more pork in Japan as well as to gain easier entry for cherries and apples. An increase in the beef quota might favor Australia more than North America, however. In addition to domestic reasons for not removing the farm quotas, Japan was reluctant to go further because that would put it ahead of its trading partners who were not prepared to do the same.

Other sectors of U.S. "attack" have been the Japanese government corporation that sells tobacco and the Nippon Telephone and Telegraph Company (NTT). The tobacco corporation has opened only a small segment of its sales outlets to U.S. cigarettes and has been pressed by the United States to open more and to permit better sales handling. Until recently NTT has preferred to deal with a small number of favored Japanese suppliers, not unlike other countries' communications utility or the American Telephone and Telegraph Company. However, under the government procurement code negotiated during the Multilateral Trade Negotiations (MTN) the United States requested Japan to open NTT bidding to foreign suppliers as it had agreed to do in 1980.[12] It is not possible to get the same quality control and service from the U.S. bidder, but bids from U.S. companies have been accepted. Companies in the United States have not displayed much interest in the new opportunity in Japan, so the NTT has sent around a team to encourage U.S. bidders.

Under both Prime Ministers Zenko Suzuki and Yasuhiro Nakasone, Japan has orchestrated several campaigns to open its market by reducing burdensome import regulations or health and safety standards as well as by easing some of its remaining import quotas and tariffs.[13] These have lacked the dramatic impact of the steps urged by U.S. or Canadian officials and will not change the trade patterns very much for some time. Rather than indicating the impenetrability of the Japanese economic and social systems or the recalcitrance of the Japanese government, these actions may indicate the genuine puzzlement of Japanese officials as to how any market-opening steps can really meet the objectives of Japan's trading partners for some massive change in its trading patterns. Since Canada's economy is comparatively small, complying with some of its requests probably would not cause much disruption. This might, however, be a precedent that would make it difficult to deal with the much greater dissatisfaction of Japan's two main partners, the United States and the European Community (EC). Japanese officials also genuinely believe that much of the trade dissatisfaction of Japan's partners was due to the severe recession of the early 1980s and poor productivity, which make it difficult for their products to compete in world markets.

Although Canada does not have a trade deficit with Japan as does the United States, Canadian officials have pressed vigorously to increase manufactured and high-technology exports on behalf of the industry in central Canada. Because its production is small and wages and taxes are comparatively high, its manufactured exports are apt to be less competitive than those of the United States. Also, Canadian business people have not been aggressive in Japan, preferring the easier U.S. market. Japan is Canada's second-largest trading partner but the trade is only a tenth the size of Canada's U.S. trade. Canada is an important source of some minerals such as coking coal or uranium but only a moderate-sized market for important Japanese exports like motor cars. Canada's chief value to Japan is as an alternate supplier that can assure a steadier supply of the essential raw materials that Japan mostly obtains elsewhere.

Economic Security for Japan

Japan has displayed a keen sense of vulnerability; it is virtually bereft of most of the essential raw materials for a modern industrial economy such as oil or uranium.[14] It has been successful in obtaining steady supplies of these from North America since the return of peace after the Pacific War although subject to severe embargoes at the beginning of that war. The United States is an important source of food and other essential commodities; in addition, its large market for Japanese exports enables Japan to earn the foreign exchange to pay for purchases there and the huge trade surpluses enable Japan to finance a big part of its oil bill with the Middle East, an area that cannot absorb many Japanese exports.

Although Japan is the largest or one of the largest buyers of U.S. and Canadian farm products and both North American countries would like to sell far more such products to Japan, they have not always been fully reliable suppliers. In 1973, when the demand for soybeans was high, there was fear in the United States that there would not be enough for domestic needs, so a sudden embargo was placed on the export of soybeans. Fearful that its supply might also be exhausted, Canada followed suit without consultation of its best customer, Japan. This blow from its most reliable suppliers is still referred to in Japan as the "soybean shock." The readiness to use food as a political weapon against the Soviet Union because of its invasion of Afghanistan (the grain embargo) reminded Japan once again of its resource vulnerability. The sudden reversal of that policy by the Reagan administration for the sake of the farm vote did little to reassure Japan of the steadiness of its supplier.

The availability of fish is a matter of great concern to Japan, as fish occupies the same place in the Japanese diet that meat does for North Americans. Consequently Japan is one of the greatest fishing nations of the world. The 1977 emplacement of two-hundred-mile economic zones by the large coastal states, which gave control over fisheries, was another severe blow to Japan. Canada and the United States, as well as the Soviet Union, did so, and Japan reluctantly followed. In the outcome Japan was able to negotiate access to some of the fishing in these new areas that were previously the open seas and vigorously undertook to form joint operations with many coastal states and to exploit new species and new areas. Despite its success in maintaining its large catch and satisfying supply needs, Japan keenly felt its vulnerability.

Both Canada and the United States are accustomed to conducting domestic politics without sufficient thought or sensitivity to the very unsettling international impact on their closest allies and trading partners. In 1977 Canada began an embargo of uranium for nuclear-reactor fuel to Japan and Western Europe that lasted for over a year, mainly to force very severe safeguards on its customers. This embargo proved to be a popular sort of peace policy in domestic affairs and was also a reaction to India's explosion of a nuclear device with some use of Canadian technology or U.S. materials. Japan's distress at being cut off from approximately 40 percent of its supply can well be imagined, although it did not result in a shutdown of its power plants. The long period of use for fuel rods or the ease of stockpiling considerable nuclear fuel makes the power source much more reliable than oil- or coal-fired plants. When Canada was vigorously advocating the purchase of its heavy-water technology and nuclear reactor for Japan, the Japanese desire for greater independence from North America prompted a decision to develop its own advanced thermal reactor. Canada's failure to sell its reactor was a severe blow to pride in its new technology and to hopes of selling manufactured and high-technology exports to Japan. The purchase was vigorously supported by the normally very influential MITI, significantly because the trade minister hoped it would ensure more reliable future supplies of nuclear fuel from Canada as well as a possible share in Canada's oil and gas resources.

Japan has also wished to enhance its energy security through the development of a complete fuel cycle and the reprocessing and reuse of nuclear materials. Like the Western Europeans who must import nuclear fuel, Japan is eager to proceed to the use of advanced reactors that can even produce plutonium that in turn becomes new fuel and thus greatly economizes on the amounts needed to be imported. Canada and the United States, which have plentiful fuel supplies of their own, are more concerned with the possible use as weapons of such nuclear materials. The Carter administration's delay of some developments in Japan for several years—an effort to postpone advances for which Japan was eager—was a conflict between Japan's desire for greater energy security and the U.S. desire for more stringent safeguards against possible diversion or use of nuclear materials for some weapons purpose.[15]

Japan has also sought access to Alaskan North Slope oil, which would be a more secure source than the Middle East, on which it is still overly reliant. Acquisition of the Alaskan oil would make a sizable contribution to the reduction of the large trade deficit of which the United States so loudly complains. The oil is also surplus to U.S. West Coast needs, and expensive shipment to the Gulf Coast is necessary, since Congress has required that the oil be reserved for U.S. use. The Reagan administration would be willing to request some diversion to Japan in return for taking western U.S. coal from as yet undeveloped West Coast ports. With the industrial slowdown in the early 1980s and oversupply of oil and coal Japan is reluctant to enter new obligations to the United States. Japan has already become involved in developing new mines in northeastern British Columbia in Canada and in diverting some of its purchases there, away from the good-quality but expensive U.S. East Coast coal. It also has long-term agreements with Australian coal producers. The reason for some of the diversion to two Canadian West Coast coal outlets was the prolonged strikes in both Australia and the United States in 1981 that temporarily cut off Japan from two of its largest suppliers. The Japan National Oil Corporation, together with other private firms, has had a share in the exploration of Dome Petroleum in the Beaufort Sea off of Canada's Arctic coast as well as an interest in the Canadian tar sands in Alberta in hopes of sharing in future supplies. Japan is also involved in liquefied natural gas (LNG) to be supplied from western Canada by Nissho-Iwai trading company and Dome Petroleum.

Thus, Japan has sought to diversify the sources of its essential supplies and to diversify among different energy types, as well as to participate in energy exploration and development in order to share in future output and to ensure steady supply. Both Canada and the United States are important suppliers of Japan's energy commodities. Even though they have not always been fully reliable sources and insist on meeting their own needs first, they are probably more reliable than many of the other areas of the world. As members of the International Energy Agency they are bound by informal pledges to assist and share with each other and other member nations in emergencies that interrupt energy supplies and thus are important elements in Japan's economic security. For Canada it is desirable to diversify its customers for a commodity such as coking coal rather than to be wholly at the mercy of Japan as its only major buyer. By selling LNG to Japan, Canada diversifies somewhat from relying on the United States as its only customer.

Japan's Military Security

The Nixon shocks of the early 1970s, which signified a less cordial patron-client relationship with the United States by virtue of such economic sanctions as the import surcharge or soybean embargo, launched Japan upon a somewhat more independent course in its foreign policy. Some of the defense-minded conservative politicians like Nakasone, who later became prime minister, assumed that Japan would probably soon replace its security treaty with the United States with a looser arrangement whereby Japan would take on more of the burden of its own defense.

In 1972 the withdrawal of U.S. forces from Vietnam, the cordial relations with China established by both Japan and the United States, and the Kissinger-Nixon détente with the Soviet Union greatly reduced tension in the East Asian region and reduced fears within Japan of being dragged into hostilities by virtue of U.S. bases in Japan and Japan's status as a U.S. ally. In addition the U.S. return of Okinawa (the Ryukyu Islands), which the United States had been administering, proved to be very popular in Japan. These changes almost snuffed out the antiwar agitation by Japanese opposition groups over U.S. Vietnam War involvement, so that the automatic extension of the Japan-U.S. Security Treaty in 1970 occurred with almost none of the large-scale protest movement that had taken place in 1960 or 1969.

The sudden and unexpected catastrophic collapse of the Saigon government in 1975, without any attempt by the United States to reverse the outcome of communist expansion in Indochina, sent a chill of apprehension throughout the East Asian region. In both the Philippines and South Korea, harsher regimes tolerated less dissent and sought to strengthen their governments against either external or internal communist pressures. As for Japan, its leaders reemphasized the older policy of close alliance with the United States, with no further suggestions from among the ruling conservative Liberal-Democrats of drawing away from such close ties.

In contrast to its long-standing opposition to the Japan-U.S. Security Treaty and to U.S. bases, China welcomed U.S.-Japanese military arrangements as an obstacle to the Soviet advance which it had so greatly feared for itself since the Soviet intervention and domination of Czechoslovakia in 1968. The Japan-U.S. Security Treaty obligates Japan to permit use of U.S. bases in that country for military operations to defend the Nationalist regime on Taiwan and the Republic of Korea in South Korea. The new friendliness between the United States and China rendered any hostilities over Taiwan quite unlikely for the time being, so the Japan bases ceased to be a threat to China. In the favorable climate, China pressed for a peace and friendship treaty with Japan to reinforce its ties and to make it more difficult for Japan to be friendly with the Soviet Union.

The danger of renewed hostilities between North and South Korea remained. The hopeful talks between the two Koreas that began in 1973 broke off in May 1975 with renewed verbal attacks on the south by the north. This termination occurred at about the time of the South Vietnam collapse. As U.S. military strength and influence in the region was declining, Japan returned to the former emphasis on the U.S. alliance for its security rather than striking out on a more independent course to strengthen its defense forces or to take on a regional defense role alone or with other regional countries.[16]

President Carter, who took office in 1977, had pledged in his election campaign to withdraw U.S. troops from Korea. In 1978, 3,400 military personnel were to be withdrawn and 2,600 more in 1979, leaving only 7,000 army and 9,000 air personnel in 1981 and 1982. Japanese leaders were quite alarmed at the weakening U.S. involvement in regional military affairs, even though the U.S. government intended to strengthen South Korean forces before the planned withdrawals. Japan then joined with South Korea in pressing for Carter's reconsideration, as did influential groups in Congress, the U.S. military, and the bureaucracy. When the long-pending scandal over Korean bribery of U.S. members of Congress subsided, it became feasible for Carter to visit South Korea. There he announced the temporary suspension of the withdrawal plans. In Tokyo shortly afterward he said that troops would not be withdrawn until the relations between the two Koreas improved, thus substantially giving up the whole idea.[17] U.S. intelligence estimated that North Korean forces were much larger than thought earlier, and South Korean forces comparatively weaker and possibly inviting North Korean aggression. This increased the need for the U.S. troops. The growing Soviet forces were tipping the balance against Japan, South Korea, and China. For the first time Japan's Defense Agency chief, Ganri Yamashita, visited Korea to inaugurate informal security consultations.

On August 12, 1978, Japan finally concluded in Beijing a friendship treaty with China, despite the intense opposition of the Soviet Union, which wanted to attract Japan into its orbit with its own friendship treaty. Such a Japanese-Soviet treaty would have had to directly or indirectly acknowledge Soviet possession of the disputed four northern island territories seized in 1945. The Soviets regarded the Sino-Japanese Treaty as directed against it because it contained a clause denouncing hegemony in the region, which was intended to refer to the USSR. The angry Soviets quickly signed an alliance treaty with Vietnam on November 3, 1978, giving it military aid, whereupon Vietnam opened airfields and ports to Soviet military forces. Vietnam then attacked, drove the anti-Hanoi and pro-China regime into the mountains of Cambodia, and installed another compliant communist regime in its place.

By January 1, 1979, the Carter administration had extended full diplomatic recognition to China, received Deng Xiaoping in the United States, and repudiated the Taiwan government. Closer ties with the United States emboldened Deng to attack Vietnam in a vain attempt to dislodge Vietnamese forces from Cambodia. Added to all this sudden fallout from the tipping of the balance was the longer-term effect of the declining number of U.S. naval vessels in full commission, as the Soviet Union continued to increase not only its blue-water navy in East Asia but also its air and land forces, especially on the disputed islands to the north of Japan. A U.S. carrier group based in Japan is now operating most of the time in the troubled Gulf region, which may help to ensure some security for the Japanese oil lifeline from that area, but the forces available in Japan's own vicinity are now spread even thinner. The desire for closer defense coordination was symbolized by joint naval exercises near Hawaii in 1980 in which not only Japan and the United States but also Canada, New Zealand, and Australia participated.

Under Prime Minister Masayoshi Ohira defense planning took a serious turn. A new term, *comprehensive defense,* emphasized Japan's traditional reliance on economic and diplomatic means to compensate for its lack of military effort. Japanese economic aid, which continues to grow, is heavily concentrated in the East Asian region. There it serves to strengthen and stabilize friendly governments, thus contributing to their ability to increase their military efforts. An example is the loans and credits extended to South Korea. Because of continuing domestic constraints on the Japanese defense effort, it is difficult to acknowledge that helping Korea acts as a defense for Japan as well as strengthening Korea. Such relations express the intent of the Japan-U.S. Security Treaty, although they are somewhat veiled by the rather general language of the document. Despite the more open defense debate within Japan, government statements that suggest regional involvement or stronger military effort are apt to produce minor storms in the press and the Diet.

Prime Minister Suzuki, addressing the National Press Club in Washington, D.C., in May 1981, said Japan would try to assume responsibility for defense of the sea-lanes extending one thousand miles from Japan. This was understood by U.S. officials as an intention to share in military tasks of the security in a more substantial fashion. It was not intended to go as far as the role suggested by Defense Secretary Caspar Weinberger, who said, "If Japan undertook the defense of the sea-lanes, the United

States would be able to throw more forces into Southeast Asia and the Indian Ocean theaters."[18] Japanese officials expect to participate in something like defending sea-lanes or mining the three straits to the Sea of Japan, in order to bottle up the Soviet fleet, in joint operations together with U.S. forces, not to act alone. They do not expect to participate in some kind of wider global or regional collective security action with the United States. That is considered to be forbidden by Japan's peace constitution. Japan does not possess the military equipment to undertake such tasks by itself even in its own immediate defense. It does not have the radar or types of antisubmarine vessels, to say nothing of the required air cover, to defend sea-lanes for one thousand miles from Japan. The prime minister even took such sharp objection to the use of the word *alliance* to describe the Japan-U.S. defense relationship in his communiqué with President Reagan that Foreign Minister Masayoshi Ito, who approved of it, had to resign to take responsibility for it.

Prime Minister Nakasone, a former naval officer who has always favored a stronger defense force for Japan, is willing to use the word *alliance*. On his January 1983 visit to Washington, D.C., he said Japan would mine the straits and act as a kind of national aircraft carrier (erroneously translated as an "unsinkable aircraft carrier") to repel the formidable Soviet Backfire bombers. That statement aroused the predictable outburst of criticism within Japan and the comment from a high Soviet official that the Soviet Union would sink that aircraft carrier in a few minutes. Nakasone's statement was intended to deflect or reduce the current trade friction by finding something to please U.S. officials, who welcomed the new forthright prime minister. Nakasone had already pleased both Korean and U.S. leaders by his trip to Seoul, where he resolved the long-standing deadlock over economic aid to Korea by agreeing to $4 billion in credits for the economic plans of the Chun Doo Hwan regime. He was also the first Japanese prime minister in office to visit South Korea.

The Mid-Term Defense Program from 1983 to 1987 to upgrade Japanese defense capabilities has not been able to keep up with the projected expenditures. In fiscal year 1983, with the tightest budget in thirty years, the Japanese government did agree to increase military expenditures by 6.5 percent when the overall budget declined by 3.1 percent. The result is that those expenditures are not keeping up with the plan, and it looks doubtful that they will catch up. Thus, even more defense-minded Prime Minister Nakasone may not be able to upgrade his forces sufficiently for the program envisaged in 1976, let alone expand Japan's regional defense role in any significant fashion. He did move decisively to enable Japan to transfer new technology that has military applications to the United States, despite the previous interpretation that considered such an action illegal under the Export Trade Control Ordinance and the three principles against weapons exports.

Trends in the 1980s

Relations between the two superpowers have deteriorated steadily in the early 1980s as the United States tries to meet the challenge with substantial improvement in both nuclear and conventional forces. In East Asia the Soviet Union has greatly upgraded its forces, both conventional and nuclear, and established a closer alliance with its ally in Southeast Asia, Vietnam. U.S. East Asian forces are being slowly upgraded but are spread thin with added commitments in the Middle East. Japan's protection is weakened by the adverse trends in the regional balance already described, which are apt to continue for some time until the U.S.-Japanese effort is upgraded or the Soviet Union can be persuaded to agree to disarmament. The unfortunate incident in which an unarmed Korean passenger plane was shot down in the late summer of 1983 near Sakhalin Island was a salutary reminder of the enormous danger from the excessive reliance of the Soviet Union on military power. Even in Japan where the danger of confrontation with the Soviet Union is less feared than in Washington, D.C., the incident may serve to strengthen the hand of the prime minister in increasing Japan's defense effort. Japan's Mid-Term Defense Program will increase Japan's own capability during the decade to a modest extent, but it probably will not increase its independent regional security role nor much affect the military balance in the region. That will be affected more by the extent to which the United States beefs up its forces there and the priority it assigns to East Asia in comparison to the Middle East or the Atlantic in terms of likely contingencies. The balance will also depend on Soviet and Chinese actions and policy.

It seems certain that during the 1980s Japan will cooperate more closely with the United States in the practical sphere of more adequate coordination in joint operations with U.S. forces as well as in the provision for operating needs in case of conflict of a conventional sort. Both public opinion and even the opposition political parties are more tolerant of modest conventional defensive plans than in past decades. Japan may go somewhat beyond past policies that have only permitted it to cooperate in defense to the minimum agreeable to the United States. It is also likely that defense cooperation will continue to ameliorate friction over trade.

The principal way that Japan has responded to the trade friction has been to limit the most controversial exports when these seem to provoke its partners to an extreme degree. Unless severe unemployment continues in North America, the friction should subside as the most sharply affected industries undergo some improvement both in Canada and the United States. In the case of automobiles, renewed production should lessen the problems of the industry even if there turn out to be some redundant workers who are no longer needed and who will have to be absorbed by other industries. It has proved to be much more difficult to increase

North American exports to the Japanese market, where there seems to be strong political influence protecting the agricultural sector and strong bureaucratic resistance to dismantling the health and safety standards or difficult rules. The chief obstacles to increased entry to Japan's market seem to be the relatively high cost or low productivity of the foreign exports, and the limited extent to which they would be able to penetrate Japan's market even if tariff and nontariff regulations were all removed. Japan will probably gradually continue to reduce those barriers, and market entry will gradually lose its saliency as an important issue as the decade proceeds.

The economic imperative that has thus far governed Japan's ties with North America has been the need for access to raw materials and markets for Japan's manufactured exports. This need has been strong enough to induce a moderate degree of defense cooperation against a strongly entrenched pacifism among a significant proportion of the Japanese community. For the United States, the value of Japan as a strong position for its East Asian regional and even global military strategy continues and has helped to moderate the economic conflict. For Canada, access to Japan's market for its commodity exports and some processed goods continues to be important even against the pressure for protection from less competitive industries in central Canada. The commitment of both the Canadian and the U.S. governments to liberal trade is also an important check on the influence of domestic protective forces, which would otherwise produce more tension and friction that could have very disruptive consequences. The continuation in the early 1980s of many of the governing factors from earlier decades, even with the shifting of the military strategic balance, seems likely to continue the same kinds of economic and security ties between North America and Japan for the rest of the decade. Japan presumably will continue to be a valuable ally and trading partner and the economic tensions will be contained, even if Japan does not take on an expanded regional role or even reach a much higher level of military preparedness.

Notes

1. Gary R. Saxonhouse, "The World Economy and Japanese Foreign Policy," in Robert A. Scalapino, ed., *The Foreign Policy of Modern Japan* (Berkeley, Los Angeles, and London: University of California Press, 1977), p. 284.

2. G. C. Allen, *Japan's Economic Recovery* (London, New York, and Toronto: Oxford University Press, 1958), pp. 170–173.

3. R. N. Rosecrance, *Australian Diplomacy and Japan, 1945–1951* (London and New York: Cambridge University Press/Melbourne University Press, 1962), pp. 196ff.

4. Frank Langdon, *The Politics of Canadian-Japanese Economic Relations, 1952–1983* (Vancouver and London: University of British Columbia Press, 1983), pp. 53–64.

5. Chalmers Johnson, *MITI and the Japanese Miracle, The Growth of Industrial Policy, 1925–1975* (Stanford, Calif.: Stanford University Press, 1982), pp. 209ff.

6. I. M. Destler, Haruhiro Fukui, and Hideo Sato, *The Textile Wrangle, Conflict in Japanese-American Relations, 1969–1971* (Ithaca, N.Y., and London: Cornell University Press, 1979), p. 8.

7. "Freer Trade Sought by Japan, Canada," *Vancouver Sun,* September 15, 1971, p. 2.

8. I. M. Destler and Hideo Sato, eds., *Coping with U.S.-Japanese Economic Conflicts* (Lexington, Mass., and Toronto: Lexington Books, 1982), p. 2.

9. Ibid., table 1-1, p. 4.

10. Donald I. Meltzer, "Color TV Sets and U.S.-Japanese Relations: Problems of Trade Adjustment Policymaking," *Orbis* 87, no. 12 (Summer 1979), p. 426.

11. Hideo Sato and Timothy J. Curran, "Agricultural Trade: The Case of Beef and Citrus," in Destler and Sato, *Coping,* p. 23.

12. Timothy J. Curran, "Politics and High Technology: The NTT Case," in Destler and Sato, *Coping,* pp. 185–241.

13. Frank Langdon, "Japan–United States Trade Friction, The Reciprocity Issue," *Asian Survey* 23, no. 5 (May 1983), pp. 656–660.

14. Saburo Okita, "Japan's High Dependence on Imports of Raw Materials," in Sir John Crawford and Saburo Okita, eds., *Raw Materials and Pacific Economic Integration* (Vancouver: University of British Columbia Press, 1978), pp. 218–228.

15. Ryukichi Imai and Henry S. Rowen, *Nuclear Energy and Nuclear Proliferation, Japanese and American Views* (Boulder, Colo.: Westview Press, 1980), p. xiii.

16. Marlis G. Steinert, *Le Japon en quête d'une politique étrangère* (Geneva: Institut Universitaire de Hautes Études Internationales, 1981), p. 53ff.

17. Chae-jin Lee and Hideo Sato, *U.S. Policy Toward Japan and Korea* (New York: Praeger Publishers, 1982), p. 190; and Chong-shik Lee, "South Korea 1979: Confrontation, Assassination, and Transition," *Asian Survey* 20, no. 1 (January 1980), p. 73.

18. Research Institute for Peace and Security, *Asian Security 1983* (Tokyo: Research Institute for Peace and Security, 1983), p. 237.

2
Japan and the European Community: An Uneasy Relationship

Marlis G. Steinert

The nature and intensity of Euro-Japanese relations have varied strikingly over time. After nearly a century of intensive commercial and religious intercourse with Portugal (1542–1639), there followed a severe period of seclusion of over two hundred years when only the Dutch succeeded in maintaining a small trading station on the tiny island of Deshima in Nagasaki harbor. Few Japanese had an occasion to meet any of the Dutch, who were considered to be "very strange creatures."[1] It was only after the appearance of Commodore Matthew C. Perry's black ships in 1853 and after a short period dominated by the desire to expel the intruders—the "barbarians"—that Europe became the preceptor of Japanese "modernization." British, French, and German institutions and know-how served as a model for many sectors of Japanese political and economic life, but most of Japan's social values and traditions remained intact.

To the Europeans, Japan was fascinating culturally and aesthetically but was of little interest politically and economically. The exception was the British, who perceived Japan as an important military ally in the Far East. Today the respective images have been more or less reversed.[2] For many Japanese, Europe has become a kind of a historical and cultural curiosity with much less relevance as a model, whereas more and more Europeans resent the Japanese as intruders, due to the stunning success of Japanese goods in their markets.

These perceptions are quite recent and are the product of various interlocking variables. In order to better understand these changes, and to correctly place the Japanese-European relationship in the overall framework of Japanese and European foreign policies, a short review of the essential features of the global and regional environments seems necessary before analyzing the structures and contents of their bilateral ties.

The Global Context

It is in the bipolar cold war context that Europe and Japan had been reinserted into international politics. Two years after the termination of the most destructive of all wars, the devastated West European economies had been rescued by the United States. It was the Marshall Plan that laid the basis for intra-European cooperation. This step was followed by the creation of the Council of Europe, which generated intergovernmental cooperation; the Schuman plan, which inaugurated a functionalist Europe with a slight supranational touch; and finally the European Economic Community (EEC) and the European Atomic Community (EAC). The EEC represented a partially integrated and partially coordinated association of six states (Belgium, France, West Germany, Italy, Luxembourg, and the Netherlands) for the execution of new political, economic, and social tasks in the modern world.

Postwar Japan appeared on the international scene after the conclusion of a peace treaty in 1952 with its former enemies—with the exception of the Soviet Union and China—and after the conclusion of a defensive alliance with the United States. Between 1953 and 1964, Japan joined the major international economic organizations and the United Nations.

During the 1950s and 1960s, while the Japanese and the European economies expanded rapidly, the United States was losing part of its former unchallenged strength and superiority. The changed international climate was dramatically highlighted by two declarations of the U.S. president in 1971, the first announcing his visit to the People's Republic of China and the second setting forth a "new economic policy," disconnecting the dollar from gold and imposing a 10 percent import tax on all goods. These two developments marked a major turning point in postwar international relations. Not only did they deal a blow to the international economic order, known as the Bretton Woods system, but they also changed the international configuration of forces. The emergence of a new world system was further emphasized by the demand of the developing world for a new international economic order (NIEO), a demand that found dramatic expression in the use of the oil embargo of October 1973 by the Arab countries.

All these events marked the beginning of economic instability. The catchwords of the 1970s were the North-South dialogue and stagflation. Despite the creation in 1973 of the Trilateral Commission (a nongovernmental organization designed to foster cooperation and understanding among the United States, Japan, and West European countries), the pressure of high oil prices, economic recession, inflation, and growing unemployment heightened trade frictions and tensions. The most important aspect of the uneasy tripartite relations was the growing trade deficit of the United States and European countries with a more and more dynamic Japan.

Politically, the beginning of the 1970s had been marked by the replacement of the cold war by détente. But the end of that decade and the beginning of the next witnessed a number of localized conflicts in Africa, Iran, Iraq, and Afghanistan that resulted in the deterioration of East-West relations. The Polish crisis, the Euromissiles controversy, and the shooting down of the South Korean plane by the Soviets further worsened the general climate. The international scene in the 1980s is thus characterized not only by growing East-West and continuing North-South tensions, but also by North-North frictions and difficult South-South relations. Economically and politically the outlook is gloomy, recalling for many the specter of the great economic crisis of the late 1920s and early 1930s and its disastrous economic and political consequences.

Regional Environments

The EEC since 1958 has had three major developments in its ongoing evolutionary process. First, it has become a major actor in the international system with an economic clout comparable to that of the United States and Japan. Second, it has enlarged its responsibilities and membership. The fusion of the EEC with the Coal and Steel and the Atomic communities and its enlargement with the inclusion of Great Britain, Ireland, and Denmark have given it a physical dimension comparable to other major powers. Third, the treaties of Yaoundé (1963 and 1969) followed by two Lomé Conventions (1975 and 1980) have made it possible for the EEC to establish a wide network of institutionalized relationships with sixty-three African, Caribbean, and Pacific countries (ACP) that is unprecedented in the annals of the contemporary world. Compounding this, the EEC is imbedded in a zone of highly developed countries that are linked together by a horizontal division of labor, that belong mostly to the same defense organization, and that benefit from a close interdependence with each other. All this has established a stable "inner full trading circle"[3] consisting of the European Community (EC), the European Free Trade Area (EFTA), and ACP as well as many of the Mediterranean countries.

Japan's regional environment is strikingly different. Located at the fringe of the Asian continent and a universe by itself, it had until recently no industrial neighbors in similar stages of development. Its biggest immediate neighbors are socialist countries with planned economies: the People's Republic of China and the Soviet Union. Paradoxically, although Japan is the only nonwhite country belonging to the club of highly industrialized democracies, it is included in the United Nations in the Afro-Asian bloc. To some extent, Japan thus often feels like the odd man out, associated with blocs it does not belong to. Japan's reinsertion in the world system under the protective umbrella of the United States resulted in a major reorientation of the Japanese trade pattern. Instead of neighboring China and East Asia, Japan's principal partners became North America and Southeast Asia. Since then, Japan's economic interdependence with these countries has risen considerably, especially with the Association of Southeast Asian Nations (ASEAN) countries, which have become a sort of Japanese hinterland.[4]

After the normalization in 1972 and the conclusion of the peace treaty with the People's Republic of China in 1978, the policy of the *seikei bunri* (separation between economics and politics) was abandoned and old trade patterns seemed possible again. But so far the huge expectations placed in the vast China market have not been fulfilled, whereas Japan's relations with Hong Kong, South Korea, and Taiwan have become extremely close, to the extent that some authors argue that they resemble those of the prewar colonial situation.[5] In fact, these newly industrializing countries (NICs) present a growing danger not only to Japan in its foreign and domestic markets but also to the West. In 1970, the Asian NICs had roughly a 10 percent share of Japan's imports of manufactured goods; by 1980, this had risen to 25 percent. Correspondingly the EC share over the same period fell from 25 percent to 20 percent, and the U.S. share fell from 40 percent to 30 percent.[6] There have even been suggestions for the creation of a common market among the United States, Canada, Japan, and Australia. For the moment, they seem to have no more chances of success than the propositions made for the granting of a STABEX-system (stabilization of export earnings) to the ASEAN countries or those of Kyoshi Kojima for a Pacific Trade Area, which were conceived of as a counterbalance to the economies of the EC countries.

Japan and the European Community

Decision-Making Processes

If some parallels can be drawn between the reinsertion of Europe and Japan into the postwar world, there are fundamental differences not only regarding their place and role in their respective environments but also in their internal settings, particularly in their decision-making processes. An examination of these differences should help us to understand some of the misunderstandings and problems that exist in their mutual relationship.

The first fact is that the EC is a regional organization of ten states (Greece became a member in 1982) that have ceded parts of their sovereignty to the Community. Any outside power wishing to develop relations with them would therefore have to interact (1) with individual states (matters of high-level policy, strategy, finance); (2) with a mixed group of Community representatives as well as the national states (concurrent competence and European Political Cooperation—EPC); and (3) with the EC exclusively in trade matters (Article 113 of the Rome Treaty). The foreign relations of the EC are thus based on a variety of legal and procedural competences expressing themselves in three different ways and passing through a number of interlocking channels.[7] It is not surprising that this complicated decisional pattern often results in a stalemate and incites countries to give preference to relations with member states and not to the EC as a whole.

This has been the case of Japan, which rapidly realized that "member Governments remain the ultimate source of power and decision"[8] in the European Community. "What kind of authority do they have and what are they up to?" asked Nobuhiko Ushiba, state minister for external economic affairs, in a speech before the Harvard Club in Tokyo. He continued, "In fact the Commission cannot move at all without being given a mandate from the member countries, and the Commission has no authority to tell the member countries to do anything. This is the strange position it has and it is with that body I must negotiate."[9] Clearly for Ushiba the Europeans remain "very strange creatures."

On the other hand, Japan—though a unitary, homogeneous, and highly centralized state with a political system modeled after U.S.-British institutions—has upheld certain continuities between the prewar and the postwar system. The most outstanding feature of this is the need to arrive at decisions by consensus. A strong emphasis is placed on personal relations among the members of the tripartite elite governing the country: the ruling party, the bureaucracy, and the business circles. In this "interlocking decision-making"[10] a "bureaucratic leadership structure" has emerged in the realm of foreign economic relations, as exemplified by the role of the Ministry of International Trade and Industry (MITI) in maintaining a constant dialogue with the business community in cooperation with the powerful Ministry of Finance, the Ministry of Agriculture and Forestry, the Economic Planning Agency, and the ministries of Transportation and of Health and Welfare. The Ministry of Foreign Affairs, the Gaimusho, is more concerned with overall political questions. Frequent conflicts therefore often surface in which all of them are varyingly involved.

The coordination and modulation among these different bureaucratic actors and the different elements of the power trilogy is a lengthy process with an excessive influence of the domestic political forces, thereby making the formulation of long-range foreign policies equally difficult. A number of authors have stressed the ad hoc, pragmatic, and sluggish nature of such a procedure. But as none other than Henry Kissinger has stressed, once a decision is taken, "execution is rapid and single-minded."[11]

Pluralist inertness and the lack of integrated decision making are thus common to both the actors, but they are clearly more pronounced and more complex in the European Community where coordination and modulation have to take place not only among national elements within member states but also among community organs, among these organs and national administrations, and finally among states themselves. Thus a whole process of institutionalized bargaining among all the appropriate organs has to be effectuated before finally the EC arrives at a common position on a given matter. It should be noted that once a common position has been elaborated, the negotiating power of the world's most important commercial bloc is indeed sinewy.[12]

What deprived the Community of its real negotiating power with Japan was the absence of a common industrial policy, whereas the existence of a rational and viable industrial policy was at the root of the Japanese success. Another handicap was the existence of two opposite schools of thought among the Community members. On the one side were the partisans of free trade (Great Britain, the Federal Republic of Germany, Denmark, the Netherlands); on the other were the supporters of a more "managed" trade (France and Italy); Belgium and Ireland stood in the middle. Furthermore, all European countries have displayed a secular trend of establishing a social-welfare state with reduced working hours and high salaries, low productivity, extended holidays, and early retirement. In contrast, extended working hours, short holidays, iron discipline, high productivity, frugality, poor housing, and a weak social-service sector are considered as the trademarks of the Japanese way of life.

Bilateral Interaction

From the foregoing analysis of the most important determinants of Japan-EC relations one can extricate some fundamental traits:[13] (1) Japan and Europe owe their resurrection to the United States, with both having stronger overall links with the United States than with each other; (2) the two parties increasingly depend on the resources and the markets of the Third World; (3) the Community's involvement in its regional environment is more pronounced than that of Japan; and (4) their geographical distance, combined with their characteristics, is accentuated by their different styles of life. What renders the relationship even more difficult is the fact that both actors are highly industrialized and lack natural resources. Japan clearly is in a more difficult position than Europe: Although Japan, in 1979, produced only 11 percent of its energy needs, the EC produced 45 percent. Half of Japan's imports consist of oil and other energies against only one-third in the case of EC. Hence for the two of them it is imperative to develop competitive export industries. As Europe and Japan represent "workshops" for the transformation of primary materials and have to some extent comparable production structures (heavy, high-technology, and capital-intensive industries), rivalry is inevitable in Third World markets as well as in other developed countries. A high level of adversarial relations is generated by this rivalry, much more than with the United States, which also exports primary materials to Japan.

As long as the world economic system was in constant expansion and as long as Japan's production was absorbed primarily by its own domestic market, the EC-Japan exchanges were minimal. At the creation of the

EC, Japan ranked twenty-eighth in the EC's external relations. A viable interaction therefore hardly existed, though a certain hostility was none-theless present due to Japan's evident potentialities in the economic sector (exemplified when it joined the General Agreement on Tariffs and Trade—GATT—in 1955). Fourteen countries, including Britain, France, Belgium, and the Netherlands, refused to establish full GATT relations with Japan by invoking Article 35 of the agreement. The same attitude was adopted later on by former British, French, and Belgian dependencies. This "second-class treatment" was deeply resented by the Japanese. To overcome the impasse, Japan started bilateral negotiations, first with Britain and then with France, which centered on the question of how to grant most-favored-nation rights to Japan and of how to incorporate safeguards in the agreements against disruptive imports. The breakthrough occurred in 1963 with the conclusion of a commercial treaty with Great Britain. The agreement included two types of safeguards: The first permitted, after consultation, the imposition of restrictions on the imports of the other country, in case these imports caused or threatened serious injury to domestic productions; the second consisted of a list of sensitive items allowing Great Britain to maintain certain restrictions. Furthermore, Japan agreed to the "orderly marketing" of certain products. The British example was quickly followed by France and the Benelux countries (Belgium-Netherlands-Luxembourg) all of which revoked the application of Article 35.

Although regular consultations between European and Japanese foreign ministers were inaugurated in 1963, thereby establishing the precedent of bilateral relationships with the member states of the EC, the estab-lishment of a common commercial policy according to Article 113 of the Rome Treaty was delayed by internal decisional difficulties and by external involvement with the Dillon and Kennedy rounds of the Mul-tilateral Trade Negotiations (MTN). It was finally the Japanese who took the initiative in 1969 in asking the EC for new negotiations in the framework of the Long Term Trade Agreement on cotton textiles. Fearing the impact of the future enlargement of the Community, the Japanese clearly wanted to establish a good relationship. The successful conclusion of an agreement and high-level Japanese visits spurred the European Commission into asking the Council of Ministers for a mandate on exploratory negotiations for a trade agreement. As the exports from Europe to Japan between 1958 and 1970 had increased by 609 percent and Europe's imports from Japan by 953 percent, the Council of Ministers gave the necessary authorization to the commission.

The story of these negotiations reads like a tragedy.[14] The major stumbling block was the European insistence on the inclusion of a safeguard clause, applicable to Japan, whereas the Japanese maintained that Article 19 of the GATT agreement provided sufficient guarantees. From 1972 on, sectoral agreements increasingly replaced the trade agreement, and some member countries resorted to unilateral import restrictions. With the start of the new MTN (the Tokyo Round), the trade agreement was shelved for the time being. The only positive step taken was the installation of semiannual high-level consultations. Despite the suggestion for triangular cooperation among the United States, Japan, and the EC made in April 1973 by Soames, the EC commissioner for external relations—an exhortation already voiced by Prime Minister Ikeda in 1971—no substantive triangular relations developed.

Thus for the second time, the Europeans missed an opportunity. The first time was at the end of the 1950s, in the beginning of the 1960s, and again in the late 1960s with the prospect of the first enlargement. By dropping some European restrictions and by exploiting the Japanese desire to escape the one-sided relationship with the United States, Europe could have obtained Japanese concessions on further market liberalizations, since Europe still had a positive image. The reasons for this neglect are quite simple: Trade with Japan at the time was fairly marginal for Europe, whereas trade with Europe and especially with Great Britain in the 1950s and afterwards with Germany was quite important for Japan.

After the oil shock in 1973, European exports to Japan fell even more while Japan heightened its export offensive. EC-Japanese relations since 1976 thus have been in a constant state of crisis. The European complaints against the flooding of their markets by Japanese goods (steel, textiles, cars, ball bearings, television sets) and their protestations against Japanese nontariff barriers (NTBs) obstructing the imports of European pharmaceuticals, processed food, cigarettes, chemicals, cars, and capital goods into Japan were critically voiced during the visit of Keidanren's president Doko in Europe in autumn 1976. After what is now commonly called the Doko shock, efforts were made to lessen the Japanese export drive by voluntary restraints, some tariff cuts, and procedural simplifications for some imports. Japanese domestic infighting impeded the implementation of a more consistent scheme. Despite some drastic European countermeasures, numerous high-level consultations, and even a short détente in 1978—mostly due to the revaluation of the yen— the trade gap between the two partners continued to widen and the European dissatisfaction further heightened. In 1976 the EC trade deficit had amounted to US$4.1 billion, in 1977 to $5.1 billion, in 1981 to $10.4 billion, and in 1982 it reached $14 billion.

In 1979, a confidential paper of the Directorate I (External Relations) of the European Commission was leaked to the press.[15] After a thorough and sober analysis of the situation, the paper threatened selected import controls and contained passages treating Japan as "a country of workaholics who live in what Westerners would regard as little more than rabbit hutches. . . ." This insulting language and inelegant gesture might be considered as a reaction to Ushiba's aforementioned remark on the EC. Although expressing the growing impatience and exasperation of certain high-placed Eurocrats, it accomplished nothing.

In 1980, the European Commission attempted to inaugurate a new commercial policy. It submitted a paper to the Council of Ministers in which it asserted that the Community was twenty years out of date because it had failed to recognize Japan's importance as the third economic power in the world. It urged the removal of quantitative restrictions and individual member states safeguard clauses in exchange for temporary Japanese restraints in sensitive European sectors, the removal of Japan's quantitative restrictions on certain goods, and the lowering of high tariffs on processed agricultural products.

After some consideration by the Council of Ministers, the commission paper was sent to the committee of the permanent representatives of the EC member states (COREPER) for further study, where it encountered strong resistance from some of the member states: from France for abandoning restrictions, from others because of their opposition to the practice of voluntary restraints (Germany, Denmark, Netherlands). After a new round of haggling among the member states, the Council of Ministers finally agreed in November 1980 to authorize the European Commission to inaugurate a wide-ranging dialogue with Japan, based on a common strategy. The dialogue, conducted again at a high level, proved as disappointing as the former experiences. It is not surprising that strong reactions by member states were expressed through the imposition of unilateral import restrictions. The measures against Japanese car imports[16] or the funneling of Japanese video tape recorders through a small customs station at Poitiers are cases in point.

In 1981, the EC resorted to the introduction of "statistical controls" of certain Japanese goods and finally decided in 1982 to bring the whole problem before a special arbitration panel of GATT, according to the provisions of Article 23, Paragraph 2. This measure induced the new Japanese administration, under Yasuhiro Nakasone, to take the European complaints more seriously and led to Foreign Minister Shintaro Abe's visit to different European capitals and to Brussels.

A Japan–European Community symposium on industrial cooperation in the fields of technology, investment, research, and development was also organized in Brussels in January 1983. In his opening address, the president of the European Commission, Gaston Thorn, listed three special causes for the friction between the EC and Japan: "the chronic nature of the deficit between the two partners . . . , the concentration of Japanese exports in sectors considered 'sensitive' . . . , and the minimal opening of the Japanese market to manufactured products from Europe."[17]

Thorn added that the Community was under strong pressures from its member states and if no negotiated solution resulted, they would themselves take appropriate measures. As a follow-up to the symposium, a high-level meeting took place in Tokyo in mid-February 1983 between the Japanese ministries of International Trade and Industry and of Foreign Affairs and Vice-Chairmen Etienne Davignon and Wilhelm Haferkamp of the European Commission. An agreement was finally reached for a Japanese autolimitation on ten sensitive points. The final outcome, however, was quite disappointing for the Europeans: The number of Japanese exports of cars, television sets, and video cassettes increased during the first eight months of 1983, thus augmenting the deficit by 8 percent. Only imports of video recorders and motorcycles declined.[18] For the video recorders the ceiling of 4.55 million units had been fixed by mutual agreement against 4.35 million in 1982. Further annual "previsions" are planned for 1984 and 1985.[19]

In view of the ongoing frictions, the European Commission has maintained its request for establishing a working party of GATT members under the provisions of Article 23, Paragraph 2. For the moment, the GATT council has postponed a decision, thereby giving the parties another chance for further consideration of the dispute. In pursuing its efforts to explore all possibilities of cooperation, the European Commission has proposed to the Council of Ministers to enter into negotiations with the Japanese government in order to conclude a framework of agreement on scientific and technological cooperation.[20] But as the "Japan-EC Trade Imbalance [is] Worsening Again,"[21] a joint warning regarding the risks of a growing deficit has been addressed by all the EC ambassadors in Tokyo to the minister of international trade and industries.[22]

Conclusions and Prospects

The main reasons for this uneasy Japan-EC relationship are mostly *structural* and therefore difficult to eliminate.

First, the relationship is *primarily economic*. The political and security aspects have been neglected to such a point that they do not constitute a sufficient countervailing force to the difficulties generated by the trade imbalance. Therefore in recent years some efforts have been deployed to strengthen political cooperation.

The Japanese, for example, backed the Europeans in their opposition to the U.S. embargo on the furnishing of steel pipes to the Soviet Union. After a period of hesitation they adopted the same measures against Iran as the EC countries; also they joined many Europeans to boycott the Olympic Games in Moscow and followed them to condemn the invasion of Afghanistan. The EC Venice declaration in favor of a Palestinian participation in any peace settlement in the Middle East was supported by members of the Japanese government. Even the fate of Poland, clearly nearer to the hearts of the Europeans, induced Japan to support Western protests against the overwhelming Soviet pressures.

These political gestures toward Europe had some military counterparts, even though timid. In September 1980 and in February 1983 the Japanese Navy held joint exercises respectively with the British and the French navies.

A visit to Tokyo in May 1980 by a delegation of the North Atlantic Assembly was reciprocated by Japanese parliamentarians in November

1980 and by the head of the Liberal-Democratic party's Security Affairs Research Council. Direct contacts between the Japanese Self-Defense Agency and North Atlantic Treaty Organization (NATO) headquarters in Brussels have also been established.[23] Japan also contributed $100 million to the aid package to Turkey of the Organization of Economic Cooperation and Development (OECD). Finally, on his trip to Europe in January 1983, Foreign Minister Abe proposed an informal arrangement with NATO. As this was opposed by France, Prime Minister Nakasone decided to intensify consultations directly with the big three of the EC: Great Britain, France, and Germany.[24] Clearly, an adequate consultative mechanism on security matters is lacking in the Euro-Japanese relationship. Since the EPC also deals with security aspects, one possibility would be that the EC member country in charge of the chairmanship would regularly inform the Japanese government on all questions of common Western interest. The Community already has an arrangement of this kind with the United States and with China.

A second reason is that the respective European and Japanese *decision-making processes* are cumbersome and suffer from major drawbacks: (1) a lack of clear-cut political leadership and (2) considerable bureaucratic infighting (even if—as Albrecht Rothacher has rightly pointed out—bureaucratic politics not only represent parochial interests but are able to induce more elements of rationality and predictability and use an increased information input).[25]

The lack of clear-cut politics is more rampant in the Community, where the ten member states have to agree. Inevitably under such circumstances the decisions are either delayed or taken at the lowest common denominator. The EC Council of Ministers is quite aware of the necessity of a reform of the Community, and propositions to this effect were made at the Stuttgart summit of June 1983. The Japanese government on its side has come out in favor of a policy that will "educe the private economic vitality and potential by allowing the widest possible freedom of private economic activities and minimizing all sorts of legal or administrative restraints and limiting the governmental functions to a minor supplementary role."[26]

Third, the fundamental dilemma of the Japan–European community relationship is the *lack of complementary economies.* Both actors have to rely heavily on manufactured exports to pay for their imports of primary goods, but many of their exports substitute for, and directly compete against, one another. Japan finds itself in even a more difficult position with its relatively small domestic market to absorb foreign manufactures, whereas the Community already possesses a continental market with 270 million consumers, which will increase to 320 million after its enlargement through the inclusion of Spain and Portugal. As the prospect of a viable integration of the Japanese economy in its regional environment seems dim, "whatever action she takes will touch the delicate nerve of other nations."[27]

Fourth, economic and military *interaction* between Japan and the United States is much greater and much more crucial for the survivial of the former. A similar argument can also be adduced regarding U.S.-European relations. The United States thus still remains the fulcrum of the trilateral world; in the event of major tensions among the three partners, Japan and the EC would tend to give priority to the resolution of their dispute with Washington even to the detriment of their bilateral relationship.

Given this basically unfavorable situation, what practical measures could be taken by both sides in order to achieve a more balanced and positive relationship?

EC Actions

If Japanese economic inroads are not limited to Europe but encompass the whole planet, the Europeans themselves are to be blamed. Their declining shares of the Asian, U.S., and other markets stem from low productivity in key export industries (steel, ships, cars, electronics, textiles) due to low levels of investment in new technology and equipment, high labor cost, and labor unrest. In many sectors the European producers are clearly lagging behind the Japanese counterparts, both in quality and in price. Considerable efforts therefore have to be made to catch up with the high standards of key Japanese industries in order to become competitive again, not only nationally but also in long-term Community strategies for a vigorous industrial policy of investment in growth sectors of the future (technology and knowledge-intensive industries, microchip electronics, computers, satellites, medical equipment, pharmaceuticals). There is an urgent necessity to invest in the Japanese market (joint ventures, company takeovers, after-sales services), to promote export activities, and to acquire greater knowledge of Japan in Europe. Furthermore, existing quantitative restrictions against Japanese imports have to be removed as quickly as possible, especially if Japan continues to agree to practice voluntary export restraints for highly sensitive sectors.

Japanese Actions

The most important effort on the Japanese side would be to further accept the international division of labor, allowing higher imports of manufactured goods. According to the latest OECD report these imports were practically stagnant during 1981 and 1982.[28] A report submitted in June 1983 by a special panel to the Japanese Trade Conference Organization (a top official trade-promotion advisory board) admitted that "Japan's imports of manufactured products, though steadily increasing in recent years, is still a far cry from those of America and the EC countries." But on the other hand it also stressed that "Japan's markets for manufactured goods are fully accessible to foreign competitors, if they really mean to enter them."[29] A study done by private researchers for the Ministry of Foreign Affairs came to the same conclusion.[30]

The establishment of the Office of the Trade Ombudsman (OTO) to examine the complaints against complicated control measures on imported goods is certainly an important step toward the opening of the Japanese market. To pursue the same line of argument it could be suggested that Japan should review its policies toward protected sectors, give foreign companies the same opportunities for takeover as Japanese firms enjoy in Europe, allow foreign banks the same facilities as Japanese banks have in Europe, and fully liberalize the capital market and the insurance sector.

As to the export side, Japanese companies should avoid "torrential downpours" of exports in sensitive sectors. An increased Japanese investment in the manufacturing sector in Europe might also help the Europeans to overcome their social problems, especially unemployment, which actually amounts to 11.7 millions in the European Community. Despite a notable increase of Japanese investment in the manufacturing industries (from 2.0 percent in the period 1951–1961 to 11.5 percent during 1976–1980), direct investments still remain relatively feeble.[31]

To sum up: To redress the balance, sustained efforts have to be undertaken by both sides in short-, medium-, and long-term time frames. The already existing ties have to be intensified in a spirit of good will and mutual comprehension; otherwise there is a danger that not only some of the member states but the Community itself may resort to protectionist measures in order to preserve Europe's "social acquisitions" and quality of life and to gain time to restructure its economies. But neither seclusion nor open or veiled protectionism are suitable means to overcome the consequences of a prolonged recession in an interdependent world.

Notes

1. Donald Keene, *The Japanese Discovery of Europe, 1720–1820* (Stanford, Calif.: Stanford University Press, 1969), p. 17.

2. Endymion Wilkinson, *Misunderstanding: Europe Versus Japan* (Tokyo: Chuokoron-sha, 1981), pp. 19–157.

3. Masamichi Hanabusa, *Trade Problems Between Japan and Western Europe* (New York: Praeger Publishers, 1979), p. 33.

4. Bernard K. Gordon, "Japan, the United States and South East Asia," *Foreign Affairs* 3 (1977), p. 582.

5. S. J. Park, "Japan's Strategies Toward a NIEO: Some Critical Views on Japan's Development Aid Policy" (unpublishsed paper presented at the workshop "Japan's Policy Strategies in a Trilateral Context," Geneva, 1982).

6. Endymion Wilkinson, "The Economic and Non-Economic Dimension of the European-Japanese Relationship" (unpublished paper presented at the workshop "Japan's Policy Strategies in a Trilateral Context," Geneva, 1982), p. 22.

7. Marlis G. Steinert, "The External Relations of the European Community," in *Policy Responses of the Changing International Environment,* edited by I. Dobozi and H. Matejka (Budapest: Hungarian Scientific Council for World Economy, 1981), pp. 77–78.

8. Albrecht Rothacher, *Economic Diplomacy Between the European Community and Japan 1959–1981* (Aldershot, Hampshire: Gower Publishing, 1983), p. 34.

9. *International Herald Tribune,* 10 February 1978, quoted in ibid., p. 243.

10. Expression introduced by Kawanaka, quoted by Chalmers Johnson, *MITI and the Japanese Miracle: The Growth of Industrial Policy, 1925–1975* (Stanford, Calif.: Stanford University Press, 1982), pp. 51, 45.

11. Henry Kissinger, *The White House Years* (London: Weidenfeld and Nicholson and Michael Joseph, 1979), pp. 324–325.

12. Marlis G. Steinert, "Un exemple de diplomatie de groupe: les activités de la Communauté économique européenne à Genève," *Relations internationales* 32 (1982), p. 547.

13. This section is based upon Marlis G. Steinert, *Le Japon en quête d'une politique étrangère* (Geneva: Centre Asiatique, Institut Universitaire de Hautes Études Internationales, 1981), pp. 125–134.

14. Rothacher, *Economic Diplomacy,* pp. 125–130.

15. *Financial Times,* 30 March 1979; *Guardian,* 30 March 1979.

16. Frank Langdon, "Japan Versus the European Community: The Automobile Crisis," *Journal of European Integration* (Canada) 1 (1981), pp. 79–98.

17. Communauté européenne, *Lettre d'information du Bureau de Genève* 2 (1983), p. 1.

18. *Neue Zürcher Zeitung,* 6 July 1983, p. 19; *Le Monde,* 23 September 1983, p. 34.

19. Organization for Economic Cooperation and Development (OECD), *Etudes économiques 1982–1983. Japon* (Paris: OECD, July 1983), p. 59.

20. *Bulletin des Communautés Européennes* 5 (1983), p. 59.

21. Headline of the *Japan Economic Review,* 15 July 1983, p. 9.

22. *Le Monde,* 23 September 1983, p. 34.

23. Rothacher, *Economic Diplomacy,* pp. 268, 269, 276; *Japan 1981/82, Politik und Wirtschaft,* edited by Manfred Pohl (Hamburg: Institut für Asienkunde, 1982), p. 91–92; Reinhold Drifte, "The European Community and Japan," *Journal of International Affairs* 1 (1983), pp. 159–160.

24. Frank Langdon, "Japan and West Europe," *Current History* 490 (November 1983), pp. 376–379, 395.

25. Rothacher, *Economic Diplomacy,* p. 320.

26. *Japan Economic Review,* 15 July 1983, p. 6.

27. Robert S. Ozaki, "Japan's Trade Controversy with West Europe," *Current History* 441 (1978), p. 186.

28. OECD, *Etudes économiques 1982–1983,* p. 12.

29. *Japan Economic Review,* 15 July 1983, pp. 6–7.

30. Consulat général du Japon à Genéve, *Nouvelles du Japon* (May-June 1983), pp. 1–2.

31. OECD, *Etudes économiques 1982–1983,* p. 50.

3
Japan and Oceania:
Strained Pacific Cooperation

Alan Rix

Japan is undeniably a powerful Pacific nation of the 1980s. For Australia and New Zealand, two small but sometimes influential countries of the region, Japan is also a dominant economic partner. The clichés about interdependence and a mature partnership that have been persistently used by governments to describe Japan's relations with its Oceanic neighbors have worn thin: Market prospects in Japan are poor for agricultural goods and raw materials, the core of Japan's trade with Australia and New Zealand; Australia's bilateral trade surplus with Japan is in decline; Japan's domestic economic changes have occurred far more quickly than Australian or New Zealand trade patterns have been able to adjust to them; and, in Australia's case at least, the growth of the bilateral trade in energy goods expected a few years ago has not occurred. As trade patterns shift and domestic recession continues in Australia and New Zealand, the balance of power and scope for initiative in each relationship seems to be moving firmly to Japan's advantage.

Conversely, the ability of Australia and New Zealand, as exporters of primary products and intermediate goods, to diversify and intensify the relationship with Japan is limited by the decline in Japanese demand and by competition from other suppliers. This chapter assesses recent difficulties in Japan's relations with Australia and New Zealand and their implications. These difficulties are a result of changing bilateral trade structures, depressed world market conditions for resources, specific Japanese economic-security policies, problems of the domestic management by Australia and New Zealand of diversifying Japanese demand, and a new Japan-centered balance of costs versus benefits in each economic relationship. The key issue in Japan's ties with Oceania is whether small states like Australia and New Zealand can exert any control over the direction of bilateral relations. That control effectively lies within the scope of Japanese policy, especially in trade, regional cooperation, and even political linkages. Australia and New Zealand are highly vulnerable as two of Japan's suppliers: Japan's global policies of resource supply diversification place Australia and New Zealand in a dependent position vis-à-vis Japanese demand, even though Australia is a major supplier of some commodities.

Past Prosperity and Optimism

Until the economic turbulence of the mid-1970s, Japan had enjoyed largely smooth and mutually beneficial ties with Australia and New Zealand. The relationship with Australia had been built up since World War II on the basis of complementary trade in Australian raw materials (wool, coal, and iron ore, in particular) and Japanese manufactured goods. By 1970/1971 Japan was Australia's largest trading partner. In New Zealand's case, bilateral trade with Japan also grew rapidly, although the complementarity was less obvious, and Japan was an unreliable market for New Zealand until certain raw materials such as aluminum and forest products became more important after the mid-1960s. The Japanese market for agricultural commodities was never entirely predictable, and Japan was not as important a market or source of supply to New Zealand as it was to Australia during the 1960s.

That decade was a period of great optimism, and the main concern of all three nations was to see trade flowing smoothly, political issues controlled, and levels of interdependence (at least in the Australia-Japan case) and cooperation raised. The attainment of these objectives by the early 1970s was facilitated by assiduous Japanese policies promoting economic growth and regional cooperation and by Australian willingness to develop its mines rapidly and to export raw materials. Limited Japanese investment in Australian resources, car assembly, and manufacturing was complemented by the ability of New Zealand and Australia to meet Japanese demand for agricultural products. Finally, government commitments in all countries paved the way for friendly but predictable relationships. Stability became the watchword, and this was possible as long as expectations of trade growth were met on both sides, which they were until about 1973 or 1974.

It was not simply the downturn in world economic growth after the oil crisis that broke this spell; government policy on both sides forced waiting issues to surface. For one thing, the politics of Japanese agricultural protectionism brought about the Japanese embargo on all beef imports in February 1974; this severely affected Australian exporters who provided over 80 percent of beef quota at the time.[1] Policies in Australia were also at issue. The Labor government's energetic commitment to strengthening national sovereignty over mineral resources worried Japan; Australia developed stricter controls over the export of, and foreign investment in, its minerals. The Japanese were further unsettled by the instability of Australia's foreign-investment and resources policies during the three years of Labor government up to 1975. Declining Japanese demand for some commodities exacerbated tensions, and by 1975 relations in the coal and iron-ore trades, for example, were bitter.[2] In New Zealand, the

Japanese beef embargo was also taken as a warning of Japan's unreliability. It planted the seeds of a practical and tough New Zealand policy toward Japan that was first articulated officially in 1976.[3]

Japan has always placed far greater emphasis on its economic and political relations with Australia than on those with New Zealand. In 1981 an official of the Japanese Ministry of Foreign Affairs stated that "frankly, it is difficult for Japan and New Zealand (unlike Australia) to develop an interdependent relationship as equal partners. The difference in scale of the New Zealand and Japanese economies is too wide."[4] Likewise, in Australia's economic (especially export) considerations, Japan has a more dominant place than it does in New Zealand: In 1971 for example, Japan took 27 percent of Australia's total exports and was its major export market; Japan took only 9 percent of New Zealand's export trade and was only its third-best customer. As a source of imports, however, Australia relied on Japan only slightly more (13.8 percent) than New Zealand (10.3 percent).[5]

The growing complexity of Japan's dealings with Australia in the 1970s accompanied growing (but slightly nervous) political and business confidence. Australia's diverse relationship with Japan was reflected in conscious and rapid broadening of its official dealings with Japan into cultural and political realms. By contrast, New Zealand's attitude to Japan after 1975 was based on more tenuous economic links. New Zealand had less with which to negotiate and higher short-term stakes, and its recognition of weakness led to a belligerent and product-centered policy toward Japan.

New Zealand's reversion to conservative government at the end of 1975 contributed to greater confrontation and argument with Japan over intractable trade issues. The Australian Labor government, dismissed in a domestic political crisis, was also defeated at election in December 1975 and replaced by a Liberal-Country party coalition. This change brought a more sober and stable—but no less nationalistic—Australian policy toward Japan, and the Japanese appreciated promises of predictability and reliability. The new Australian approach represented a desire to mollify Japanese criticism of a lack of "responsibility" in trade. As it happened, Japan has benefited greatly from its ties with Australia since 1976, for Australia's policy over market terms and conditions in the resources trade was inconsistent and wavered under pressure from Japanese buyers. The Australian position was slow to adapt to the longer-term adjustments in the trade relationship evidenced by realignments in the strength and direction of Japanese demand.

Trade Structures

Japan's experience in trade with both Australia and New Zealand since 1975 has been strained and has involved conflicts. Japanese diplomatic rhetoric remained placid and reassuring,[6] but structural changes away from heavy industry in Japan brought about a noticeable decline in its demand for raw materials and a realignment of bilateral trade. Australia's trade surplus with Japan shrank slightly after Australian fiscal year 1975/76 as Australian import costs rose more quickly than its export revenues.[7] The Japanese deficit was in fact halved between Australian fiscal years 1980/81 and 1981/82 to A$823.9 million. This is of great concern to Australia: Its imports of those commodities for which Japan is the prime source (electrical machinery, communications equipment, certain types of motor vehicles, iron and steel, and metal manufactures) are rising most quickly. Likewise for Japan's trade with New Zealand: The rapid increase in Japan's exports of electrical goods, cars, and trucks brought about a slight trade surplus in favor of Japan in calendar 1981 of US$24.9 million. The number of cars imported from Japan doubled, going from forty-one thousand to eighty-one thousand between 1979 and 1981. Demand in Japan for New Zealand's major exports to that country (aluminum, lumber, and wool) slipped, although the demand for lamb increased slightly.

The policy implications for the two Oceanic nations are highly significant. Japan's agricultural protectionism and policies to provide self-sufficiency have continued to incur the ire of Australia and New Zealand and of other governments. At the same time, Japan's industrial policy has reduced the demand for raw materials, supported a strong export drive, and thereby fundamentally altered the nature of Japan's economic relationship with its developed neighbors in Oceania.

Japanese demand for primary products was the original basis for Japan's postwar economic relations with both Australia and New Zealand. The ties built up (which had strong roots in prewar trade in wool and textiles) produced a firm commitment to bilateral trade by government and the private sector in all three countries. Such commitments were not, unfortunately, always permanent or unequivocal. As an example, the new conservative government in Australia sought in 1976 to consolidate and expand trade with Japan, to encourage broader and more stable ties, and to inject more Australian initiative into the relationship. Japanese agricultural import policies upset that strategy. In 1976 it appeared that Japan's beef import quota for the second half of the fiscal year would be cut from 45,000 to 20,000 tonnes as a result of a Japanese general election in December of that year. Australian pressure on Japan to maintain quota levels (which included some veiled threats by Australian ministers to deny port access to Japanese fishing vessels) was partly successful, but because of the political rigidities in Japan, Australia was really at the mercy of Japanese policy decisions. Japan responded more readily to an approach in a multilateral context and concluded an agreement with Australia in April 1979, as part of the Multilateral Trade Negotiation settlement, to assure a total of 135,000 tonnes of beef imports per annum by March 1983.[8]

Japan has made no fundamental revisions to its beef import policy since that time, although Australia's position has worsened. As far as

Japan is concerned, having a high percentage of a commodity trade held by one country is a source of insecurity that should be reduced: This course has been adopted in food as in raw materials. In addition, the segmentation of the Japanese domestic market for beef has allowed Japan to accommodate pressure from the United States at the expense of Australia: Rising demand in the high-quality beef sector of the market has been satisfied by imports from the United States, and Australia's share of the total beef market has declined from "an average of 83 percent over the three-year period 1975–77 to 71 percent in 1981."[9] More recent quota distributions have seen Australia's share go even lower, with increases in the U.S. and New Zealand shares.[10]

Australia relied (vainly, as it turned out) on its minerals trade with Japan as a buffer against a changing balance in the relationship, but Japan faced a more stubborn approach from New Zealand on agricultural imports. New Zealand had a sharper perception of its own clearly subordinate position with respect to Japan, and from 1976 on Japan faced a tenacious bargaining stance by Robert Muldoon, New Zealand's prime minister. Muldoon sought better access for New Zealand timber, dairy products, and meat to Japan in exchange for valuable tuna fishing rights in New Zealand waters. Japan had to be forcibly moved, as it was not prepared to accede to polite requests from a minor supplier like New Zealand.

Japan was certainly taken aback by Muldoon's abrasive and abrupt style. The New Zealand approach brought results at the time, for in July 1978 Japan agreed to trade access concessions in return for lifting the ban on the licensing of Japanese fishing vessels. Fearing flow-on demands from other countries, Japan insisted that parts of the agreement (for example, relating to beef access) remain confidential.[11] The apparent success of New Zealand's demands was due primarily to Japan's wish to preserve fishing rights. Nonetheless, placation of a minor trading partner like New Zealand carried fewer risks for Japan (especially when part of the agreement was secret) then a similar deal with a more significant supplier such as Australia.

Resources bargaining has not been an Australian policy and, as a result, Japan has generally found Australia rather eager to please. One exception—which caused the most rancorous Japan-Australia trade dispute since the mid-1970s—concerned Japanese imports of sugar and showed how difficult it is for all government and commercial interests in trade disputes to be satisfied. The issue at stake was a December 1974 long-term (five-year) contract between the Australian negotiators, CSR Limited, and Japanese sugar refiners that called for a fixed price based on a world price—a world price that was halved in the next six months. The owners of the sugar, the Queensland government, and CSR refused Japanese requests for price cuts and shipment deferrals, and government intervention was required to keep the commercial parties negotiating. The sight of sugar-laden ships riding at anchor in Tokyo Bay while the

Japanese refiners refused to accept, let alone unload or pay for, the sugar was testament to the gulf between Japanese and Australian views over the sanctity of written contracts. The dispute was resolved in October 1977 after both governments had pressed for compromises. Negotiations began in 1980 on a new long-term contract with a more complex price formula.

Japan's overall position as Australia's main trading partner has eased in recent years toward a lessening of Japanese dependence on Australian commodities: Australia could do little to exert much influence in trade. While the share of Australia's exports going to Japan fell (from 34 percent in 1976/77 to 27 percent in 1982/83), Japan's share as a supplier of imports to Australia did not drop. It remained at 21 percent, with a temporary fall to 16 percent in 1979/80. As a basis for understanding Japan's economic and political relationship with Australia, therefore, the notion of "interdependence" is of less relevance to both countries in the 1980s. Trade complementarity is not as strong and, at government level in Japan, Australia presents an important policy problem in that the level of the relationship is being scaled down, and effective management of that decline is required.

Japan's economic structure determines that this reduction is unavoidable over time, since Japan's domestic industries most relevant to trade with Australia are undergoing long-term readjustment. Many of Australia's major exports to Japan are locked into sectors of the Japanese economy that are declining in relative importance. For example, the Japanese steel industry is not likely to expand greatly in the future. Aluminum smelting is officially designated a "structurally recessed industry," as are spinning and pulp and paper. The bad news for Australian wool producers (who provide about 80 pecent of Japan's raw wool) is that the key to revitalization of the Japanese textile industry is said to be in large producers of synthetic fibers. The slower growth in demand for electric power means that, whatever forecasts are used, predictions for steaming-coal demand are not so optimistic as to see the energy trade as a new basis for trade revival.

The Australian government has recognized these developments, but has been far slower than the New Zealand government in attempting to gain a part of Japan's new and growing markets. When New Zealand took an unyielding stance on access for some goods, it also saw a need for enterprise in marketing, whereas Australia remained confident that Japan would continue to come to it for resources. New Zealand has been successful in selling Japan its fiberboard, fish oil, fruit and vegetables (including cherries and onions), flowers, and—with the greatest long-term potential—tourism.[12]

Japan's policy toward Australia and New Zealand has centered on trade, mainly in resources and raw materials. Japan's policies for the Pacific region have also focused on resources, for reasons of long-term economic security. One difficulty is that, apart from the trade and economic-security aspect, neither Australia nor New Zealand has meant much more to Japan in terms of its major political interests. Neither country in Oceania was essential to Japan's international diplomacy in the 1970s and, unless Japan launches a major Pacific-based policy (which admittedly is not out of the question), will not become so in the 1980s. Australia and New Zealand are friendly, safe, and, by and large, predictable; furthermore, Japan now has, for the most part, the upper hand in these economic relationships, barring perennial minor skirmishes over raw-materials issues.

The Resources Link

It has been over the resources trade with Australia that Japan has experienced greatest difficulty in its Oceania policy. Japan's postwar relations with the region, although not founded on resources, grew most quickly in the 1960s because of Japan's demand for the high-quality and low-cost raw materials that Australia (and later, in a smaller way, New Zealand) could provide: iron ore, coal, bauxite, alumina, woodchips, metals, wool, and foodstuffs. It was over those resources that the most serious and lasting rifts occurred with Australia, particularly over Japan's contractual obligations as a buyer. This was a clash made inevitable by the changing composition of Japan's requirements.

The most intractable issues relate to demand by the Japanese steel industry, in which production dropped in fiscal 1982 for the third consecutive year.[13] Australia has long been the major supplier of coal and iron ore to that industry, and its raw-materials export industry relies overwhelmingly on the Japanese market. Australian industry and government are therefore loath to see the market share in Japan dwindle, particularly for the benefit of U.S. or other exporters. Third-country pressure on Japan in the 1980s to buy more coal—such as that from the West Coast of the United States—is politically easier for Japan to accede to, especially when demands are made in the context of the large bilateral trade deficit with the United States.

Japan's major interest is in diversifying its sources sufficiently to cushion its own security of supply and to ease further adjustments over the longer term. A 1980 Japanese report on the Japan-Australia relationship was blunt in stating that "to reach appropriate prices and secure necessary imports in unforeseen circumstances, it will be necessary for Japan to diversify her import sources beyond Australia. In particular, when those import sources are either developing or Asian-Pacific countries, resources development can link up with Japan's policies of economic cooperation to promote development in those countries. This makes diversification of sources of supply all the more important."[14]

Japan's assurance to Australia of a 46–47 percent share in Japan's iron-ore purchases[15] is certainly higher than the 35 percent of 1970, but is equal to the share in 1973 and comes at a time when Australia's dependence on Japan as an iron-ore market is rising again (from 72.4 percent in 1978/79 to 76.5 percent in 1980/81). After the return to a bilateral rhetoric of trade stability in 1976, the Australian government was under continued pressure from its own exporters to achieve better prices and sustained tonnages of coal and iron ore—not an easy task when Japanese demand was itself falling. Japan continued to give formal reassurances to Australia, but always with a polite but pointed reminder about Australia's need to remain "internationally competitive." The Australian government in October 1978 even tried to enforce government pricing guidelines in a bid to cartelize exporters to achieve a tougher Australian bargaining stance, but internal political differences in Australia (minerals-producing state governments opposed the national government) defeated it.[16]

Japan will continue to be a flat market in the 1980s for coking coal and iron ore. Since the mid-1970s individual Australian companies have faced progressive price and quantity falls. Japanese buyers now appear to have informally placed ceilings on Australia's share of the market—thus an upper limit of 48 percent for the iron-ore market in Japan. Likewise, for coking coal, Australia's share is declining and in 1981/82 was down to 38 percent,[17] although optimistic forecasts of Australia's share in 1990 generally predict between 40 and 49 percent.

A more subtle approach has been adopted by Japan over its requirements for energy goods. It was only as recently as 1979 that officials in both Australia and Japan were predicting a boom in the bilateral energy trade. Since then, expectations of rapid growth have been dampened by world recession and by more sober Japanese assessments. Reduced Japanese interest in energy goods affects not only steaming coal but also uranium and liquified natural gas (LNG). Japanese energy utilities are both investors and buyers in Australia's North-West Shelf gas project, but the Japanese have diversified the sources of their supplies widely, and natural-gas demand forecasts are not buoyant by any means.

Development of steaming-coal production in Australia in recent years was predicated on Japanese forecasts of energy consumption that were, for Japanese domestic policy reasons, consciously inflated and that have been revised downward since 1976. At that time, for example, Japan was forecasting imports of 102 million tons of coal and 42 million tons of LNG in 1985. In the 1979 figures these quantities had dropped to 101 and 29 million tons respectively, and in 1982 and 1983 they were again revised. The new projections were partly the result of formal Australian government and industry complaints about unrealistic figures, but there is still some degree of uncertainty. The 1983 predictions show a demand for upwards of 90 million tons of imported coal in 1990, and 37 or 38 million tons of LNG in the same year.[18]

Japan has been circumspect in its dealings with Australia on uranium, taking much time and care before agreeing in 1982 to strict Australian requirements (introduced in 1977) for a uranium safeguards agreement.

Japan was at first unwilling to agree to Australian demands for controls over reprocessing and other stages of the nuclear fuel cycle, in spite of several relevant circumstances: Without an agreement Australian exports of uranium to Japan would have been forbidden, Australia had concluded similar agreements with several other countries including France, Japan had sufficient reserves of uranium until 1990, and the outlook for nuclear-energy demand in Japan continued to worsen. Japan was distinctly reluctant to accept Australian policy on this issue and clearly preferred to retain as free a hand as it could in its resources procurement.

In these and other ways, resources is a policy area in which Japan has been very careful to maneuver, and Japan is strong enough in many resource markets to be able to sidestep crude forms of resource bargaining. New Zealand's maritime resources diplomacy between 1976 and 1978 was touted as a successful gambit at the time. It was only partially successful, for "assured and stable access agreements" on several commodities were not achieved. In a 1981 visit to Japan, Prime Minster Muldoon was still pressing for improved access for dairy products and sawn timber.[19] By contrast, the Australian approach was not one of blunt resources bargaining—its experience was generally that such methods brought only short-term remedies, and its policy of eschewing such resources bargaining has certainly kept tension in the relationship at a lower level. But Australia did seek gradually to exclude Japanese tuna long-liners from the Australian Fishing Zone over a period of years after the zone was proclaimed on 1 November 1979. A series of annual negotiations reduced Japanese access significantly to aid conservation of southern bluefin tuna stocks, to allow the Australian fishing industry greater areas of operation, and to gain access for Australian-caught tuna to the Japanese domestic market. A tripartite arrangement now includes New Zealand in discussion about managing the tuna resource, which passes through both Australian and New Zealand waters in its migrations.

In the fishing negotiations with Australia, the Japanese carefully ignored Australian arguments about the links between fisheries access and the "wider economic relationship." Overall, it was not a linkage pushed hard or consistently by Australia and the absence of resources trade-offs in the fishing talks suggests that Australia recognized the difficulty of using a relatively minor issue in the relationship to alter entrenched Japanese agricultural import policy. New Zealand, however, had a less diversified relationship, and fishing was not a minor matter. As a result bargaining had to be taken to a fairly extreme form.[20]

The resource trade, therefore, reflects fundamental structural changes in the Japanese economy and industry—changes to which resource buyers and suppliers alike in Australia and New Zealand have had difficulty in adjusting. It is obvious that rational Japanese policies of import diversification and lessening of particular dependences (such as in coal and iron ore) have had severe effects on Australian raw-materials industries. Australian government efforts have not halted the so far slight decline in Australia's importance to Japan. For Australia this decline will ultimately be of benefit in reducing its overreliance on its major trading partner, but efforts need to be made by Australian resource producers either to offset the loss of demand due to Japanese policies or to take advantage of new opportunities in the Japanese market for other commodities.

Political Management of the Relationship

Tensions in the economic relationships between Japan and its two neighbors in Oceania impose political costs on all three nations. One response by all has been to seek to widen the scope and content of bilateral dealings: first, into political and cultural spheres, and second, into a regional framework. This is a common enough practice in international relations, particularly in an era of complex transnational ties. Japan eagerly supported moves over the 1970s to dilute the economic bias in its policy toward Australia and New Zealand, something which it did as part of a general policy of "cultural diplomacy."

Japan has been an enthusiastic promoter of the cultural-relations aspects of its internationl diplomacy. Increased intercultural contact by itself cannot rectify economic disputes, but it can divert attention from the immediate effects. However, Australia was more concerned to lay a basis for a relationship that could be insulated from the bitterness of economic confrontation and some lingering memories of the war. New Zealand, likewise, recognized in a more practical vein that "an accurate perception of each other's culture has importance for the material relationship."[21] All three countries, therefore, had slightly different reasons for extending the scope of the relationship: Japan, to dilute the reality of economic dependence; Australia, to protect its high but sensitive levels of trade; and New Zealand, to expand its limited opportunities in Japan.

The most far-reaching Australian initiative in the political relationship was the broad bilateral Basic Treaty of Friendship and Cooperation, first proposed in 1973 by Australia's Prime Minister Gough Whitlam and signed in June 1976 by his successor, J. M. Fraser. Although in the negotiations Japan unsuccessfully attempted to gain retrospective most-favored-nation treatment in entry rights, the treaty is an important formal commitment by both countries to policies and standards of cooperation and fair dealing. But the treaty is also criticized for being little more than a general statement of principles and intent. Japan gives Australia, for example, an undertaking of cooperation in the resources trade, but this and other key economic clauses are couched in the form of "best endeavors" rather than hard commitments. The treaty is a symbolic political document and has rarely been invoked in economic disputes between Australia and Japan.

The basic treaty represented a conscious Australian policy of injecting more Australian content into the relationship. Perceptions and fears can become relevant in international relations, and Australian fears of being dominated by Japan have been a powerful spur to some very firm policies. Such policies characterized not only the political relationship and the resources area, but Australia's foreign-investment guidelines as well. One of Japan's major concerns up until 1975 was the strident "economic nationalism" of the Labor Party government of 1972 to 1975, and the Japanese therefore welcomed the change of government. In the foreign-investment area, however, Fraser's conservative administration held to its pledge to Japan of "predictability and stability" by retaining the essence of its predecessor's tough scrutiny of foreign-investment proposals.

The policy, said the new government, was to be nondiscriminatory and nonpreferential. Japan wanted preference given to Japanese investors to aid Japanese investment in resource projects, but the Australian government held to its nondiscriminatory stance. Market conditions, rather than government policy, have affected Japanese investment flows since 1976; portfolio investment and institutional loans from Japan to Australia have increased to take advantage of high interest rates, while direct investment has slowed. This has matched similar trends in investment from the United Kingdom, the United States, and the Association of Southeast Asian Nations (ASEAN). An interesting pattern is the unusually low rate of Japanese investment in the mining industry (Japan owned only 3.3 percent of the Australian mining industry in 1981/82), a higher but fluctuating investment in manufacturing, but a most rapid rise in "other" industries, notably finance, wholesale and retail, and property. In 1981/82, the levels of Japanese investment were $118 million, $291 million and $768 million respectively in the mining, manufacturing, and "other" industries.

The most intensive Japanese investment in Australia since the mid-1970s, with wide political and economic effects, was in the car industry. Australia has not experienced the direct external threat of Japanese auto imports in the same way as the United States and Europe, because Japanese firms were persuaded to invest in manufacturing plants in Australia in 1976, after some years of assembling. The companies were told by the Australian government that establishing local manufacturing operations was preferable to increased Australian import restrictions, and the Japanese firms agreed. This large-scale investment has led to Japanese dominance of the Australian domestic car market. Three of the five manufacturing firms are now Japanese (Toyota, Nissan, and Mitsubishi, which took over Chrysler's operations in 1980), and half of the passenger cars sold in 1980 were Japanese-designed or -built. That figure has been forecast to rise to 65–75 percent by 1985;[22] in other categories of motor vehicles (trucks, light commercials, and off-road vehicles) the picture is similar.

Political diversification in relations with Japan, therefore, has not been easy for Australia, and a speech by Australian Prime Minister Hawke in August 1983 suggested that attempts to provide a buffer for economic

difficulties have not been successful. He pointed out the "virtual transformation of the economic basis of the relationship" and made the strong
point that "what is needed to develop the Australian trading relationship
with Japan is hard work, resourcefulness and imagination. . . . The
complacency of the past, engendered as it may have been by the extent
and depth of the Japanese relationship, must now give way to a constructive
exploration of ways of carrying the relationship forward. . . . Constant
attention must be given to the fundamentals if our mutual interests are
to be furthered."[23]

Japan's political ties with New Zealand are limited to cultural-exchange
policies and regional consultations. Japan has become wary of the potential
for sudden politicization of trade with that country. Of course Japan's
own trade restrictions are partly to blame (especially its delays over the
import of sawn timber), but it is anxious to avoid stimulating anew the
feeling of desperation that dominated New Zealand policy from 1976
to 1978. It is perhaps indicative of Japan's view of New Zealand's
approach that an official Ministry of Foreign Affairs report on Japan–
New Zealand relations in 1981 should conclude with recommendations
that all related to cultural affairs and none to bilateral trade.[24]

The Pacific

One policy issue that has touched all three nations is that of the
Pacific Community. This was originally a Japanese initiative, which has
since very successfully entered the mainstream of public debate on the
future of the Pacific region. As a result, Japan's relations with both
Australia and New Zealand have been strongly influenced by the possibility
of formal regional cooperation. Also, both Australia and New Zealand
have benefited from the clearer view of long-term Japanese objectives in
the region that the Pacific Community concept has brought to the surface
in the last five years.

Japan's active support for discussion of the Pacific Community concept
had its origins in the 1950s and 1960s, when many academics and
officials in Japan were discussing appropriate directions for Japan's postwar
economic diplomacy. Takeo Miki, as foreign minister in the late 1960s,
pressed so far as to make a proposal for Pacific regional cooperation. It
was not taken up at a high political level again until 1978, when
Masayoshi Ohira made it part of his foreign-policy platform before
assuming office as prime minister. Others in Japan had also rekindled
the idea, particularly in the context of Japan's "overall security," and
an official report prepared for Ohira in 1980 was heavily weighted to
the resource and food security aspects of Pacific cooperation. Although
much of the report was overlain with discussion of cultural and educational
issues, suggesting a Japanese preference for playing down the overt
economic approach, the resources focus highlighted the basic objectives
of Japanese thinking.

The Pacific Community idea rapidly gained regional political support in 1979 and 1980, when Ohira visited Australia and New Zealand and won the backing of Australia's Fraser and New Zealand's Muldoon for a government-sponsored but private seminar on the subject. The seminar was subsequently held in Canberra in September 1980. But the more the possibilities of a formal Pacific grouping were discussed, the greater the potential difficulties of "Pacific" cooperation that emerged. It was seen to threaten the interests of existing regional groupings like ASEAN (to which Australia was very sensitive) and the South Pacific Forum (which neither Australia nor New Zealand wished to see endangered). Also unresolved was the question of leadership and responsibility for carrying the concept further politically. Predictably, Japan decried any active role in promoting the idea, preferring others such as Australia and South Korea to test the political waters first. In the end Australia shied away from going into those waters too far, and formal Pacific cooperation awaits another political initiative that, in an increasingly tense trans-Pacific economic and defense climate, would not be well-timed.[25]

The political challenges of a Pacific policy are particularly complex and taxing for Japan. Not only must Japan thread a careful path between bilateral trade difficulties with Australia, New Zealand, and its larger Pacific trading partner, the United States, but questions of defense and security are growing in importance to Japan's regional responsibilities. The Pacific Community concept was for Japan primarily a further means toward its national comprehensive security. Japan's reluctance to take the lead on the issue is therefore not surprising, but at least Japan was one of the few countries involved with a clear set of economic and political objectives based on the community concept. The New Zealand and particularly the Australian governments were wedded to vaguer ideas of regional cooperation in several policy areas. The availability of structured resource markets in the region would have produced benefits, although they exist in any case in a less predictable form. Australia's and New Zealand's interests would be served best by improved levels of consultation and communication at government level, something that high levels of Pacific transnational interaction already render necessary.

The implications of Japan's security policies are not limited to regional economic arrangements; they also have a military dimension. The recent expansion of Japan's Self-Defense Forces and its commitment to a wider regional security role have forced a rethinking in Australia of its approach to Japanese defense policy. Both Australia and New Zealand have, over the years, supported Japan's limited defense role. Since all three nations possess formal security-treaty links with the United States (Australia and New Zealand in the ANZUS [Australia–New Zealand–United States] Pact, signed on 1 September 1951, a week before the U.S.–Japan Mutual Security Treaty), there existed a level of common commitment to Pacific security. There has been political support in Japan for the steady expansion of Japan's defense budget under conditions of fiscal rigidity since 1980. This has involved a quite rapid increase in the ratio of defense expenditure to gross national product (GNP) from 0.90 in fiscal 1980 to 0.98 in fiscal 1983. Prime Minister Nakasone's policy of cooperation with the United States against a perceived Soviet threat has taken rhetorical form but has also led to concrete commitments such as providing military technology to the United States, extending sea-lane defense and upgrading joint defense maneuvers. This cooperation has altered Pacific defense arrangements.

In 1981 Australia's former Prime Minister Fraser publicly backed the U.S. position that Japan should take greater responsibility for its own defense.[26] No Australian minister under his government said any more than this, and Australia's new ambassador to Japan in December 1982 admitted that Australia had no clear policy on Japan's defense buildup. However, the Labor government that came to office in March 1983 enunciated a detailed policy toward Japanese defense. During a visit to Tokyo in July 1983, Foreign Minister Tom Hayden expressed Australia's interest in a harmonious U.S.-Japan defense relationship. But he warned that "Australia would be concerned if—either as a result of external pressure or internal decision—there were a shift in Japan's basic defence posture, or a dramatic acceleration of defence spending. . . . Australia would also be concerned if Japan were to attempt to develop a regional security role. This would have a destabilising effect on the Asia-Pacific region."[27] Hayden emphasized that a more effective Japanese role could lie in its nonmilitary contributions to regional security, through aid and its political and diplomatic activities.

Japan has a modest level of defense cooperation with Australia and New Zealand, principally in the area of combined naval exercises and regular official defense discussions. Australia wants to maintain these contacts, and Japan wishes to keep as strong as possible defense ties with its important regional trading partners. The real question for Japan is whether and to what extent an increased defense capacity will entail more extensive regional defense cooperation and an independent Japanese defense presence in the Southeast Asia–Oceania region. This is unlikely to involve Japanese defense activities in Oceania: Rather more likely is a form of Australian and New Zealand support for a Japanese Pacific naval presence, sea-lane defense, or regional peacekeeping activities. Present Australian policy would preclude such support, but it is not clear that Japanese policy rules out regional defense activity. Japan has agreed to patrol waters up to one thousand nautical miles from Tokyo, and the *Defense of Japan 1982* (the official English translation of the 1982 White Paper) states that "Japan must protect her sea lanes to ensure the import of essential commodities."[28] The 1983 Defense White Paper extends this to claim that Japan has a right to defend foreign ships with a cargo for Japan.[29] Japanese defense activity is likely, therefore, to be closely aligned to its economic interests. Australia is already a part of that economic-security framework, and the Japanese foreign minister was recently reported as describing the Japan-Australia relationship as "an economic alliance."[30] Japan's security thinking seems to pervade its economic diplomacy.

The 1980s

Japan's relations with Australia and New Zealand are in some ways quite vulnerable. Despite high levels of economic interdependence in the past and efforts by all three countries to broaden the political and cultural base of their policies, neither Australia nor New Zealand has strongly influenced Japanese goals and policies. There is a danger, therefore, that Japan could easily alienate people in both countries as the harsher realities of changing trade structures become apparent. That has already happened to New Zealand once, and that country's trade compromise with Japan in 1978 required the terms to be secret before Japan could accept New Zealand's demands for better trade access.

Japan cannot, however, rely on a foreign economic policy anchored to secret trade deals. For Australia's part, the need to revitalize trade with Japan is clear and accepted, but Japan appears to have rejected initial Australian attempts to place trade on a longer-term footing.[31] Even Japanese ministerial assurances about isolating the Australia-Japan trade from third-country pressure are a little hollow when U.S. demands for Japan to accept more U.S. coal play off one Japanese ministry (the Foreign Ministry) against another (the Ministry of International Trade and Industry—MITI).[32] In that sense, Japanese decision-making processes cannot necessarily be relied on to provide coherent policies in the short term. The balance of Japan's bilateral political and trade interests can change quite rapidly, and the ultimate arbiter in Japanese decisions will be different ministries' views about Japanese security. In the end, of course, Japanese policy will serve Japanese interests, not those of its trade partners.

To the extent that Japan's interests lie in a Pacific Community, it is important for it to reach acceptable trade terms with Australia and New Zealand. This is largely because both those nations will have a significant influence over developments toward regional trade and security arrangements and because friction in raw-materials trade will inevitably increase in the coming few years, until Australia consolidates its alternative markets and achieves a long-term competitive position in the Japanese market. Japan would therefore gain by broadening as far as possible its political, cultural, and defense contacts with both countries.

The implication here is that Japan's traditionally cooperative and beneficial ties with Australia and New Zealand could be undermined by an excessive Japanese preoccupation with its broad security interests. It is essential for Japan that its national pursuit of security does not lead to feelings of exploitation or, even worse, suspicion and fear on the part of Australians and New Zealanders. This would be an unfortunate, but not unpredictable, reaction.

Japan's objectives in regional cooperation will likely continue to dictate that Australia and New Zealand not be alienated. Especially because of Australia's regional role as a resource and food supplier (now including oil exports on a small scale), Australia will be pivotal to the debate about regional cooperative arrangements in the 1980s. Australia and New Zealand will be necessary in any Pacific cooperation that, given Japan's emphasis on the importance of stability, predictability, and security in its foreign economic policy, will never be far from Japan's principal goals in the region.

Notes

1. For a discussion of this, see D.C.S. Sissons, "Japan," in W. J. Hudson, ed., *Australia in World Affairs 1971–75* (Sydney: George Allen and Unwin, 1980).

2. The 1975 coa negotiations had left, said one Japanese industry journal, "a stain on the histoιy of Australia-Japan relations." *Australian Financial Review,* hereafter *AFR,* 28 January 1976.

3. Juliet Lodge, "New Zealand Foreign Policy in 1976," *Australia Outlook* 31, 1 (April 1977), pp. 88–89.

4. Gaimushō ōakyoku, *80 nendai no wagakuni taiyōshū gaikō* [Ministry of Foreign Affairs, Japan's relations with the Pacific in the 1980s] (Tokyo, 1981), p. 137.

5. Statistics in this chapter are drawn from the Australian Bureau of Statistics; Australia-Japan Economic Institute, *The Australia-Japan Relationship: A Statistical Review* (Sydney, 1980); Sixteenth Foreign Policy School 1981, *New Zealand and Japan* (Dunedin: University of Otago Extension, 1981), pp. 61–62; and Ministry of International Trade and Industry, *White Paper on International Trade* (Tokyo, 1982).

6. As in the Ministry of Foreign Affairs' report, *80 nendai no nichigō kankei* [Japan-Australia relations in the 1980s] (Tokyo, 1980).

7. All years are calendar years except those in the form 1975/76, which are Australian financial years (July through June).

8. For a detailed analysis of the period 1976 to 1980, see Alan Rix, "Australia and East Asia: Japan," in P. J. Boyce and J. R. Angel, eds., *Independence and Alliance: Australia in World Affairs 1976–80* (Sydney: George Allen and Unwin, 1983), pp. 189–206.

9. Aurelia George, *The Changing Patterns of Japan's Agricultural Import Trade: Implications for Australia,* Pacific Economic Papers no. 100 (Canberra: Australia-Japan Research Centre, 1983), p. 16.

10. *The Australian,* 24 June 1983.

11. According, at least, to the New Zealand prime minister in Robert Muldoon, *My Way* (Wellington: Reed, 1981), pp. 122–123.

12. Graham Kitson, "Prospects and Perspectives in New Zealand/Japan Trade," in Sixteenth Foreign Policy School, *New Zealand and Japan,* pp. 69–70.

13. *Nippon Steel News* 161 (October 1983), p. 2.

14. Ministry of Foreign Affairs, *Japan-Australia Relations in the 1980s,* p. 47.

15. *AFR,* 22 October 1982.

16. Rix, "Australia and East Asia."

17. Economist Intelligence Unit, *Coal in Australia: Prospects to 1990* (London: Economist Intelligence Unit, 1983), p. 26.

18. The 1976 and 1979 figures are from official MITI forecasts. The 1983 figures were reported in *AFR,* 23 August 1983.

19. See *Asahi Shimbun,* 16 and 18 April 1981.

20. G.W.P. George, "Linkage Diplomacy: New Zealand's and Australia's Fisheries Access Negotiations with Japan," *Australia Outlook* 36, 1 (April 1982), pp. 39–45.

21. New Zealand's Foreign Minister Brian Talboys, "New Zealand and Japan," in Sixteenth Foreign Policy School, *New Zealand and Japan,* p. 9.

22. *AFR,* 2 January 1981.

23. R. J. Hawke, "An Australian View of the World," speech to the 50th Anniversary Conference of the Australian Institute of International Affairs, 26 August 1983.

24. Ministry of Foreign Affairs, *Japan's Relations with the Pacific in the 1980s,* pp. 142–143.

25. The best collection of papers on the Pacific Community concept is Sir John Crawford and Greg Seow, eds., *Pacific Economic Cooperation: Suggestions for Action* (Selangor: Heinemann Asia, 1981).

26. *AFR,* 6 July 1981.

27. Minister for foreign affairs, press release, 27 July 1983.

28. Defense Agency, *Defense of Japan 1982* (Tokyo: Defense Agency, 1982) p. 58.

29. *AFR,* 29 August 1983.

30. Australian Foreign Minister Tom Hayden, in transcript of his Tokyo press conference, 25 July 1983.

31. *AFR,* 29 August 1983.

32. *AFR,* 25 August 1983.

Part 2

Socialist Countries

4
Japan and the Soviet Union

J.A.A. Stockwin

The usual stereotype of relations between Japan and the Soviet Union is that they are bad, getting worse, and unlikely to improve. Indeed, relations between the two countries since the slight thaw of the early 1970s give few grounds for an optimistic assessment. A recent article by Chalmers Johnson even goes so far as to argue that "during 1983 . . . it became at least possible that an American–Japanese–South Korean entente will confront the Soviet Union and replace the Sino-Soviet dispute as the most important security configuration in East Asia."[1] The argument, however, that will be developed in this chapter is that although there are strong historical, political, and strategic reasons why relations between Japan and the Soviet Union are unlikely to become warm and friendly in the foreseeable future, there are also factors that could conceivably draw them closer together. The problem in assessing possible future trends is to strike a balance between the factors that tend to pit the two nations against each other and those that might tend to restrict the scope of their antagonism.

On the face of it, it would be surprising if the two nations were anything but cool and suspicious toward each other. Historically they have been rivals for supremacy in Northeast Asia and have fought each other in big and small wars during this century. Toward Russians, Japanese experience little of the cultural sympathy many of them feel toward Chinese, and the social, political, and economic systems of the two countries appear to have little in common. Japan's long-standing security relationship with the United States, its links with the Republic of Korea, and its 1978 Peace and Friendship Treaty with the People's Republic of China appear to place Japan and the USSR in antagonistic security blocs, and the dispute over the "northern islands" continues to inhibit improvement in the relationship. Moreover, a heightening of tensions is manifest since the Soviet invasion of Afghanistan, with enhanced fortification of Soviet territories to the north of Japan. The shooting down over Sakhalin of a Korean Airlines jumbo jet in August 1983 was a shocking reminder to Japan of Soviet willingness to use violence.

On the other hand, successive Japanese governments have made efforts to improve, or at least to avoid worsening, their relations with the USSR. The latest such efforts were talks on 12–13 March 1984 between the two sides at the level of deputy foreign minister.[2] Moreover, if only the politics were right, Japanese industry would be excellently placed to participate in the development of the resources of eastern Siberia, and actual trade between the two sides, although far below the level of what might be economically possible, remains far from negligible. Perhaps most important, despite Japan's clear security ties with the United States, there remains a substantial and influential body of opinion in Japan that feels uncomfortable with a situation in which Japan–U.S. security linkages uniquely define the Japanese foreign policy and defense position.[3]

Let us therefore examine in more detail the factors creating ill feeling and inhibiting a working relationship before going on to discuss factors that have tended or might tend to inhibit escalation of conflict.

Factors That Exacerbate Conflict

Territoriality

The nineteenth century saw the expansion of the Russian empire into the eastern part of Siberia and the early Japanese colonization of Hokkaido and islands to its north. This inevitably brought the two nations into direct contact and later into conflict. The Russo-Japanese war of 1905–1906 was a major war by the standards of the time and established Japan as the first Asian participant of significance in a European-dominated international system. Russia was simultaneously exposed (a trifle unfairly, perhaps, because the war had scarcely been a walkover for Japan) as an inefficient and ramshackle empire. When the Bolsheviks took control of Russia, the conservatively minded Japanese government joined with several others in sending troops to support the "white" forces. Japan's Siberian Expedition was to last for four years, from 1918 to 1922, and undoubtedly etched into the Soviet mind an enduring suspicion of the Japanese.

Even though the Soviet Union and Japan refrained from fighting each other between 1941 and 1945 under the terms of the neutrality pact of 1941,[4] Stalin's entry into the war in its final week following a secret Allied agreement at Yalta led to the swift collapse of Japanese forces on the mainland of Northeast Asia. It also subsequently came to rest in the Japanese folk memory as an act of perfidy comparable to the way Pearl Harbor has been regarded in the West.[5] Large numbers of Japanese prisoners, captured by the Red Army during the final week of the war, were held in Siberia until the 1950s and were released into Japanese society only following intensive indoctrination.

Fisheries and fishing grounds have been a regular area of contention between the two countries, while the long-running dispute over three islands and one group of islands to the northeast of Hokkaido has been a constant reminder of unfinished business inherited from World War II. The failure to reach accord on the territorial dispute has prevented the conclusion of a peace treaty, thus leaving Japan and the Soviet Union technically in a state of war.

Divergent Socioeconomic Systems

The differences between them, however, go far beyond unhappy historical memories and an unresolved territorial dispute. Their social, political, and economic systems diverge in fundamental ways. The Soviet Union operates a severely authoritarian[6] political system in which the Communist Party of the Soviet Union (CPSU) functions according to the Leninist principle of "democratic centralism." This principle embodies a vertical command structure in a bureaucratically organized hierarchy, with severe restrictions on horizontal communication and extreme limitations in practice on the extent to which lower echelons are able to influence higher echelons of the hierarchy. Fundamental to the system is the fact that there are at least two parallel bureaucracies, that of the party and that of the state. In the running of industry, for instance, the bureaucratic structures under the control of government ministries have parallel party structures at every level whose role is to check on performance, ensure that party policy and directives are being carried out, and generally impart dynamism to the work that is being performed. In addition, the armed forces and the security services play a powerful political role, though maybe it is wrong to suggest that they are in any real sense "independent" of the CPSU. Indeed, one of the key features of the system is the interlocking nature of the various political structures, especially at top levels. The top party leadership, through its *nomenklatura* procedures, determines a very wide range of lower-level appointments throughout the system.

Several features of the Soviet system, some of them stemming directly from its formal organization, need to be noted. The first is that at least in its traditions, ideology, and rhetoric, the Soviet Union is "goal oriented." That is to say, the principles that guide the regime are fundamentally concerned with planning, goal setting, guidance, and control and accord little legitimacy to the unstructured free play of human endeavor. The regime justifies this approach in terms of the merits it sees in large-scale coordination and economy of effort, whereas its critics point not only to the low level of individual freedom but also to stifling bureaucracy and inefficiency stemming from the crushing of individual or group initiative. Second, although nominally "democratic" procedures of election are followed, in practice at all elections in the USSR a single slate of candidates is presented, all of whom are endorsed by the CPSU, and the electoral turnout is close to 100 percent. This suggests that the purpose of elections to "legislative" bodies is that of providing a show of legitimacy for decisions taken elsewhere rather than allowing the electorate to influence decisions in any way. Third, the system has a serious problem in effecting and legitimating top leadership succession, the determination of which is in any case surrounded by great secrecy (as are many political activities in the USSR). Succession to central power at the apex of the system seems to be largely determined by the ability of an individual to attract majority support in the Politburo of the CPSU. In recent years, however, this has placed at the very top of the regime men of advanced age and infirm health whose capacity for innovative, dynamic leadership is questionable. And fourth, the path of political power in such a secretive and closed system is inevitably through the cultivation of informal structures of support that may be referred to as cliques or factions, though such terminology probably oversimplifies a highly complex reality.

When we turn to Japan the differences are obvious enough. In a fundamental sense Japan enjoys an open political system, with free competitive elections regularly conducted for legislative bodies at national and local levels, and a cabinet formed by the majority party or parties in parliament, to which it is responsible. The press and other media are free to criticize the government and virtually any of its policies and do so with considerable determination and skill. The management of economic activity is largely in private hands, and industrial enterprises compete with each other keenly. The Liberal-Democratic party (LDP), continuously elected to power at the national level in free elections since the 1950s, is broadly liberal-conservative in its orientation and talks a political language sharply distinct from that of its Soviet counterpart. Political parties in opposition to the LDP operate freely, and their policy preferences have on occasion been influential, though obviously far less so than if some combination of them had been able to attain power.

In the making of policy, particularly economic policy, the government bureaucracy exercises a powerful role. This is partly because of a tradition of bureaucratic power and effectiveness stemming back to the prewar period, partly because the party in office has not changed so that continuity of bureaucratic influence becomes possible, and partly a result of links established within an elite that includes representatives of industry as well as government officials and politicians. The relatively weak (though not entirely negligible) political role of organized labor also conspicuously strengthens the hand of government and industry in developing economic policies designed to promote economic efficiency and competitiveness, even if the politically powerful agricultural lobby has been able to exercise political influence that has often distorted economic rationality. In stark contrast to the Soviet Union, however, Japan has managed to develop a politico-economic system combining a large measure of political openness with a dynamic, thrusting economy. Indeed, the Japanese gross national product (GNP) is believed to have surpassed that of the Soviet Union (hitherto second only to the United States) sometime in the early 1980s. It is also worth noting that one of the problems commonly mentioned by Japanese industrialists attempting to do business with their Soviet counterparts is that excessively bureaucratic and unreliable procedures on the Soviet side make the conduct of negotiations unusually frustrating.[7]

Strategic Relationships

When we turn from socioeconomic contrasts to the Japan-Soviet strategic relationship, we see again that the situations and attitudes of the two regimes could scarcely be more different nor, it may well be argued, the prospects for their mutual accommodation more dim. At the level of geostrategic conditions the contrast is most marked. The Soviet Union (under whatever regime) is fundamentally a land-based power, blessed with generous natural resources of its own, many of which as yet are undeveloped. A policy of economic autarky is possible to an extent unimaginable for Japan. The land area of the Soviet Union is actually more than twice the size of Canada, the second-largest country in the world. Moreover, unlike Canada, the USSR has historically been cursed with the longest land borders in the world, traditionally difficult to secure against hostile powers. The attempt to secure naturally indefensible borders has generated a belief common to most Russian rulers that still further extension of the borders (or failing that, extension of areas over which the empire has direct influence) is the most effective means of security. It is arguable that the establishment of a Communist regime following the Bolshevik revolution of 1917 ended up reinforcing traditional notions of national security, though the catastrophic Soviet losses in the war against Hitler served further to reinforce these perceptions. The USSR is now a nuclear superpower engaged in a nuclear arms race with the United States and spending perhaps 15 percent of its GNP on defense.

Japan, by contrast, is a nation almost without natural resources, a mere one and a half times the size of Great Britain, surrounded on all sides by sea, and forced to make optimum use of the one resource it has in abundance—skilled and readily organizable manpower. The "catch-up" mentality so deeply embedded in the Japanese consciousness since the opening of the country to the outside world in the middle of the nineteenth century ensured a dynamic economy, whereas the attempt to carve out an empire and thus control markets and sources of supply for its industries collapsed catastrophically in 1945.

Japan went ahead from the 1950s to make a virtue out of necessity by creating what is now perhaps the most competitive and dynamic economy of the contemporary world. Admittedly, in the earlier stages this was excessively reliant on cheap resources of oil. When the era of expensive oil emerged, much rethinking of economic strategy was required. Essentially, though, the principal aim was maximization of economic security, and in this, though oil remained problematic, a remarkable degree of success was achieved. The strategy involved development of maximum flexibility in respect of markets and sources of supply. In the case of the latter, the cultivation of multiple sources of supply so that any one source could be written off if necessary was pursued with considerable success except in the case of oil, where dependence on the Gulf area remained uncomfortably high. In respect of markets, the basic aim has been to keep Japanese manufactured products so desirable to the foreign consumer that protectionist policies introduced by the foreign countries as a result of the very success of Japan's export drive would be blunted in their impact. The development in the past few years of Japan-based multinationals, increasing Japanese overseas investment, and the sophisticated international communications networks set up by the Japanese trading companies may all be regarded as aspects of Japan's emergence as a global economic superpower.

It is immediately apparent that this approach is almost the exact reverse of that being pursued by the Soviet Union. Whereas the USSR has staked its security on the maintenance of enormous military strength, both nuclear and conventional, Japan—enjoying U.S. security guarantees, but subject to a constitutional restriction on military development itself— has accorded far lower priority to defense spending, instead deploying human resources and technological flexibility to the maintenance of a viable and dynamic economy. The early 1980s, however, witnessed some reassessment of these priorities in favor of more positive policies toward defense.

The strategic relationship between Japan and the Soviet Union has experienced significant change since the early 1970s. If we take the period from approximately 1974 to 1984, we can say that in very broad terms Japan has developed greater activism in its foreign policies, but that if anything it has reaffirmed its alignment with the United States and with other states similarly aligned. The Soviet Union over the same period moved from the short-lived détente with the United States to much more uncompromising confrontation (in part forced upon it by hard-line U.S. policies that in turn were a reaction to actual and perceived Soviet military buildup). There was some evidence that the Soviet Union was beginning to take the rise of Japan as constituting a potential threat on its eastern flank, or at least that it was coming to regard this as something that needed to be dealt with by a show of military strength in the regions of its territory close to Japan.

Various developments during the period underlined this trend. Perhaps the most significant was the Peace and Friendship Treaty between Japan and the People's Republic of China (PRC) signed in 1978, together with a trade agreement early the same year. The negotiation of the final document had been held up for several years because of Chinese insistence upon the inclusion of an "antihegemony clause" directed against the Soviet Union, and Soviet indications that should Japan sign a treaty including such a clause it would be regarded by the Soviets as an unfriendly act. In the end a compromise was reached.[8] Indeed, for Japan improved relations with China unaccompanied by perceptible improvement in relations with the USSR ultimately spelled the end of a policy of "equidistance" that Japanese governments had been attempting to pursue during the 1970s. Equidistance made sense in the context of a policy that sought to minimize political involvement and confrontation while pursuing primarily economic ends. If it had proved possible to improve relations with both China and the Soviet Union simultaneously, such a policy would no doubt have remained viable. In the event, however, the Soviet government made it clear to Japan by a series of actions that it was not prepared to play the game according to rules devised in Tokyo. From the viewpoint of Moscow, in any case, the Japanese attitude was hardly geniune. Japan maintained a close security link with the United States, which permitted the Americans access to bases in Japan, and the strenuously maintained Japanese claim to the Northern Territories was a constant irritant that rendered Japanese professions of goodwill inherently suspect.

Japan's rapprochement with China also affected Japanese policy toward the USSR in another and more subtle way. Up to the early 1970s when an opening to Beijing became possible, a disproportionate amount of Japan's foreign-policy effort went into the complex task of attempting a solution to the so-called China problem. The difficulties of arriving at a mutually acceptable *modus vivendi* with the PRC continued to preoccupy both foreign-policy makers and the mass media until the signing of the Japan-China Peace and Friendship Treaty. China, for cultural and historical reasons, was a highly emotive issue seriously dividing politically aware opinion, and other issues had come to be closely linked with it. In particular, the U.S.-Japan Mutual Security Treaty, when portrayed by those hostile to it as directed against China, opened a gap within the Japanese polity that required effort and ingenuity to bridge. The idea that the Americans were holding on to Japanese territory (Okinawa), forcing Japan to conform with U.S. aims through the security treaty, and inhibiting a Japanese rapprochement with China added up to a powerful nationalist argument on the left in the 1960s, but this tended to evaporate during the 1970s with the return of Okinawa and the conclusion of the treaty with China. These issues all consequently lost salience, and the one issue outstanding, relations with the Soviet Union, loomed larger as a result. For Japanese defense and foreign-policy makers, relations with the USSR came to be "the problem," in part because of the disappearance of other perceived sources of security threat.

This is not to neglect the actual deterioration of Japan-Soviet relations from the late 1970s. Several events contributed to a cooling of the atmosphere, including one in 1976—the landing at Hakodate, Hokkaido, of a MiG 25 aircraft piloted by a Soviet defector. The Soviets strongly objected when the Japanese authorities allowed the U.S. military to inspect the aircraft before it was returned to the Soviet Union. Japan's support for U.S. sanctions following the Soviet invasion of Afghanistan marked a distinct hardening of anti-Soviet policy by Japan under the Ohira government, which was continued and even strengthened under his successors. Japanese participation in combined naval exercises in the Pacific, the exposure of a Soviet spy network in Japan, visits by Prime Minister Nakasone shortly after his inauguration to Seoul as well as Washington, D.C., and his statement that Japan was a "large aircraft carrier," that Japan might transfer military technology to the United States, and that in case of war Japan might be prepared to consider closing the straits between the Japanese islands, when taken together with the gradual increasing of the defense budget, could be regarded as a new policy departure.

Similarly on the Soviet side a general reinforcement of military capacity in the region was under way in the early 1980s and manifested itself in such provocative gestures—to Japan—as the fortifying of the disputed Northern Territories and the idea of placing SS20 missiles in the eastern part of Siberia. The increase in strength of the Soviet navy, which worried Western policymakers generally from the 1970s on, necessarily involved Japan because of the geography of the northeastern Pacific. From the Soviet point of view access to the open Pacific required control of the Kurile islands, and the prospect of a blockade conducted by the Americans and Japanese was obviously unacceptable. The shooting down of the Korean airliner in 1983 marked a particularly low point in Japanese-Soviet relations.

Factors Inhibiting Conflict

Hitherto we have concentrated on the factors that have tended to blight relations between the two countries, and in any assessment of recent developments these must be regarded as dominant. There is, however, an alternative set of considerations that might lead us to modify this picture to some limited extent.

It is true, as noted above, that the history of the Japanese-Soviet relationship is an unfortunate one, but that in itself need not be an insuperable barrier to improvement. Contemporary attitudes of French and West Germans toward each other would have been hard to predict from the perspective of 1945. Japan itself has experienced a spectacular turnaround from its relations with the United States in not distant memory, as well as with China and some East and Southeast Asian nations more recently. These examples were brought about by some combination of mutual economic advantage, mutual strategic advantage (for instance, the perception of a common enemy), the fortunes of war, and goodwill, or at least willingness to compromise. In the contemporary world the establishment of a working economic partnership has proved a particularly promising way of overcoming previous hostilies, at least in certain instances.

The conspicuous failure of such an approach hitherto between Japan and the USSR reflects not simply the gulf between their respective social and political systems, since that ultimately has not inhibited the pragmatic mending of fences between Japan and the PRC. Indeed, comparison of Soviet and Japanese politics shows that although there are enormous differences, there are at least four kinds of similarity, though these are rarely acknowledged by either participants or observers. The first is political continuity, brought about by the fact that in both countries, though for different reasons, a single party has monopolized power over a long period. This in turn goes some way to explaining the second area of similarity, the phenomenon of bureaucratic policy control, which is admittedly far more pervasive in the Soviet Union than in Japan. Third, political advancement in both societies is mediated by informal structures of power known as cliques or factions, which ultimately determine to a large extent leadership succession. Even though succession to the prime ministership is more highly institutionalized in Japan than is succession to the general secretaryship of the CPSU, both depend on the cultivation and maintenance of alliances involving personal loyalty to the leader. Fourth, there is a considerable degree of "goal orientation" in the Japanese government's approach to economic policies, though the extent of this is controversial.[9]

It would be wrong to make too much of these similarities, but it is worth noting that both the USSR and Japan differ conspicuously in their political arrangements from the United States or from many of the states of Western Europe or Australasia, where alternation in power is fairly normal, where bureaucratic power is tempered by this, where leadership succession results essentially from open and formalized electoral competition, and where policy is supposed to result from a pluralistic set of processes. It would be too much, perhaps, to expect a meeting of minds to result from these similarities, but we believe that they have been unduly neglected in discussions of Japanese-Soviet relations.

Returning to the economic relationship, there was ample evidence during the early 1970s, when relations between Japan and China were dramatically improving, that Japanese businesspeople were also attracted by the prospect of lucrative participation in the development of Siberian resources. Demonstrably in the case of China, and no doubt also in the case of the Soviet Union, early expectations concerning trade potential were exaggerated, but it is interesting that despite all the reassessments that have subsequently been forced on Japan about trade with China by Chinese cancellation of contracts and apparently arbitrary changes of policy, Japanese industry is accustomed to consider development from a long-term perspective and has pressed on with its involvement. The history of Japanese trade since the 1950s shows that even where relatively modest gains are anticipated, sections of Japanese industry are likely to be interested.

This indeed may be seen as part of the general approach taken by Japanese government and industry toward the conduct of international economic relations, that so far as possible trade, investment, and other economic relationships should be given precedence and ideological or strategic objections to a particular regime or set of policies by another government should not be allowed to get in the way. This has long been evident in Japanese policies to southern Africa, and even in Korea, where Japan has close economic relations with the south, this has not prevented the development of an (admittedly far smaller) trading relationship with the north. Another interesting example is the Middle East, where recent quite serious Japanese attempts to mediate in the Iran-Iraq war are plainly motivated by concern that the supplies of oil from the Gulf should not be interrupted and that the spread of political instability in a volatile region of crucial economic importance to Japan should be inhibited. The point is that economic motivations remain primary and that the absence of any military involvement by Japan renders it an acceptable negotiator for both sides.

It is with the Soviet Union that this approach has come up against a barrier more impenetrable than any that has confronted Japan in recent years. It is therefore worthwhile examining the nature of this barrier to see whether there is any chance that at some time in the future Japan might find some way of breaching it by the application of its time-honored economic diplomacy, perhaps in an updated version.

Northern Islands Dispute

The first thing to be considered is the notorious northern islands dispute. This is not the only territorial dispute that Japan has been engaged in since 1952, but it is the only one that has so far proved intractable. Japan's most serious territorial problem concerned Okinawa and the Ryukyu Islands, administered by the United States after the end of World War II. It was the most serious because nearly a million ethnically Japanese people inhabited the islands and because of the issue of U.S. bases. The Ryukyus, including Okinawa, were returned to Japan in 1972. The issue of the Senkaku (Tiao yu tai) islands, which involved Japan, the PRC, Taiwan, and residually South Korea, threatened to become serious in the early 1970s, but was allowed to fade into the background after the restoration of diplomatic relations between Japan and the PRC in 1972. The similarly uninhabited Takeshima (Dokdo) Island has long been in dispute between Japan and South Korea, but in recent years it has not been allowed to impede constructive economic intercourse.

The northern islands question is therefore the great exception, in that hitherto no progress whatsoever has been made in resolving it to the satisfaction of both sides. Its history is too complicated to relate in detail here[10] and goes back to the period when both Russia and Japan were attempting to establish their influence in a bleak and sparsely inhabited area of islands that lay beyond the farthest extent of their respective territories. Japan officially claims the islands of Etorofu (Iturup),

Kunashiri (Kunashir), Shikotan, and a group of islands called Habomai. All are close to the Nemuro peninsula of northeastern Hokkaido, and all of them (together with the rest of the Chishima [Kurile] chain, and the southern part of Karafuto [Sakhalin]) were captured by the Soviet forces in the last days of the war. Shikotan and Habomai, however, are in a different category from the others, because they used to be administered by Japan as part of Hokkaido (that is, part of Japan proper), whereas Etorofu and Kunashiri were administed as part of Chishima. It seems probable that had Japan been prepared to settle for the return of Habomai and Shikotan during the Japanese-Soviet negotiations of 1955–1965, those islands would have been returned and a peace treaty would have been signed also. In the event, however, the Japanese negotiators, hampered by lack of a coordinated or consistent stance on the part of the Japanese government, held out for Etorofu and Kunashiri as well.[11]

The Soviet government for some years after this continued to hold out the possibility of returning Habomai and Shikotan on the conclusion of a peace treaty, provided that Japan would renounce its claim to the two southern islands of the Chishima chain, but in 1960 Nikita Khruschev added a further condition for their return: Japanese renunciation of the U.S.-Japan Mutual Security Treaty. When Kakuei Tanaka visited Moscow in 1973 an assurance was allegedly obtained (according to the Japanese version) from the Soviet side that the territories were one of the issues left over from World War II that still needed to be solved. The Soviet side, however, subsequently refused to concede that any such assurance had been given, and since at least the late 1970s the USSR has cleaved to the position that the issue is settled and that the northern islands are Soviet territory with which it may do what it wants.[12] The signing of the Japan-China Peace and Friendship Treaty may well have been the stimulus that prompted the Soviets to embark on a program of fortification of the disputed islands, which in turn has significantly contributed to a heightening of Japanese concern about Soviet intentions. The issue is also further complicated by the fact that both Japan and the Soviet Union are major fishing nations and the right to fish in sea areas near the disputed territories is a matter of regular negotiations between the two sides.[13]

Soviet policy on the northern islands may simply be regarded as an aspect of the generally tough policies maintained over the years by the Soviet authorities toward Japan, on the grounds, presumably, that there was no realistic prospect of developing a close and fruitful relationship with Japan on anything approaching acceptable terms for the Soviet Union. In addition to this, however, Soviet intransigence over the northern territories may well have a logic of its own, quite apart from its relevance for policy toward Japan. As I suggested early in this chapter, the Russians have historically sought to expand their borders as a principal means of defending them. The expansion of the borders of the Soviet Union around 1945 (including the extension of territories under its effective, but not sovereign control) was massive and involved in particular the redrawing of the map of central and eastern Europe. With its extreme sensitivity about boundaries, the Soviet leadership is extremely loath to set a precedent by the return of territory that it acquired at that time, and apart from a few minor pieces of territory relinquished in the 1950s soon after the death of Joseph Stalin, no piece of land has in fact been returned.[14] There were a few signs that in the rather more relaxed international atmosphere associated with détente in the 1970s, the Soviet government might be willing to take a slightly more lenient line as a result of the recognition that Western powers were prepared to give to the status quo in central and eastern Europe. Nothing, however, came of this, and with the return of cold war conditions in the 1980s no sign of flexibility remains.

There is obviously no likelihood that the Soviets will return the northern territories (in whole or in part) to Japan except as part of a much wider settlement that would involve either Japanese concessions to the Soviet Union or else the development of a much more substantial program of economic cooperation than anything seen hitherto. This, however, must lead us to speculate about the reasons for the Soviet hard line as such. From some angles, Soviet tough-mindedness and insensitivity toward Japan appear quite irrational, assuming that Soviet policymakers have their own national interest primarily in view. Whereas with India the Soviets have established an apparently durable relationship of mutual tolerance providing some mutual benefits, no attempt has been made— at least on terms that Japan could remotely accept—to do this with Japan. Why then does the Soviet Union not attempt realistically to play the Japanese card?

A standard Soviet answer to this question would be that, unlike India, Japan is a thrusting capitalist country with a conservative government, closely aligned with the United States (as well as with South Korea and latterly with China) in an unholy alliance against the Soviet socialist state. My own reading, however, of Japanese foreign-policy perceptions and actions in the recent period suggests that if the Soviet Union had been reasonably flexible and accommodating, it might well have encountered a similarly flexible Japanese response. There were indeed some signs of this developing in the early to middle 1970s. Such an approach by the Soviet Union could have tended to neutralize (or render relatively innocuous) any Japanese threat to Soviet interests in the area by allowing Japanese industry to become involved in the economy of eastern Siberia to an extent likely to generate pressure from Japanese industry against government moves to jeopardize relations with the USSR. Plainly, however, the Soviets have drawn very different conclusions from their reading of the current realities and intentions of Japan. A vicious circle is also involved, in the sense that the tough Soviet line has tended to drive Japan closer to U.S. foreign policies despite the disquiet widely felt in Japan about Reaganite foreign-policy formulas.

Japanese policy toward the northern islands issue has been correspondingly uncompromising. The question has exercised the political parties, and various pressure groups exist whose purpose is the return of the islands to Japan. A Northern Islands Day is celebrated with varying degrees of enthusiasm in different parts of the country. The government is careful to include a demand for the return of the islands in any negotiations with the Soviet authorities and repetitiously receives a similar rebuff on each occasion. Both nationalist conviction and calculations of domestic political cost disincline Japanese governments to modify their long-standing position that not only Habomai and Shikotan but also Etorofu and Kunashiri are Japanese territory and that the Soviets occupied them illegally at the end of World War II.

In any case elementary bargaining principles would suggest that there should be no retreat from a maximalist position in advance of actual entry into negotiations. The difficulty, however is that in recent years the Soviet Union has not showed the slightest sign of being prepared to enter into negotiations on what it regards as a closed issue. Variant proposals by those in or close to government are rare, but one example deserves to be noted. In 1974 the late Kazushige Hirasawa, who was at the time an adviser to the prime minister, Takeo Miki, suggested in an article published in the U.S. journal *Foreign Affairs* that even though Japan should not renounce its claim to the islands, the whole issue ought to be postponed until the twenty-first century.[15] The proposal met a largely negative response in the Ministry of Foreign Affairs, and no action was taken in the direction that Hirasawa proposed. In the early 1980s the Japanese government has been similarly negative about Soviet proposals that the two countries should negotiate a treaty of good neighborly and friendly cooperation or alternatively implement confidence-building measures, thus bypassing the linked problems of a peace treaty and the islands.[16]

To sum up on the northern territories, it is reasonable to conclude that no significant improvement is likely except in the context of a major change for the better in Japanese-Soviet relations, and the prospects of this seem remote at present. Nevertheless, it also seems sensible to remark that if Japan and the USSR were capable of dealing with each other on a reasonable neighborly footing, or even on a basis that placed primary emphasis on rational calculations of national interest, a compromise solution of the islands dispute ought to be quite feasible. Much as in the case of the textile dispute between Japan and the United States in the late 1960s and early 1970s, where an issue of limited national importance for each country was allowed to sour the relationship as a whole, so it is arguable that on an objective assessment either side could afford to make concessions on the islands question without jeopardizing its vital interests. To say this, however, is very far from saying that the two sides are likely to act on such a prescription in the foreseeable future.

The impasse, indeed, is as much a result as a cause of the general lack of Japanese-Soviet rapport, but its perpetuation also serves certain purposes for each government. For the government of the USSR, the irredentist campaign within Japan provides propaganda evidence of resurgent Japanese nationalism, and an excuse therefore to strengthen its armed forces in eastern Siberia. For the government of Japan the refusal of Moscow to budge over the islands despite repeated Japanese representations provides evidence of Soviet intransigence that can be translated into justification for increased military spending and strengthening the national resolve against the "Soviet threat." It also helps the government to resist pressure both from the Soviets and from Japanese business interests for excessively rapid and extensive involvement in the economic development of Siberia. In this way, for each government, despite its protestations, the existence of the territorial dispute provides a convenient excuse for pursuing policies that it is determined upon for other reasons.

Trade Relationships

Trade between the two countries may be more briefly dealt with. Remembering that Japan's economy is large, growing, and oriented toward international trade, whereas the Soviet economy is less dynamic and based on autarkic principles, it is interesting to note that in 1981 Japan accounted for 63.5 percent of Soviet trade with the Far East, whereas trade with the Soviet Union in the same year amounted to a mere 2.1 percent of Japan's total exports and 1.4 percent of its imports.[17] This suggests a considerable capacity for economic leverage by Japan in certain circumstances. It is true that in the early 1970s, when the grandiose Tyumen oil pipeline scheme was under active consideration, the Japanese government was anxious not to become excessively dependent on Soviet supplies of oil and was working for U.S. participation in the project as a safety guarantee. Since the collapse of the Tyumen scheme, however, the degree of actual and potential economic leverage has been heavily in Japan's favor.[18]

The volume of Japanese-Soviet trade increased quite rapidly during the early and middle 1970s, and since the late 1970s has continued to increase but at a slower rate.[19] The balance of trade has been roughly three to two in Japan's favor, and it has exhibited unambiguously a pattern whereby Japanese manufactured goods (principally steel manufactures and machinery) are exchanged for Soviet raw materials and energy fuels (timber, coal, oil and oil products, nonferrous metals).[20] Since the establishment in the 1960s of Japanese-Soviet and Soviet-Japanese economic committees in Japan and the Soviet Union respectively, a number of bilateral development projects have been established for the development of the resources of Siberia. These include, among others, various forest projects, the development of coking coal in Yakutia, natural-gas exploration in the same area, the exploration and development of natural gas and oil of Sakhalin Island, and the Vrangel port-development project. The main projects for the development of energy resources began in the middle 1970s and involved the extension of considerable amounts of government-financed credit by Japan. The impetus behind these projects, however, has definitely slowed since the late 1970s, reflecting in part Japanese participation in economic sanctions against the USSR following the invasion of Afghanistan and in part, as Kinbara argued, the fact that Soviet development priorities lie currently more in western rather than eastern Siberia.[21] Nevertheless in economic terms there appears to be considerable potential for expansion of a mutually beneficial collaborative economic relationship between Japan and the Soviet Union. Indeed in economic terms the prospects are probably more favorable than they are between Japan and China, which by comparison with the Soviet Union still has a Third World economy. Some observers regard recent moves to get the economic relationship moving again as significant.[22]

Conclusions

Many Western analyses of Japanese-Soviet relations are based on two assumptions. The first is that the Japanese side of the picture is the only one worth taking seriously: Soviet attitudes are "ideological," disingenuous, or both. The second is that in assessing the Japanese approach, U.S. interpretation of it ought to prevail. Thus those Japanese pressing for an "evolution" of Japanese defense policy in the direction of increased military spending and greater "contribution to the defense of the Free World" are highly evaluated. The alternative of holding military spending at relatively lower levels is dismissed as "Japan taking a free ride on the Security Treaty," not of course without reason from the standpoint of the U.S. taxpayer.

Putting it somewhat crudely perhaps, it follows from these two propositions that any possible rationale for Soviet policies toward Japan in terms of Soviet perceptions of present and future Japanese expansionism is ignored or dismissed, whereas Japanese interests in relation to the USSR are assumed to coincide more or less with those of the United States. I wish, however, to argue that neither Soviet nor U.S. mainstream thinking about Japanese foreign policy has fully grasped the principles on which it has been based over the past two decades or more (or, alternatively, while conceding that such principles are expressed, neither the Soviets nor the Americans have been prepared to take them seriously). The principles, though they may have developed in an ad hoc and even chaotic fashion, are in essence that given Japan's geostrategic position and the current state of military technology, Japan is an extremely difficult country to defend or from which to deter a hostile power. Given the extreme difficulty of mounting effective deterrence, the best that can be reasonably pursued is a kind of rolling economic security, conceived of as maximizing flexibility in markets and sources of supply, as being so far as possible nonprovocative of neighbors, and as becoming economically indispensable internationally by virtue of technological superiority.

These policies have obtained not inconsiderable success generally, but have had rather little success in relation to the USSR. The fact that the USSR has not responded as other countries have may now even threaten the integrity of the policy itself. The Soviet Union frequently makes a Marxist equation of Japanese economic advance with the inevitability of Japan becoming a military threat to Soviet interests. The Soviets have always been hostile to the U.S.-Japan Mutual Security Treaty, but recently the Japanese rapprochement with China, the gradual upgrading of the Self-Defense forces in response to U.S. pressure, and enhanced military collaboration with the United States and its allies in the region have no doubt set the alarm bells ringing anew in Moscow. Fortification of the northern territories and other deployments in the far eastern region of the USSR need to be seen in this light as well as in terms of Soviet global strategy. The USSR certainly wishes to "neutralize" Japan so far as possible (though the alternative term Finlandize could scarcely be appropriate to the Japanese case, given the discrepancy in international importance between Japan and Finland). Perhaps because of its Marxist blinders, however, the Soviet Union has gravely miscalculated both the rationale behind Japanese foreign policy and the real possibility of neutralizing Japan.

The underlying current of anti-Soviet feeling within Japan, its enhancement since the late 1970s because of events both internationally and in the vicinity of Japan, and increased national self-confidence and nationalist aspiration for the return of the disputed territories have further served to tip the balance of Japanese foreign and defense policies in a direction being urged upon Japan by the United States. In retrospect the exceedingly hard line taken toward Japan by the Soviet Union on political issues since the late 1970s appears designed to achieve virtually the exact opposite of what may reasonably be regarded as the Soviet national interest.[23]

There are few present grounds for optimism that the improvement in relations between Japan and China will be repeated between Japan and the USSR in the near future. Potential for trade and development collaboration, however, is quite considerable. Japan has much to offer the USSR in the high-technology area, and Soviet energy resources are not irrelevant for Japan's energy problem. It is probably too much to hope in present circumstances that Japan, following the rationale of its postwar foreign policies, might be able to contribute significantly toward a solution to what is still the most problematical international-relations conundrum of our age: how to bring the Soviet Union—in so many ways still a pariah state—into full and responsible membership of the comity of nations.

Notes

1. Chalmers Johnson, "East Asia: Another Year of Living Dangerously," *Foreign Affairs* 62, no. 3 (1984), pp. 721–745, at p. 723.

2. *Nihon Keizai Shinbun*, 13 March 1983; 13 March 1983 (evening).

3. For an interesting "revisionist" perspective, see Yonosuke Nagai, "Beyond Burden Sharing," in the Program on U.S.-Japan Relations, Center for International Affairs, Harvard University Annual Review 1982–83, *U.S.-Japan Relations: Towards a New Equilibrium* (Cambridge, Mass.: Harvard University, 1983), pp. 17–29. See also by the same author, "Can Japan Have a Strategy?" ibid., pp. 117–130.

4. See George Alexander Lensen, *The Strange Neutrality: Soviet-Japanese Relations During the Second World War 1941-1945* (Tallahassee, Fl.: Diplomatic Press, 1972).

5. In Ibid., p. 191, Lensen maintained that Japan itself had considered breaking the neutrality pact.

6. "Severely authoritarian" is a term used by Peter Reddaway in "Dissent in the Soviet Union," *Problems of Communism* 32, no. 6 (November-December 1983), pp. 1–15, at p. 1. It seems preferable to the problematic "totalitarian."

7. See, for instance, David I. Hitchcock, Jr., "Joint Development of Siberia: Decision-Making in Japanese Soviet Relations," *Asian Survey* 11, no. 3 (March 1971), pp. 279–300.

8. The antihegemony clause was included, but another clause was inserted, specifying that it was not aimed at any particular country. For an assessment of the effect of the Japan-China treaty on Japanese-Soviet relations in the late 1970s, see Peggy L. Falkenheim, "The Impact of the Peace and Friendship Treaty upon Soviet-Japanese Relations," *Asian Survey* 19, no. 12 (December 1979), pp. 1209–1223.

9. Chalmers Johnson, *MITI and the Japanese Miracle* (Stanford, Calif.: Stanford University Press, 1983), and review of the same book by Kozo Yamamura in *Journal of Japanese Studies* 9, no. 1 (Winter 1983), pp. 202–217.

10. See John J. Stephan, *The Kurile Islands: Russo-Japanese Frontiers in the Pacific* (Oxford: Clarendon Press, 1974); and John J. Stephan, "The Kurile Islands: Japan Versus Russia," *Pacific Community* 7, no. 3 (April 1976), pp. 311–330. For a concise summary, see Wolf Mendl, "The Soviet Union and Japan," in Gerald Segal (ed.), *The Soviet Union in East Asia: Predicaments of Power* (London: Heinemann, 1983; and Boulder, Colo.: Westview Press, 1983), pp. 50–69, at pp. 65–67.

11. See Donald Hellmann, *Japanese Foreign Policy and Domestic Politics: The Peace Agreement with the Soviet Union* (Berkeley and Los Angeles: University of California Press, 1969).

12. See, for instance, "Japan-USSR Senior Working-Level Consultations," *Japan* no. 269 (London: Japan Information Centre, 22 March 1984), p. 1 (quoting Soviet Vice Foreign Minister Mikhail Kapitsa).

13. See Takashi Inoguchi and Nobuharu Miyatake, "Negotiation as Quasi-Budgeting: The Salmon Catch Negotiations Between Two World Fishery Powers," *International Organization* 33, no. 2 (Spring 1979), pp. 229–256.

14. See Stephan, "The Kurile Islands: Japan Versus Russia," p. 320, for a persuasive analysis of this aspect of Soviet motivations.

15. Kazushige, Hirasawa, "Japan's Emerging Foreign Policy," *Foreign Affairs*, October 1975, pp. 155–172.

16. "Japan-USSR Senior Working-Level Consultations."

17. Kazuyuki Kinbara, "The Economic Dimensions of Soviet Policy," in Segal, *The Soviet Union in East Asia*, pp. 102–128, at p. 102 and p. 111. See also Kazuo Ogawa, "The USSR's External Economic Relations and Japan," *Japanese Economic Studies* 12, no. 1 (Fall 1983), pp. 26–53.

18. Kinbara examined and rejected the view that Japan may become dangerously dependent on energy sources from Siberia. "The Economic Dimensions of Soviet Policy," p. 109.

19. Ibid., table 8.1 (p. 104); Ogawa, "The USSR's External Economic Relations," table 1 (p. 29).

20. Kinbara, "The Economic Dimensions of Soviet Policy," table 8.2 (p. 110); Ogawa, "The USSR's External Economic Relations," table 2 (p. 32) and table 3 (p. 33).

21. Kinbara, "The Economic Dimensions of Soviet Policy," pp. 112–113.

22. Keisuke Suzuki and Ken'ichirō Yokowo. "Japan's Trade Mission to Moscow, February 1983: What Did It Accomplish?" *Japanese Economic Studies* 12, no. 1 (Fall 1983), pp. 54–70.

23. The contrast between Soviet policies toward Japan and India is instructive and deserves further research.

5
Japan and COMECON

Joseph Richard Goldman

1982 was the third year in a row in which the world economy performed poorly; the recession that began in 1980 was the longest since the Great Depression of the 1930s.[1] As one of the leading industrial powers, Japan felt the pressure throughout its worldwide market system as its exports dropped in 1982.[2] Overall, Japan's prosperity was affected only slightly compared with its peers among the Western industrial states. However, certain regions and marginal economies in the developing countries were squeezed hard to avoid losing ground financially. The structural problems contributing to this period of relative economic stagnation for most nations seemed to be carry-overs from the 1970s. Among these were the worsening account balances of all oil-importing countries, the protracted economic downturns of the United States and West Germany, the growing heavy debts owed by Eastern Europe and industrializing Third World states, and increasingly uncertain political outcomes caused by mounting tensions between the United States and the Soviet Union.[3]

As Japan was a superpower in the global economy, especially during the 1970s and 1980s, its approach to international trade, technology transfers, finance, and aid is a matter for close scrutiny in the policy councils of its many commercial customers, not just its competitors. In fact, among Japan's market countries are the socialist countries of the communist world. This chapter deals with the trading experiences of the Council for Mutual Economic Assistance (COMECON—the Soviet-sponsored counterpart to the West European Common Market) and Japan during the past twenty years and with developing trends that can be expected to persist throughout the 1980s. Specifically, I will concentrate on the East European members of COMECON (with the notable exception of the Union of Soviet Socialist Republics, which was treated in Chapter 4). The cases include the active partners in COMECON: Bulgaria, Czechoslovakia, East Germany, Hungary, Poland, and Romania. Albania and Yugoslavia present different aspects insofar as COMECON-Japan relations go. Albania withdrew completely from COMECON after 1961 when it aligned itself with the People's Republic of China in Beijing's quarrel with Moscow. Yugoslavia has been an affiliate member of COMECON since 1965, and it has been (and still is) an active trading partner with both COMECON and Japan for most of the period under consideration.

Because international trade and finance are features of increasing global interdependency and are integral to most modern nations' well-being, Japan and the COMECON countries of Eastern Europe do share one or two common interests, despite their ideological and political differences. One way to understand something about the commercial patterns existing here is to compare the industrial policy approaches that characterize each actor's political economy and then see how trade policy meshes in the relationship between capitalist Japan and socialist Eastern Europe.

Among other things, industrial policy is a deliberate by-product of political decisions to develop, nurture, expand, and protect national economic interests as advantageously as domestic and foreign conditions permit. Industrial policy is the area in which politics and economics interact through state involvement at the micro and macro levels of private and public business activity, on the one hand, and of corporate investment and individual savings, on the other, to accomplish planned or guided economic growth. The approach surrounding any state-initiated or -assisted industrial policy depends above all on the type of political system itself (i.e., liberal democratic, Marxist-Leninist, democratic socialist). Governments approach economics more or less according to their politics, and policymakers in Japan obviously employ a strategy fundamentally different from the ones operating in Eastern Europe.

In the case of Japan, Chalmers Johnson characterized the Japanese strategy as "plan rational": one that simultaneously coordinates the structure of domestic industry and promotes the economy in ways that enhance the country's "international competitiveness."[4] In order to accomplish these tasks through the plan-rational approach, Japanese experts in MITI (Ministry of International Trade and Industry) and the private sector analyze their target markets for what other nations need, can pay for, produce, and offer as future resources. For example, knowing that Romania is the largest oil-producing state in Eastern Europe (after the Soviet Union) and knowing how much the Romanians want to develop their economy from oil to a diversified economy based on, say, computer technology and similar service-related industries, the Japanese can sell modern plants and transfer technology on terms favorable to both Bucharest and themselves. The same strategy of research, information collecting, data and intelligence processing, and contracts with carefully cultivated sources in a given country or with embassy staffs based in Tokyo is likewise applied to Poland, Bulgaria, Hungary, Czechoslovakia, East Germany, and Yugoslavia on a country-by-country basis.

But there are refinements to this technique. When countries belong to a regional association such as COMECON, then marketing assumes a much different character for the Japanese. Gauging the balance between individual customers and regional ones is a tricky process, one the experts

within Japan's business community and government know how to accomplish. After the world market is factored into the equation, Japanese
planners and investors must decide where to sell what, to whom, and
when, so that unnecessary collisions between markets—Brazil and Romania, for example—will not harm Japanese interests—commercial or
diplomatic. Relying on past experiences, accurate information, careful
planning, deliberate calculation, consensus decision making, corporate
(both business and government) flexibility with respect to changing
conditions, and opportunity, Japanese policymakers act in what may be
called the "way of strategy."

The basis of this strategy used abroad is reflective of how industrial
policy really developed in Japan itself. In a sense, several factors are at
work here. First, the Japanese government and business communities
share a symbiotic relationship (only achieved in this century and over
decades) whereby they help each other to their mutual benefit. Second,
the government learned by trial and error about the marketplace through
policy manipulation, so that today Tokyo knows when business requires
political support or economic aid and under what conditions.[5] By
extrapolating this domestic pattern internationally, one can see how the
Japanese operate with the nations of Eastern Europe or anywhere else
for that matter.

In contrast, the industrial and trade policies existing in Eastern Europe
are substantively different from Japan's, particularly in terms of strategy.
Generally speaking, all communist political economies are state-owned
and -operated systems. Industrial (as well as trade) policy rests in the
hands of party politicians and bureaucratic technicians. Whereas the
Japanese state employs a plan-rational strategy for selective intervention
and assistance in the political economy, the communist state adheres to
a "plan ideological" strategy that is neither selective nor efficient.[6]

Be that as it may, many decision makers in the policy councils of
COMECON nations want their economies to succeed. Almost every
East European socialist economy has at one time or another experimented
with various political formulas in order to move from backwardness to
modernity; none now is totally committed to the Soviet model that
Stalin once dictated for each country directly under Soviet control.
Yugoslavia and Hungary developed increasingly mixed-market–socialist
economies after 1953 and 1968, respectively, and even more staid regimes
like East Germany (1962), Romania (1965), Czechoslovakia (1968), and
Poland (1980–1982) have attempted new approaches, if only to improve
upon the economic performance of the USSR.[7]

Naturally, changes in communist industrial policy usually lead to
changes in trade policy; the East European members of COMECON
are no exception. In order to acquire new technology and capital,
communist governments in this region want (and are pursuing) Western
contacts. Consequently, socialist states like the ones covered here are
dealing with Japan in whatever ways will assist their political economies.

This point can be illustrated by examining the trade patterns existing between Japan and the COMECON members of Eastern Europe.

Japan-COMECON Trade Patterns

Historically speaking, Japan's trade with the postwar communist world is generally taken to mean with the Soviet Union and the People's Republic of China. It is true that trade with other communist nations is clearly overshadowed by the proximity (and profitability) that these socialist superpowers share with Japan; however, Japanese business people and bureaucrats recognize that the lesser states in the Second World possess some value as well. Although the volume of Japan's trade with COMECON members in the aggregate is negligible compared to its trade with the Soviets or Chinese, Japanese leaders (both political and corporate) since the early 1960s have explored avenues for increasing economic ties in Eastern Europe. Obviously, this exploration is not without its political obstacles (to be discussed later). Yet the politics and economics that differentiate Japan from, for instance, Poland or Czechoslovakia do offer opportunities. Japan prospers by trade and it survives because of trade; to a growing extent this is true with most nations in Eastern Europe as they develop more rapidly. The exchange of finished products for raw materials and the sale of high-technology equipment or total industrial plant operations on credit in return for more direct market access and new investment possibilities apparently provide all parties enough benefits to outweigh costs.

In a world of rising aggressive competitors like South Korea and Taiwan, or retooling ones like the United States, Japan cannot afford to let markets go, no matter what their immediate return is, without costs to its overall well-being at some future point. This is one reason why the East European market is important to Japanese policymakers. Put quite simply, what is at stake is not profits as much as a secure share in the world marketplace. If Eastern Europe has possibilities (perhaps slight today in the 1980s but greater by 2001), then securing this region for Japan against competitors is part of shaping industrial, trade, and foreign policies by business and government officials to meet long-term national interests.

Japanese trade with Bulgaria, Czechoslovakia, East Germany, Hungary, Poland, and Romania within COMECON—as well as with Yugoslavia (technically part of COMECON on mutually acceptable terms[8])—is an uneven affair because Japan must sometimes cope with several factors at once. First of all, every communist state has an entirely different set of political and economic structures than those found in Japan, and negotiations by all parties involved always must appreciate these distinctions.[9] Second, from a Japanese perspective, these countries have little direct purchasing power of their own: All but Yugoslavia must coordinate their economic and trade policies with the Soviet Union in matters of foreign exchange, and they still restrict any large-scale penetration by Japanese firms into their territories.

On the other side of the coin, nearly all of the COMECON countries can use Japanese technical know-how, credit, aid, and whatever market Japan permits East Europeans to have in it. What kind of trade exists between these communist-bloc nations and Japan, and how significant is it for both sides, especially in the 1980s and beyond? To answer those questions, I will present relevant data and discuss trends.

Characteristics of Japan's Trade with COMECON

For the first decade after the war (1945–1955), Japan was actively rebuilding its shattered economy. Whatever trade existed at that time was solely with the West, and commerce between the Japanese and all communist states stood practically at zero.[10] By the early 1960s Japan's reindustrialization and capitalization was at a threshold: Business people and bureaucrats were ready to position the nation in the world market as a competitor instead of as a client of the West. As far as foreign exchanges with the Soviet bloc during this entire period went, Tokyo followed political considerations more than economic ones in determining that little trade with Eastern Europe would be allowed (partly out of deference to U.S. wishes; partly out of the very strong conservative distaste against communism then shared by many corporate executives and politicians in the governing Liberal-Democratic party).

However, after 1961 the international climate changed when the United States and the USSR opened more lines of commercial contact between themselves; Japan quickly responded to the new situation by making its own economic gestures toward Eastern Europe. Because Tokyo hosts embassies from every country in the Soviet zone, diplomatic relations soon led to limited trade proposals and agreements among all governments interested. From the very start of Japanese-COMECON trade, however, MITI's experts were guarded in their appraisal of prospects for business with the socialist states. Many decision makers predicted that any trade "may become a one-way trade because these countries have little to offer even if Japan wanted to import goods as collateral for her exports."[11]

On the other side of the world, the nations of Eastern Europe emerged from the war either severely damaged (East Germany, Poland, Hungary, Romania, Yugoslavia, and Czechoslovakia) or moderately affected (Albania, Bulgaria) insofar as their economic infrastructures went. The Red Army occupied nearly every East European country beyond Soviet borders (with the notable exceptions of Albania and Yugoslavia) or was poised to invade (Czechoslovakia in 1948). Stalin imposed his model for industrial policy on Poland, Hungary, Romania, and Bulgaria and variations thereof for Czechoslovakia and East Germany. Only Tito's Yugoslavia and Hoxha's Albania subsequently embarked upon different paths to socialism as their relations with Moscow deteriorated over time.

Even today it is this overall Soviet model of politics and economics that more or less dominates development and trade among member states in COMECON, and COMECON's relations toward Japan are colored by this in ways that Japanese policymakers have to accommodate when they are dealing with Eastern Europe.

Before World War II, Stalin decreed a new industrial policy for the USSR that would transform the postrevolutionary economy he inherited from Lenin. This industrial policy called for rapid industrialization in order to move the Soviet Union forward in its struggle against the Western powers. Furthermore, he ordered the collectivization (or "reenserfment" of the peasantry under state auspices) of agriculture, ostensibly to generate new production and capitalization for his program. In essence, Stalin's original industrial policy remained basically unchanged until the war uprooted the Soviet economy; after 1945 Stalin reimposed this system not only on the Soviet Union but on much of Eastern Europe.

The Soviet-styled mode of industrial policy organizes politics and economics in ways quite different from those in Japan and the industrial West. In planning and developing the political economy of, say, the USSR or Poland, the orthodox strategy subscribed to by most communist regimes involves special economic policies. According to Werner Gumpel,[12] these include

1. development of labor-intensive industries and the substitution of labor for capital since labor was superabundantly available;
2. neglect of the replacement of capital assets on the one hand, and, on the other, the extensive use of write-offs to increase capital investment;
3. extensive utilization of available resources in two respects: in capital formation, through processes of forced savings carried to the limit of the population's output capacity; in the use of natural resources, raw materials, and fuels, in highly material-intensive ways;
4. assignment of priority to the development of the overall economy rather than of individual segments of the economy.

Among other things, this scheme from the 1930s might be ideologically suitable for an economy striving to achieve complete autarky, especially under the political, rather than economic, considerations that marked communist industrial policy during Stalin's heyday. However, in the 1980s this type of direction has great shortcomings (as it probably did half a century ago). Such a policy continues a nation's falling behind other states employing more advanced methods, rather than arresting and reversing the process. Certainly, it is no secret that much of Eastern Europe is retarded by an ever-apparent outmoded political mismanagement of the national and regional economies. Throughout the COMECON system, there are highly visible signs of this mismanagement by communist political and bureaucratic authorities: (1) the overuse of labor to keep employment artificially high regardless of individual productivity; (2) poor work discipline that persistently plagues managers and employees alike and that results from low morale, difficult working conditions, lack of incentive owing to few personal rewards and satisfaction for real effort, and so forth; (3) a chronic (to sometimes acute) undercapitalization of the domestic economy because resources are diverted for extravagant military outlays or nonproductive projects abroad; and (4) a low technological level of production and little development of new technologies, particularly where the consumer sector is concerned.[13]

For the Japanese there are opportunities in the difficulties that these communist countries experience. Because these nations want and need modern technology in order to advance their economies, the Japanese are in a position as traders to offer it. Since Japan is a world leader in the development and sale of high-technology equipment or processes, the COMECON bloc apparently is very interested in having more contacts (and contracts) to obtain whatever Japan will merchandise.[14] On their side, the Japanese know the basic problems that their socialist clientele have with labor and capital policies, and they market accordingly. Because most of Eastern Europe is industrializing but can only finance this with scarce capital resources, the Japanese sell and deal in a variety of ways so as to avoid losses while making business attractive to East European governments. In short, although this trade right now constitutes a tiny fraction of Japan's global volume of exchanges (slightly over 6 percent in 1982), the Japanese consider it complementary to their interests and potentially more lucrative than heretofore was the case.

Using 1963 as a starting point, Japan's trade with COMECON was expensive for the then redeveloping Japanese economy, as Table 5.1 demonstrates. Even with the sizable imbalances that favored Albania and East Germany over the Japanese, Japan's exports to Romania, Czechoslovakia, Bulgaria, Hungary, and Mongolia helped ease the balance of payments somewhat (or at least kept that account from sinking deeper into the red).

1964 and 1965 saw a gradual shift in favor of Japan, one reflective of Japan's gains in the East European COMECON market (see Table 5.2). Although the data in this table show that Japan's position as exporter improved considerably with respect to Bulgaria, Poland, and, to a lesser extent, East Germany, it was an almost zero-sum situation with respect to Romania. Czechoslovakia, however, was a good market in 1965 compared to the year before. The data for Albania reflect its self-imposed trade isolation following events occurring in the communist world more than any specific difficulties with Japan; furthermore, the statistics for 1966–1982 indicate hardly any real improvement in trade relations between Tirana and Tokyo.

During the 1960s and well into the 1970s, the Japanese drive for technical excellence in chemical, petrochemical, and other process-related industries attracted the interest of some COMECON members in Eastern Europe, especially Romania and Czechoslovakia. *Chemical Week* reported that Japan's Dainippon Ink & Chemicals and Sumitomo Shoji Kaisha

TABLE 5.1
Japan's Trade with Communist Countries, 1963 ($1000/%)

	Exports		Imports	
Japan's Total Trade	5,452,116		6,736,377	
Total for 13 Nations	254,615	100.0	299,089	100.0
U.S.S.R.	158,136	62.1	161,940	54.1
China	62,417	24.5	74,599	24.9
Cuba	2,775	1.1	22,948	7.7
Romania	8,136	3.2	7,653	2.6
North Korea	5,347	2.1	9,430	3.1
North Vietnam	4,317	1.7	10,254	3.4
Czechoslovakia	6,507	2.6	4,431	1.5
Bulgaria	2,206	0.9	1,421	0.5
Hungary	2,550	1.0	409	0.1
Poland	1,177	0.5	1,344	0.4
East Germany	590	0.2	3,221	1.1
Mongolia	456	0.2	143	0.05
Albania	1	0.0	9	0.0

Source: Japan Trade Monthly, 1965.

(a trading company) reached a trade agreement with Bucharest to build a synthetic chemical plant. Upon completion of this facility, a 51 percent controlling interest would be in the hands of the Romanian government; however, the Japanese now would have another source of products for sale anywhere and an increased market in Romania besides. In the meantime, Toyo Engineering (owned by Mitsui Toatsu Chemical) won a $23 million contract from Prague to build an ethylene plant in Slovnaft, Czechoslovakia, by early 1975. In this case, U.S. technology (the Lummus Cracking Process) was involved in the transaction.[15]

With the advent of the 1970s the states in Eastern Europe experienced new pressures on top of old problems in advancing their economies; correspondingly, these nations' foreign-trade policies needed to be adjusted to cope with rising energy prices, inflation, and the like. The Japanese observed these trends closely and at the time attributed much of this region's economic sluggishness to agriculture's poor performance.[16] Because these countries are still mixed economies for the most part in terms of industry-to-agriculture ratios (Albania and Bulgaria being the most agricultural to industrial; East Germany, Czechoslovakia, and Poland more industrial than agricultural in that order; and Hungary, Romania,

TABLE 5.2
Japan's Trade with Selected Countries of the Communist Bloc ($ million)

	Exports		Imports	
	1964	1965	1964	1965
Communist Bloc[a]	358.8	447.7	444.4	527.1
Romania	19.2	15.2	11.9	19.0
Bulgaria	7.5	10.9	5.8	6.1
Czechoslovakia	2.8	8.7	6.0	7.0
Poland	2.5	5.4	2.1	1.9
Hungary	4.0	2.3	0.6	0.4
East Germany	0.1	1.1	0.6	0.4
Albania	0.1	0.1	0.0	0.0

Source: Taizo Ishizaka, ed., *Nippon 1966* (Tokyo: Kokusei-sha, 1966).

[a]USSR and Yugoslavia are included in total Communist-bloc figures.

and Yugoslavia roughly balanced between both sectors), the costs incurred in producing, distributing, and buying food certainly affect the overall economy and its performance. Since most of these countries are experiencing a higher standard of living (compared to the 1950s, for example), tying up valuable capital, labor, and resources in less than efficient farm production does eventually impose costs on all other areas of a national economy. One way to assist this "means of socialist production" is to import the technology and equipment that will help produce more foodstuffs and fiber. Chemical- and food-processing plants were some of the things East Europeans bought from Japan, but still their economies met plan targets with difficulty.[17]

When one looks at trade figures from 1975 to 1981 for Japan and Eastern Europe, the data favor Japan's export position over imports in this corner of the world. Exports to Eastern Europe only rose by 0.1 percent (or $74 million) in 1976 compared with 1975; however, Japan cut its imports from these countries by 23.2 percent (or $213.1 million). Hungary and Poland showed large gains in their imports by 7.1 percent, and Czechoslovakia took in more Japanese goods by 6.4 percent over 1974. With respect to Bulgaria and Romania, on the other hand, Japanese merchants fared less well. Bulgaria imported 26.4 percent less than in 1974, and Romania's drop in imports from Japan was 18.2 percent. In sum, the East European percentage of total Japanese exports to the socialist bloc was 12.3 percent, a small share compared with those of China (48.2 percent) and the Soviet Union (34.7 percent).[18]

Just what were the East Europeans and Japanese trading with one another in terms of commodity groups? Table 5.3 gives some answers to this question. One can see from this table that Japan buys mostly raw materials, agricultural products, and semifinished goods from countries like Bulgaria, Hungary, and Yugoslavia, which are less industrialized. Conversely, East Germany, Czechoslovakia, Poland, and Romania sell to the Japanese not only those items but finished products such as machinery and equipment (East Germany and Czechoslovakia) or even ships (Romania). All these nations import from Japan the latest technology in plastics, machinery, and synthetics (e.g., rubber, chemicals and pharmaceuticals, textiles). Overall, the balance of trade appears to complement Japan in dollar margins, particularly for 1975 and 1978 when compared to 1970. Still, for a region like Eastern Europe, possessing little immediate capital on hand and continually striving to develop sophisticated means of production and outside distribution, there also seems to be benefit from their trade relations with Japan.[19]

Joint Venture Corporations

In discussing the ways in which trade is facilitated between Japan and Eastern Europe, one factor needs to be examined that is important to understanding the exchange process: the joint venture corporation (JVC). In a sense, the joint venture corporation is a device established between a particular socialist country (e.g., Poland) and a capitalist one (e.g., Japan) for bringing about commercial cooperation while at the same time circumventing political barriers that would hamper deals. These corporations perform a variety of tasks, acquiring foreign capital and technology for the socialist state while providing a ready market and secure licenses to trade for business people from nonsocialist nations.[20]

This idea is not new. Lenin himself authorized his agents in the early 1920s to implement joint venture organizations with Western countries to help the nearly bankrupt Soviet economy. After World War II the USSR set up its version of these companies in Eastern Europe to begin that region's economic recovery during the late 1940s and early 1950s. Throughout the 1950s and 1960s, the JVCs operated within the socialist community. However, as those economies looked for more capital and better technology to enhance their drive for modernization, the international joint venture type came into existence after 1970 as various communist governments (Poland, Yugoslavia, Hungary, and Romania) enacted laws permitting Western firms to do more business with them.[21]

Besides reducing legal and ideological barriers between East-West trading partners, the joint venture corporation directly tackles the problems of currency differentials and ownership rights that generally complicated commercial transactions in the past. Under the post-1970 JVC

TABLE 5.3
Commodities of Trade between Japan and East European Countries ($ million)

	1970 Exports	1970 Imports	1975 Exports	1975 Imports	1978 Exports	1978 Imports
East Germany	Iron & Steel 9.8 Plastics 1.5 Machinery & Equipment 1.3	Pig Iron 27.6 Machinery & Equipment 7.7	Machinery & Equipment 25.0 Iron & Steel 9.6 Textiles 7.6 Chemicals 1.3	Pig Iron 11.5 Machinery & Equipment 6.0 Chemicals 3.5 Malt 3.5	Machinery & Equipment 15.0 Iron & Steel 14.3 Textiles 11.4 Metal Manufactures 7.9	Machinery & Equipment 5.4 Chemicals 4.6 Malt 3.6
Poland	Textiles 7.4 Machinery & Equipment 4.4 Iron & Steel 4.2 Chemicals 2.9	Pig Iron 15.0 Coal 14.8 Oil-seeds 1.7 Malt 1.2	Machinery & Equipment 143.0 Iron & Steel 134.0 Textiles 27.9 Chemicals 25.5 Metal Manufactures 5.0	Coal 63.8 Malt 3.2 Textile Products 2.9 Chemicals 2.9	Machinery & Equipment 174.9 Iron & Steel 28.6 Chemicals 26.9 Textiles 17.3 Metal Manufactures 3.8	Coal 33.9 Chemicals 4.9 Aluminium 7.2 Textile Products 4.8

TABLE 5.3 (Cont.)

	1970 Exports	1970 Imports	1975 Exports	1975 Imports	1978 Exports	1978 Imports
Czechoslovakia	Machinery & Equipment 4.4	Machinery & Equipment 7.3	Machinery & Equipment 29.9	Malt 9.7	Machinery & Equipment 20.3	Aluminium 16.6
	Chemicals 2.3	Malt 2.7	Chemicals 4.1	Machinery & Equipment 6.5	Chemicals 2.8	Malt 14.2
		Nickel 1.4	Textiles 2.3	Hops 3.7		Hops 4.7
			Raw Materials & Fuels 2.2	Glassware 2.6		Glassware 3.8
						Machinery & Equipment 3.4
Hungary	Textiles 3.7	Chemicals 1.6	Machinery & Equipment 14.8	Chemicals 4.0	Machinery & Equipment 23.2	Chemicals 6.4
	Chemicals 3.5	Meat 1.4	Iron & Steel 5.2	Textile Products 1.8	Chemicals 21.7	Aluminium 3.0
	Machinery & Equipment 1.3		Chemicals 5.0	Aluminium 1.6	Textiles 1.8	Textile Products 2.3
	Iron & Steel 1.0		Textiles 4.6		Molybdenum 1.5	Meat 1.3

Romania											
Iron & Steel	16.6	Sunflower Seeds	1.0	Iron & Steel	70.2	Aluminium	15.7	Machinery & Equipment	132.8	Aluminium	29.7
Machinery & Equipment	4.0	Aluminium	0.9	Machinery & Equipment	39.2	Heavy Fuel Oil	10.8	Iron & Steel	70.2	Pig Iron	7.4
Textiles	1.5			Chemicals	10.3	Pig Iron	9.2	Chemicals	10.9	Slabs	7.2
Synthetic Rubber	1.2			Textiles	4.1	Chemicals	2.4	Textiles	5.5	Chemicals	4.0
				Rubber Products	2.9			Rubber Products	1.7	Vessels	3.5

Bulgaria											
Machinery & Equipment	7.1	Raw Silk	2.0	Machinery & Equipment	32.2	Tobacco Leaves	4.9	Machinery & Equipment	31.1	Tobacco Leaves	4.3
Iron & Steel	6.4	Sunflower Seeds	2.4	Iron & Steel	6.9	Fruits & Vegetables	2.5	Iron & Steel	8.2	Aluminium	3.6
Chemicals	2.0	Tobacco Leaves	1.7	Textiles	5.2	Wine	2.2	Chemicals	4.8	Textile Raw Materials	2.2
Textiles	1.6			Chemicals	5.0	Aluminium	1.4	Textiles	3.1	Wine	1.8
										Fruits & Vegetables	1.7

Yugoslavia											
Iron & Steel	23.8	Tobacco Leaves	0.9	Machinery & Equipment	30.5	Aluminium	6.0	Machinery & Equipment	72.7	Aluminium	6.1
Machinery & Equipment	5.0			Iron & Steel	25.5	Pig Iron	4.5	Iron & Steel	7.8	Copper	3.8
Textiles	3.4			Refined Sugar	18.2	Copper	1.4	Rubber Products	6.2	Silicon	2.0
Rubber Products	3.1			Textiles	9.2			Chemicals	5.7	Wine	2.0
Chemicals	2.8			Rubber Products	8.6			Textiles	4.5	Silver	2.0

Source: Kazuo Ogawa, "Economic and Trade Relations between Japan and Socialist Countries." In Digest of Japanese Industry and Technology 144 (1980), p.17.

system, contracts drawn between Japanese and Romanian negotiators, for example, regarding new trade or investment first agree on what currency rates are acceptable (i.e., the mix of yen to lei and value of the lei against the yen at contract time) for all parties involved. In terms of property ownership, a socialist country like Romania usually ends up with the plants themselves, while Japan is paid full value by outright lease to purchase or earns profits unencumbered by political risk and operational costs since the host government wants Japanese participation.

Romania is a good example of what Bucharest and Tokyo can accomplish together through one JVC arrangement. As was mentioned earlier, Dainippon Ink & Chemical entered into an agreement with Romanian state officials to manufacture chemical products in Romania. RONIPROT (a state corporation) combined with Dainippon Ink & Chemicals to attract Japanese investment capital and technology in exchange for another Romanian market and source of products for joint sale abroad. This international venture began making and selling synthetic oil after April 1974. The Romanians pledged 57.38 percent of the capital required to build and maintain this operation, and their Japanese partners contributed 42.62 percent in credits and hardware.[22] To date this JVC is profitable for both sides: an example of how trade complements the investments and market interests of Japan along with the development and growth of Romania in the energy industry.

Conclusion

At the beginning of this chapter it was pointed out that Japan has a worldwide market system, which includes most countries in the socialist camp. It was also mentioned that the Japanese approach to international trade, technology transfers, finance, and aid certainly affects the policy councils of Japan's numerous customers. In the examination of Japanese–East European trade relations, the discussion centered in part on how industrial policy and trade policy differ between Japan and the socialist systems of COMECON in Eastern Europe. Yet Japanese and communist policy approaches appear to share some complementary qualities.

Although real ideological and political differences exist between capitalist-oriented Japan and socialist-oriented Eastern Europe, one bridge open to both sides is commerce. Even though the traffic flow is two-way on this bridge, it is not an even affair. The East European developing countries need what Japan can invest and produce far more than what the Japanese want from their East European clients. But Japan understands possibilities quite well in this situation owing to its experience elsewhere in the world it must live and trade in.

All the participating members of COMECON in East Europe are at various stages of their economic modernization. Nations like East Germany and Czechoslovakia, for instance, are already post industrial (i.e., service-based and knowledge-intensive economies) proportionally speaking when compared to industrializing Bulgaria, Hungary, Romania, Yugoslavia, and industrial Poland. Save for Albania, every socialist state in this region is business oriented in its economic modernization today. Japan can relate to the economic transitions and demands occurring in Eastern Europe from its own historical reference points; however, there are other considerations now that Japanese policymakers must take into account when dealing with this market.

One of these considerations is the overall percentage that East European trade represents in Japan's global economy (this percentage only averaged some 6 percent between 1973 and 1982). Markets in Latin America or the Middle East are less fraught with political restrictions (such as cumbersome security procedures, bureaucratic red tape, and so on) on Japanese activity in their countries than is Eastern Europe, and these hindrances have an effect on trade volume. Another consideration is the lack of substantial hard currency in reserve and an established credit repayment record (Poland and Yugoslavia are prominent examples of these problems with their foreign creditors) with which East European governments can entice Japanese companies to do more business compared to oil-producing or other resource-rich regions elsewhere in the Third World. The list could go on, but despite those difficulties the evidence presented here does demonstrate that the Japanese and East Europeans share a complementary relationship. In a nutshell, the East Europeans are primarily buyers and the Japanese are sellers, and both sides across the table seem interested in making more deals.

With that idea in mind, what are the discernable trends for the 1980s when speaking of trade between Japan and Eastern Europe? Both the immediate past and foreseeable future show what some of these trends are and why. During the 1960s and 1970s, the East European members of COMECON imported Japanese industrial technology mostly in the forms of heavy and light manufacturing (steel making, shipbuilding, chemical and textile finishing, and the like). With modern industrialization comes computerization, and East Europeans definitely want computer technology for their economies. Romania is one of Japan's largest customers for computers and their attendant software; other countries such as Poland, Hungary, and Bulgaria are perhaps not so far behind in demand (even East Germany and Czechoslovakia are interested in acquiring whatever the Japanese have to offer if only to upgrade their already-developed computer industry). Certainly the 1980s mean the "computerization" of nearly all socialist economies in the region, and Japan appears eager to expand its market share while competing aggressively against U.S., West German, and French dealers.

Another area might be medical and health-care technology. The Japanese rival the Americans with the latest designs and equipment when it comes to diagnostic and treatment devices. Price will attract East European customers as they compare offerings by Western suppliers and Japanese ones. Transportation technology (i.e., high-speed trains, energy-efficient buses, and other vehicles) should become an important trade item on East European shopping lists, and the Japanese are leaders in this product line. Advanced telecommunications technology is another area in which Japanese companies can increase sales to most East European nations.

In short, as East European societies become more "mainstream" in their consumer demands and production systems throughout the 1980s, their governments must meet these social needs and national interests with whoever can deliver quality at reasonable exchange terms. Today Japan is in a strategic position to take more East European business; however, the Japanese are not without future strong competitors from rivals in the United States, Western Europe, and East Asia.

Specialists in East European and Japanese economic affairs are cognizant of the problems and prospects that coexist in trade relations among these nations. My survey has attempted to elucidate what some of those problems and prospects are while examining a few of the policy factors involved. Although Japanese–East European trade relations are small in volume or value when compared to Japanese–Middle Eastern or Japanese–Latin American relations, nevertheless both Japanese and East European policymakers do place a premium on their exchanges. As the 1980s wear on, this trade relationship will assume a more important role in the course of world events.

Notes

1. World Bank, *World Development Report 1983* (New York: Oxford University Press, 1983), p. 7.

2. Economic Planning Agency, *Economic Outlook Japan 1983* (Tokyo: Economic Planning Agency, 1983), p. 13.

3. Japan External Trade Organization, *White Paper on International Trade 1981* (Tokyo: Japan External Trade Organization, 1982), p. 1.

4. Chalmers Johnson, *MITI and the Japanese Miracle: The Growth of Industrial Policy* (Stanford, Calif.: Stanford University Press, 1982), p. 19.

5. Ibid., p. 29.

6. Ibid., p. 18.

7. Robert F. Byrnes, "East Central Europe: Present Situation and Principal Trends," in *East Central Europe: Yesterday-Today-Tomorrow,* edited by Milorad M. Drackovitch (Stanford, Calif.: Hoover Institution Press, 1982), pp. 18–42.

8. Richard F. Staar, *Communist Regimes in Eastern Europe,* 4th ed. (Stanford, Calif.: Hoover Institution Press, 1982), p. 301.

9. Werner Gumpel, "East Central Europe and International Economics," in Drackovitch, *East Central Europe: Yesterday-Today-Tomorrow,* pp. 107–124.

10. Taizo Ishizaka, ed., *Nippon 1956* (Tokyo: Kokusei-Sha, 1956), p. 52.

11. Taizo Ishizaka, ed., *Nippon 1961* (Tokyo: Kokusei-Sha, 1961), p. 54.

12. Gumpel, "East Central Europe and International Economics," p. 108.

13. Ibid.

14. Shigeta Shibasaki, "An Analysis of Japan's Communist Bloc Trade," *Japan Trade Monthly* 9 (September 1964), pp. 19–22; G. C. Allen, *Japan as a Market and Source of Supply* (New York: Pergamon Press, 1967), p. 99; Franklyn D. Holzman, "Foreign Trade Behavior of Centrally Planned Economies," in *Com-*

parative Economic Systems: Models and Cases, 4th ed., edited by Morris Bornstein (Homewood, Ill.: Richard D. Irwin, 1979), pp. 261–278; and Stephen Sternheimer, *East-West Technology Transfer: Japan and the Communist Bloc,* Washington Papers Series, vol. 8, no. 76 (Beverly Hills, Calif., and London: Sage Publications, 1980), pp. 28–30.

15. "Japan Cashes in on East Bloc Plant Market," *Chemical Week* 111 (November 29, 1972), p. 21.

16. Japan External Trade Organization, *White Paper on International Trade 1976* (Tokyo: Japan External Trade Organization, 1976), p. 44.

17. Ibid.

18. Ibid., p. 248.

19. Isao Maeda, "Plant Exports to the Soviet Union and East European Countries," *Digest of Japanese Industry and Technology* 144 (1980), pp. 39–41.

20. Teruji Suzuki, "Joint-Venture Corporations in Socialist Countries," *Digest of Japanese Industry and Technology* 144 (1980), p. 19.

21. Ibid., pp. 20–25.

22. Ibid., p. 30.

6
Japan and China

Walter Arnold

With the official launching of China's modernization drive in March 1978, many observers in Asia and the West began to suggest that China's modernization program would provide Japan with a comprehensive solution to its perennial "export or perish" dilemma. Indeed, China's modernization program called for raising steel production to 60 million tons per year, and a total of 120 large-scale projects were to be built throughout China, including 10 iron and steel complexes, 10 oil and gas fields, 9 nonferrous metal complexes, 8 coal mines, 30 power stations, 6 new trunk railways, and 5 harbors.[1] China's modernization drive offered a welcome opportunity for Japanese business and industry to penetrate the China market, and its potential led to euphoria in Japanese economic circles.

It soon became clear that the importation of large quantities of foreign technology and equipment was critical for this most ambitious modernization plan. As a result, China's modernization drive became linked to large-scale imports of Western and Japanese technology, equipment, and machinery. To this end, numerous Chinese technical missions were dispatched abroad to contract for machinery, equipment, and turnkey plants and to negotiate large-scale construction projects.

Japan alone received orders amounting to some $3.8 billion in 1978, and it appeared that Japan was to become the major beneficiary of China's new modernization effort. Thus, not surprisingly, with the rapid expansion of Sino-Japanese trade from 1978 onward, many analysts have pointed to the basic economic complementarity between the two countries and suggested that the future of Sino-Japanese economic relations was bright, if not of "unlimited potential." In this vein, the *Beijing Review* noted recently:

> China, with its rich mineral and other resources, and Japan, with its advanced industrial technology can share what each has and what each has not. Japan's over-all security strategy requires it to ensure the supply of fuel and raw materials from China, its close neighbor, in order to diversify its fuel and energy resources. Furthermore, with the "long-standing"

stagflation in the West, Japan finds China's vast market to be of enormous appeal.[2]

Japan's overpowering position in the China market is often viewed as a function of its high level of economic and technological development and of the basic economic complementarity in Sino-Japanese relations. Moreover, geographic proximity, cultural affinity (*do bun do shu*—"same script and same race"), and common historical experience have been frequently cited as indicators of closeness between the two countries. These and other assertions have led many to assume that Japan is certainly enjoying a favorable position in China and that there now exists a special relationship between the two countries.

The argument advanced here suggests that neither geographic, cultural, and historical factors nor economic complementarity sufficiently explains Japan's predominating position in the China market and its preeminent role in China's modernization effort. Rather, any explanation of Japan's role in the China market and its linkage to China's modernization drive must be grounded in Japan's political calculations and its long-term view of Sino-Japanese relations. With the normalization of diplomatic relations in 1972, Japan abandoned its policy of *seikei bunri* (separation of politics from economics with respect to China), and since then economic calculations have been subordinated to Japan's long-term political interests in its dealings with China. I argue in this chapter that Sino-Japanese economic relations are determined, by and large, by domestic Chinese politics (vicissitudes of modernization) and Japan's long-term political interest in a stable China, and not primarily by Japan's pecuniary interests. In fact, the chapter will show that financially Japan has fared less well in the China market than is commonly assumed. The first part discusses the current problems afflicting Sino-Japanese economic relations, the second part presents a critical examination of economic complementarity in Sino-Japanese relations, and the third part offers a brief interpretive analysis of China's plant and contract cancellations and their ramifications for future Sino-Japanese economic relations.

1982—A Critical Turning Point?

1982 marked a critical juncture in Sino-Japanese relations, because Japan and China commemorated the tenth anniversary of the normalization of their diplomatic relations. It symbolized the occasion when Chinese Premier Zhao Ziyang visited Japan from May 31 to June 5, with Japanese Prime Minister Zenko Suzuki reciprocating with an official visit to China from September 26 to October 1. Indeed, the chroniclers were quick to point out that Sino-Japanese relations and cooperation had developed rapidly in all fields from 1972 to 1982. Tourism had increased twelve times, from a mere 9,000 to 127,000 in 1980, and forty-two pairs of Chinese-Japanese sister cities had been formed.[3]

Economically, Sino-Japanese relations and cooperation were set on a solid basis with the signing of the Long-Term Trade Agreement on February 16, 1978, covering the years 1978–1985 and calling for $20 billion in bilateral trade. The agreement was intended to provide a concrete framework for the Japanese export of technology, plants, machinery, and equipment, in exchange for Chinese crude oil and coal, thus linking Sino-Japanese trade to China's modernization program. The Long-Term Trade Agreement, although it was not an intergovernmental agreement, was concluded between Liu Xiwen, vice minister of foreign trade, and Yoshihiro Inayama, the chairman of Nitchu Keizai Kyokai (Japan-China Association on Economy and Trade), it provided the foundation for the rapid development of bilateral economic relations and cooperation. In fact, by the end of 1981 the bilateral trade volume had reached slightly more than $10 billion, a tenfold increase since 1972. In March 1979 the Long-Term Trade Agreement was extended to 1990, and the amount of two-way trade raised to $40 billion.

Politically, an important breakthrough in Sino-Japanese relations occurred with the signing of the Peace and Friendship Treaty on August 11, 1978, which not only drew the two countries closer but also signaled a clear Japanese tilt toward China. Subsequently, both China and Japan seemed to concur on a variety of international issues; for example, both condemned the Soviet invasion of Afghanistan and Vietnam's invasion of Kampuchea. More importantly, since the end of 1980 China and Japan have been holding annual consultative conferences at the cabinet level to further personal contacts among senior Chinese and Japanese officials and decision makers. Furthermore, along with other frequent official exchange and meetings, the first People-to-People Conference between private individuals from China and Japan was held in Tokyo, October 7–9, 1982, to promote further understanding and cooperation between the two countries, with a follow-up scheduled in Beijing in 1983. However, these positive developments in Sino-Japanese relations could not conceal the serious problems underlying Sino-Japanese economic relations, especially the lack of economic complementarity and increasing commercial dissonance. As Japanese Prime Minister Suzuki poignantly remarked, "Japan-China relations have developed into a 'period of maturity' from a 'period of honeymoon.'"[4]

By 1982 Japan's business world became disenchanted with the course of political and economic events taking place in China. The mood of Japanese business in 1982 was different from 1978, when the signing of the Long-Term Trade Agreement brought a flood of contracts and orders in the amount of $3.8 billion, because a series of unilateral Chinese plant and contract cancellations had adversely affected Sino-Japanese economic relations since 1979. As a result of China's cancellations and suspensions in 1979 and in 1980–1981, Japan's "China fever," once pervasive in business circles, had markedly subsided; there was even a sign of an anti-Chinese mood in Japan by 1981, as indicated by an 8 percent drop of China's popularity in a public-opinion survey on diplomacy. Japanese business and industry both have learned that they can no longer "expect" much from the China market, at least not during the present phase of Chinese economic adjustment, which they assume will last until 1985.

Chinese Premier Zhao Ziyang's commemorative visit in May–June 1982 tried to restore the confidence of Japanese business in China and the China market. Zhao attempted to bring a new measure of stability and predictability into Sino-Japanese relations by enunciating "peace and friendship, equality and reciprocity and long-term stability" as the new principles underlying Sino-Japanese economic relations.[5] Moreover, Zhao tried to reassure the Japanese audience that China would continue to carry out its open-door policy in economic development and would further seek economic cooperation from Japan. In fact, Zhao asked for Japanese governmental loans totaling 90 billion yen ($410 million).[6] But prior to his visit to Japan, Zhao announced that future Sino-Japanese economic relations would focus primarily on the development of China's energy sector and on "technical cooperation" (the latter in accordance with China's new emphasis on "technical transformation of existing Chinese enterprises").[7]

Premier Zhao's outline for a new framework regarding Sino-Japanese economic interchange will have some important short-term consequences as well as some long-run ramifications for Japanese business. For example, China has now officially shifted its emphasis from importing expensive, large-scale plants to importing single, simple, and cheap industrial techniques and processes. Although this new development was welcomed by the Japan Machinery Exporter's Association (which has subsequently sent a delegation to China), this latest development in China's economic readjustment means a continuing slack in exports for Japan's plant producers and also means that lucrative large-scale projects in China might be a thing of the past. Japanese plant and equipment manufacturers and trading companies—all specialists in the transfer of large-scale technology to China—consider these developments detrimental to their interests and a serious setback. Furthermore, they anticipate that Sino-Japanese trade will suffer over the next several years as a consequence of this new policy emphasis. These fears held in Japanese economic circles were really confirmed when Beijing made an announcement in December 1982 that 36 percent—or 130 billion yuan ($592 million)—of China's total capital construction fund for the ongoing sixth Five-Year Plan (1981–1985) was earmarked for the updating of equipment in existing enterprises.[8] In fact, Japan's role has already been relegated to "technical assistance and cooperation."

From the Chinese standpoint, the practical implication of this is that China will spend little, since the upgrading of enterprises might entail only the importing of licenses, techniques, processes, some sample machinery, management methods, basic plant designs, and a part of plant equipment.[9] From the Japanese side, however, this is a far cry from the expensive large-scale imports and multi-billion-dollar deals of the buoyant 1978–1979 period.

Obviously, the "textbook controversy" developing in the summer of 1982 put considerable strain on Sino-Japanese relations, too.[10] By and large, the whole affair attested to the absence of any special affinity in Sino-Japanese relations. Nevertheless, both China and Japan chose a relatively quick diplomatic settlement of the issue when the controversy showed a propensity to endanger Sino-Japanese cooperation in general and Sino-Japanese trade specifically.[11]

No doubt, 1982 was an exceedingly disappointing year for Sino-Japanese economic relations given Japan's setback in the China market. In 1982, Japan's China-bound exports of equipment, plants, machinery, and consumer durables had dropped sharply as a result of China's continuing policy of "readjustment" to economic modernization. Sino-Japanese trade was down for the first time since 1976, with two-way trade reaching a $8.86 billion low (being off 14.7 percent from $10.388 billion in 1981). Japanese trading circles were quite alarmed at the downturn in Sino-Japanese trade, and their concern was further heightened by fears that there was little hope for Sino-Japanese trade to expand significantly in the near future, unless, of course, China would again alter its developmental priorities.

From a Japanese point of view, a significant turnaround in Sino-Japanese trade could not be expected until exports of machinery and plants could be increased and expanded. On the other hand, there were a few hopeful signs during 1982 that brightened what otherwise was a dour picture. On August 9, 1982, in an article in the *People's Daily,* Zhu Yue Ling called for attention to the importance of technology and machinery imports, and in the following months China started anew to send inquiries to Japanese plant producers and exporters.[12] And, in fact, on February 17, 1983, it was reported that Toyobo Company and Teijin were negotiating with China for the export of a synthetic-fiber plant worth 8 billion yen ($34.6 million), to be constructed in a petrochemical complex in Tianjin. However, this report was preceded by adverse news on February 16, 1983, when Japanese industry sources disclosed that China inexplicably decided to cancel its orders for plants and machinery it had planned to use for constructing a petrochemical plant at Daqing.[13]

Understandably, most Japanese plant and machinery exporters can find little comfort in these contradictory signals emanating from China. And, as a result, a high official of the Japan-China Association on Economy and Trade has recently called attention to the fact that the very nature of the Sino-Japanese Long-Term Trade Agreement has changed its original purpose of enabling China to pay for the cost of importing Japanese plants, equipment, and technology through the export of Chinese oil and coal to Japan. In essence, this view openly called into question the very basic premise of Sino-Japanese economic relations: namely, the economic complementarity—the presumed logical axis in Sino-Japanese trade—that links China's economic modernization needs to Japan's needs for markets and energy resources.

Economic Complementarity

A closer look at Sino-Japanese economic relations of the past several years reveals that the thesis of economic complementarity is scarcely tenable; moreover, the widespread argument of a natural complementarity in Sino-Japanese trade is a gross oversimplification of economic reality, and the whole notion is basically little more than a myth. This myth was originally created by Japan's long-standing interest in China as a source for energy supplies and China's initial willingness to supply considerable quantities of crude oil and coal to Japan in exchange for equipment and technology. The Long-Term Trade Agreement of 1978 helped to maintain the myth, as did the genuine search for economic complementarities by both China and Japan over the past several years.

In fact, the well-propagated economic complementarity—based on Chinese oil and coal for Japanese technology, machinery, and equipment—was aborted before it ever could become a salient factor in Sino-Japanese relations. The past record of Chinese plant contract suspensions and cancellations (to be discussed later) and China's inability to supply Japan with the originally contracted quantities of energy resources clearly indicate that for now Sino-Japanese economic complementarity is a misnomer at best. Economic complementarity in Sino-Japanese relations will most likely not come into full play until China develops its energy industry and its national economy reaches a considerably higher level of development. When this might be achieved remains highly speculative, with guesstimates ranging anywhere from eight to fifteen years.

Some of the major constraints afflicting Sino-Japanese economic complementarity are problems of logistics, infrastructure, and the general political uncertainty surrounding Chinese energy supplies to Japan. According to the 1978 Long-Term Trade Agreement, apparently Chinese exports hold the key to bilateral trade expansion, with Chinese energy resources exports paying for the Japanese technology, machinery, and equipment imports.

Nevertheless, since the very inception of the Long-Term Trade Agreement, the alleged economic complementarity has been severely compromised by China's inability to fulfill its contractual obligations. Logistically and economically it has been most burdensome for China to provide Japan with even a less-than-adequate quantity of the originally stipulated amount of crude oil and coal. As a result, Chinese energy exports fell far short of the 1978 projections, and China was forced to reassess not only its economic modernization but also its import priorities in general, which led to the suspension and cancellation of Japanese plant contracts.

Since 1979, China has repeatedly stated that it will be difficult to boost exports of energy and raw material in the short run. In fact, as one economist has pointed out, "China was unable to fulfill its commitment to export 8.6 million tons of crude oil to Japan in 1980 and had to cut its crude oil commitment to Japan by 13 percent for 1981 and by 45 percent for 1982. Under a new arrangement, China was to export 8 million tons of crude oil to Japan annually in 1980, 1981, and 1982."[14]

Chinese energy exports to Japan are impeded not only by logistical and technical problems but also by an inimical debate among Chinese decision makers over the "proper utilization" of natural resources. According to a 1981 *Jetro* report,[15] however, there seems to be a growing view in China that priority should be given to the export of resources, the argument being that it is in the long-term interest of China's modernization effort to undertake a massive development of resources and expand exports in order to earn foreign exchange to finance the import of technology and equipment badly needed to upgrade China's national economy. The pervasive view in Foreign Trade Ministry circles is that resources are certain to become a major item for Chinese exports because of a massive demand for such resources in the international market and because of rising prices for crude oil. The declining crude-oil prices of 1983 already rendered this argument obsolete (although an "oil crisis in reverse" seems very unlikely).[16]

The opposing view, which has received a great deal of exposure lately, holds that it is still premature for China to export oil and coal because much of the domestic needs and demands are still unsatisfied. However, it would be overly simplistic to reduce the entire issue of energy and raw-material exports to nothing more than competing institutional interests and bureaucratic infighting over the allocation of scarce resources. Obviously, any solution to this problem is critical for the course and outcome of the entire modernization effort, a fact the Chinese and foreign parties involved must be well aware of by now.

With the acceleration of China's modernization drive, shortages in energy supplies became rampant, and they began to create widespread bottlenecks in industry that in turn assumed alarming proportions. It did not take very long to identify energy as one of the weakest links in China's economic modernization. A combination of previous inadequate policies, inept management, and general waste due to inefficient and obsolete equipment was subsequently identified as the major cause leading to these energy shortages that are now having a devastating impact on the national economy and economic modernization. Many Chinese enterprises have been forced to determine production plans based on energy availability. Idle industrial equipment (20–30 percent) has led to astronomical losses in industrial production (70 billion yuan in one year). This situation further exacerbates the already precarious state of China's underemployment and unemployment. As a result, "energy development" (meaning the creation of new sources of supply and remedying existing obsolete user facilities) has been officially declared to be of strategic importance for China's economic modernization.[17]

Experts, however, have estimated that it will take a good ten or more years for China to develop its energy resources just to satisfy its basic domestic needs adequately. Most observers, including the Chinese, agree that the development of China's energy industry will be very slow and, above all, extremely costly. According to one official estimate, only by the end of this century will China's total energy output reach 1.2 billion tons, doubled from the 600 million tons in 1980. In the meantime, the savings of energy and sustained technological progress are to make up for the difference resulting from energy shortages and anticipated increases in industrial output.[18]

From these factors it can be deduced that the realization of complementarity in Sino-Japanese economic relations hinges primarily on the outcome of China's critical debate over the "proper utilization" of energy resources. Meanwhile, each barrel of oil exported to Japan means one less barrel of oil available for China's economic modernization. All this casts serious doubts on a further expansion of Chinese energy exports to Japan in the near future.

Originally, the Chinese had pinned their hopes for economic modernization on vast oil export revenues and the Japanese on huge exports of technology, machinery, plants, and equipment. By and large, these hopes for economic complementarity have proven to be unrealistic and unattainable. China's inability to satisfy Japanese demand for energy supplies has been hampered by technical, logistical, and, above all, domestic political problems, all of which appear unsurmountable for the next several years to come. Furthermore, Japan's role as the major source of technology for China appears utterly frustrated by the vicissitudes of China's modernization drive. This has led to a great deal of discord in Sino-Japanese economic relations, as the following discussion of China's unilateral plant cancellations shows.

Plant and Import Contract Cancellation

China's unilateral suspension and subsequent cancellation of numerous plant and import contracts with Japanese manufacturers and trading houses in 1979 and 1980–1981 greatly soured the basis of trust underlying Sino-Japanese economic relations.[19] Increasingly, Japanese economic circles have begun to express reservations about China's reliability as a trading partner, and in spite of sporadic signs of a resurgence in Sino-Japanese trade (e.g., in 1981 when bilateral trade reached the $10 billion mark), uncertainty seems to characterize this important bilateral economic relationship.

China based its modernization and massive import of foreign technology and plant purchases on mistaken projections of oil production and exports. Consequently, in 1978 and early 1979 numerous contracts for steel-making and petrochemical plants were signed with Japanese companies. By February 1979, only two months after the ground-breaking ceremony and start of construction of phase one of the Baoshan Steel Complex (a fully integrated steel mill in the vicinity of Shanghai), China informed the Japanese main contractor—Nippon Steel Corporation— that the project was suspended because of a shortage of funds. At the same time, twenty-three other plant contracts with Japanese companies and trading houses were suspended for the same reason. These contracts were worth an aggregate $2.1 billion, for which orders had already been placed with hundreds of Japanese enterprises. For Japanese business, these contracts certainly offered a means to escape from the doldrums of worldwide recession, even though the companies involved had had to drive hard bargains to win the orders. This unfortunate turn of events left Japanese economic circles shocked and outraged.

After several rounds of negotiations between officials from both governments and the concerned Japanese companies, all of the contracts (except one) were validated by China, including the multi-billion-dollar Baoshan Steel Complex. However, during the renegotiation of the contracts, promulgated targets of the Ten Year Plan for the Development of the National Economy (the blueprint for China's modernization) were severely criticized. As a result, capital investments were ordered to be drastically cut back, and a program of economic adjustment deemphasizing heavy industry was launched. This meant that all plans for new steelworks were shelved, seriously affecting the development of the Baoshan Steel Complex.

In many ways, the Baoshan Steel Complex has taken on a symbolic meaning for both China and Japan. For some of China's modernizers Baoshan has been a symbol of China's determination to introduce the most up-to-date technology and equipment needed to accelerate China's modernization drive; for others, Baoshan came to stand for gargantuan waste and inept policy. For the Japanese, Baoshan was not only a monument to their own ability but the very symbol of Japan's intrinsic linkage to China's modernization effort. Furthermore, Baoshan was also the first project to be implemented under the aegis of the Sino-Japanese Long-Term Trade Agreement of 1978. And lastly, the sheer magnitude of its size and value (close to $4 billion) made the Baoshan Steel Complex an important factor in Sino-Japanese economic and political relations. As a result of China's overambitious modernization drive, the nation soon found itself overextended in capital construction. This led to a serious drain on its finances, caused inflationary pressures throughout the land, and finally resulted in a 12-billion-yuan state deficit in 1980, to which the Baoshan project was directly linked.[20]

On November 21, 1980, China officially declared that it had decided to postpone the start of the second phase of the Baoshan Steel Complex. Then in January 1981, the Japanese business community was shocked by yet another Chinese revelation that several other plant contracts would be postponed, again caused by China's ongoing policy of economic readjustment and a general lack of funds. These cancellations amounted to $1.5 billion, a considerable sum even for Japan. They involved the second phase of Baoshan—a Mitsubishi steel rolling mill at Baoshan—and several petrochemical complexes in Beijing, Nanjing, and Shengli.

In what amounted to a series of surgical moves, China was attempting to reduce some of the large-scale projects that had proliferated during the heyday of its technology-import mania. Some of these projects were canceled outright; others were postponed indefinitely in order to bring a measure of order into China's chaotic capital construction program. Baoshan's phase two was sacrificed, according to a Japanese analyst, because of the internal difficulties Chinese decision makers encountered in their effort to reduce the overall scale of China's capital construction. By showing the nation their willingness to stop even the symbol of Sino-Japanese cooperation, Chinese leaders would be able to push forward "economic readjustment" more effectively on a nationwide basis.[21]

It seems inconceivable that Chinese decision makers did not consider the potential acrimony such actions would engender against the goodwill and trust in Sino-Japanese economic relations. It appears that Chinese domestic political considerations prevailed and, in fact, overrode China's international economic and commercial obligations. Obviously, China had taken great risks to the detriment of international economic cooperation in general and Japan's in particular. Naturally, the Japanese business community's confidence was shattered by the course of these staggering events, and there has been great resentment in Japan's steel and heavy-machinery circles ever since. Japanese business did not take these reversals lightly, and there were repeated calls for payments of stiff penalties and compensation for the losses incurred as a result of China's unilateral postponements and cancellations. Many Japanese saw China's actions as a virtual abrogation of the Sino-Japanese Long-Term Trade Agreement. Subsequently, Japanese trust and goodwill vis-à-vis China reached its nadir in the early months of 1981, and it has never really recovered to its previous state.

Due to domestic pressures, the Japanese government sent its special trade representative, former Foreign Minister Saburo Okita, to China on February 10, 1981, in order to discuss the precarious situation with Chinese leaders. Both Deng Xiaoping and Vice Premier Gu Mu, then in charge of economic affairs, assured Okita that China would accept responsibility and compensate Japan for losses emanating from China's plant cancellations in accordance with international trade practices. Most Japanese companies, however, did not have any compensation clauses in their contracts with China because they had regarded China as a reliable partner. During Okita's conversations with Gu Mu and Deng Xiaoping, it became clear that there was still a chance of reviving these contracts, since these were cancelled primarily because of a shortage of domestic funds and capital. Gu Mu and Deng Xiaoping hinted that China might be willing to reconsider the cancellations providing there was a possibility to obtain soft loans from Japan for the revitalization of the projects.[22]

On February 24, 1981, as a follow-up to Okita's call on China, a mission was sent to Japan to discuss "compensation" with the concerned Japanese companies. The talks were not successful and remained inconclusive with both parties able to agree only that compensation should be paid. The Chinese delegation subsequently demanded that the Japanese government take the necessary steps to resolve the compensation issue, in other words, that Japan should come up with a proposal for soft loans.

The 1980–1981 plant cancellation issue was finally resolved in September 1981 when, after protracted negotiations, Japan made a "final offer" to China through its ambassador in Beijing on September 6, offering China loans in the amount of $1.3 billion. The loan package's breakdown was 130 billion yen credits, 100 billion yen Export-Import Bank loans, and 70 billion yen in syndicated loans by private banks.[23] Although China had originally requested a total of 600 billion yen in order to continue construction of the Baoshan Steel Complex and the Daqing and Nanjing petrochemical complexes, the Japanese offer was accepted in principle the next day.

As a result, most of the contracts cancelled in January 1981 were revived, except for Mitsubishi's hot strip mill (contracted for Baoshan phase two) and five other plants at Baoshan. China also agreed to compensate Japanese firms, but compensation amounted only to $46 million in total or about half of that originally requested by the Japanese firms.[24] China viewed its willingness to compensate Japanese companies as a demonstration of goodwill, whereas the Japanese parties concerned regarded it as their inalienable right.

A year later, on October 14, 1982, Sun Shangquing (a prominent economist close to Zhao Ziyang) revealed during an interview that the second phase of the Baoshan Steel Mill project would not be resumed until the end of 1985 and that China would then attempt to carry out half or more of the construction by itself.[25] The most recent episode in this seemingly never-ending saga of Chinese economic and commercial retractions concerned the February 16, 1983, disclosure that China had decided to cancel an estimated 6-billion-yen ($27.3-million) order for plants and machinery contracted for its Daqing petrochemical complex.

This latest event seems even more perplexing than usual because the Daqing petrochemical complex was one of the industrial projects China intended to "revive" as a result of the September 6, 1981, loan package.[26] China, however, chose not to elaborate on the reasons for this particular cancellation.

China's unilateral plant and the contract cancellations—the largest in foreign-trade history (approximately $1.6 billion)—have put severe physical strains and psychological stress on Sino-Japanese economic relations in addition to creating an aura of dissonance and apprehension.

Many Japanese enterprises have lost considerable amounts of money in the China market as a result of the unpredictable course of China's modernization and the slack in energy exports (not to mention the losses forcing China to abandon about 40 percent of its key development projects). The erratic succession of postponements and cancellations ultimately led to the temporary collapse of the China market for large-scale projects in 1982, when not a single contract was signed with Japan. Japanese economic circles responded prudently to this turn in events and by and large continued to show a positive and cooperative attitude toward China's incessant requests for special considerations and financial assistance throughout 1983. Since the 1982 cancellations Japanese business, in collaboration with the economic bureaucracy and leadership of the Liberal-Democratic party (LDP), has managed to salvage a considerable number of the cancelled Japanese projects in China by financing some of them either with outright loans or deferred-payment schemes. It is noteworthy to point out that the Japanese government has been taking a considerable interest and played a leading role in these negotiations.

It appears that Japan's long-term perspective and prudent approach to the China market has already led to some short-term results. After the hefty 15 percent drop in 1982, Sino-Japanese trade picked up in the latter half of 1983. The 1983 advance in two-way trade received considerable impetus from China's ongoing modernization program: renewed investment in industrial equipment and the beginning of the projected technical overhaul of three thousand enterprises. Japan's steel industry experienced a 60 percent surge in sales over 1982, topping 6 million tons. On the other hand, China's exports to Japan fell 10 percent, largely because of lower Chinese oil prices.

This notwithstanding, the China fever has tremendously subsided in Japanese business circles. Many enterprises have lost interest in China entirely, and some have turned elsewhere for business and trade.[27] During his seven-day visit to Japan in November 1983, Hu Yaoban, general secretary of the Central Committee of the Chinese Communist party (CCP), tried to calm concerned Japanese business and industrial circles by declaring that Sino-Japanese economic relations were now on a firm foundation and that any problem in the past (alluding to the plant cancellations) should be viewed as peripheral.[28]

Prospects

In any event, what are the prospects for Sino-Japanese economic relations? Most would probably concede that their future hinges primarily on the success of China's modernization effort. Ostensibly, only the Chinese themselves can modernize their country. By the same token, China depends on the import of foreign technology and capital for a great many of its infrastructure and energy-development projects that are critical for the very success of its modernization efforts. In the past several years, China has come to view Japan as a principal supplier of technology, capital, and assistance as well as a market for its own exports.

Since the Sino-Japanese diplomatic normalization in 1972, and particularly with the inception of China's modernization in 1978, both China and Japan have developed strong and important economic relations. Japan ranks first among China's foreign-trade partners and provides China with about 25 percent of China's total imports. At the same time, Japan is rapidly becoming the most important market for Chinese raw materials and finished products, which resulted in a staggering Japanese deficit of $1.84 billion in 1982.

On the other hand, Japan's economic stability and prosperity are far less contingent upon the China trade than is often assumed. China ranks only fifth among Japan's trading partners with bilateral trade reaching $10.3 billion in 1981, $8.86 billion in 1982, and $9.6 to $10 billion in 1983. Moreover, China has been unable to provide Japanese industry and commerce with a stable market for their products or to supply large quantities of energy resources to Japan. Both China and Japan have had to concede that the high hopes for economic complementarity in 1978 had been unrealistic and presumptuous from the beginning. And as a result, the very basic premise of Sino-Japanese economic relations, "presumed economic complementarity," has been changed into a diminished private-sector interest in China and an increased role and function by the Japanese government in this important bilateral relation.

The increasing importance the Japanese government attaches to Sino-Japanese relations is primarily of a political nature and stems mainly from considerations of "high politics." Japan strongly believes that Chinese economic viability and political stability are essential for Asia's stability and economic prosperity, and it appears that the Japanese are taking seriously Deng Xiaoping's dictum that (economic) modernization will make or break China. Thus, it might not be difficult to see that Japan's ultimate motives to assist China and cooperate in its modernization effort are based on a long-term political conception of China's role in Asia, where Japan has its greatest political and economic stake because of its geographic proximity. It is precisely for these political reasons that one can rationalize the Japanese government's continuing willingness to actively participate in China's modernization effort by granting loans and arranging for technical assistance. On the other hand, Japanese big business, industry and commerce in particular, have shown decreasing enthusiasm about China as a marketplace.

In conclusion, what lessons can be learned from the past experience in Sino-Japanese relations? The record of the past five years shows that Sino-Japanese economic relations have been increasingly complex, politically and economically exacting, and at times outright difficult. Although always "correct," this important bilateral relationship has never been really smooth. Both sides have been driving hard bargains, with Japan yielding in many cases. At the same time, both China and Japan have shown a great deal of flexibility in their mutual dealings and a capacity to compromise (e.g., Baoshan).

In the short run, it is reasonable to expect that China's economic readjustment policy will take far longer than originally anticipated, Chinese energy exports to Japan will not develop as desired, and the commercial discord between segments of Japanese big business and the Chinese government will continue. Moreover, China's ability to deal effectively and efficiently with the huge influx of foreign technology and loans will improve only slowly. In the long run, however, China will find the Japanese government a responsive partner in its modernization drive, because the Japanese decision makers are basically taking a long-term view of Japan's economic relations with China and, for the time being at least, have subordinated economic considerations to politics.

And, finally, both China and Japan are hopeful that economic complementarity will eventually be realized as China proceeds with its modernization program. Whether—or when—this might be accomplished remains to be seen, for the outcome of China's modernization will depend primarily on Chinese domestic politics, with Japan playing only a tangential role.

Notes

1. *Beijing Review,* no. 10, March 10, 1978, pp. 18–26.
2. *Beijing Review,* no. 40, October 4, 1982, p. 12.
3. Ibid.
4. *Jetro China Newsletter,* no. 40, September-October 1982, p. 18.
5. *Beijing Review,* no. 24, June 14, 1982, p. 6.
6. *Far Eastern Economic Review,* June 11–17, 1982, p. 14.
7. *Jetro China Newsletter,* no. 40, September-October, 1982, pp. 20–22.
8. *Beijing Review,* no. 15, December 20, 1982, pp. 12–13.
9. *Beijing Review,* no. 7, February 14, 1983, pp. 14–18.
10. Japan's vacillating attitude and generally dismal performance throughout the textbook affair were nearly excelled by Chinese insinuations about rising militarism and rightward inclinations in "certain" Japanese circles. This was quite astonishing, since China previously asserted that Japan should increase its defense appropriations in order to counter Soviet hegemony jointly with China.
11. The controversy finally was put to rest with Prime Minister Nakasone's statement on February 18, 1983, admitting that the 1937–1945 Sino-Japanese war was a "war of aggression" started by Japan; the statement was welcomed by China.
12. *Kogyo Nikkan Shimbun,* October 29, 1982, p. 4.
13. *Japan Times,* February 26, 1983, pp. 9, 11.
14. See Chun-yuan Cheng, *China's Economic Development* (Boulder, Colo.: Westview Press, 1982), p. 483.
15. *Jetro China Newsletter,* no. 38, May-June, 1982, pp. 6–8.
16. It was anticipated that Japan would buy less oil from China and would pay a lower price for it in 1983 than 1982. See *Wall Street Journal,* March 25, 1983, p. 26.
17. *Beijing Review,* no. 5, January 31, 1983, pp. 16–20.
18. Ibid.

19. This entire part is based on my readings of Nitchu Keizai Kyokai Ho, no. 94, *Nitchu Puranto Mondai Kankjei Nisshi,* May 1981, and no. 95, *Chugoku Puranto Keizoku de Seifu Shakkan o Yosei,* June 1981.

20. See Keitaro Hasegawa, "Yatsuppari, Hasanshita Chugoku Keizai," *Bungei Shunju,* no. 59, April 1981.

21. *Jetro China Newsletter,* no. 29, December 1980, pp. 3–5.

22. *Jetro China Newsletter,* no. 31, March-April, 1981, p. 3.

23. *Jetro China Newsletter,* no. 34, July-August, 1981, p. 27.

24. *The China Quarterly,* no. 87, Quarterly Chronicle Documentation, p. 734.

25. *Nihon Keizai Shimbun,* October 14, 1982, p. 6.

26. *Japan Times,* February 26, 1983, p. 11.

27. For example, Toyota Motor Co. and the Taiwan-based China Steel Corp. signed a joint venture agreement on December 23, 1982, and Sanyo Electric Co. disclosed on February 21, 1983, plans to begin production of video tape recorders in Taiwan the same year. Moreover, the Soviet Union replaced China as the second-largest export market for Japanese steel in 1982.

28. *Beijing Review,* no. 49, December 5, 1983, p. 6.

Part 3

Developing Countries

7

Japan and ASEAN

Willard H. Elsbree
Khong Kim Hoong

Japan's defeat in 1945 ended its political and military role in Southeast Asia; its presence and influence were virtually wiped out. However, with its miraculous economic recovery, Japan has slowly repenetrated the region, not through force of arms or manipulative diplomacy but through economic means, and today it is the area's dominant economic power. Japan's success is even more astounding when one considers that the nation has had to work against historical patterns. The countries of Southeast Asia had very strong economic links to their previous Western colonial masters (although nominally independent, Thailand's economy may be said to have been essentially a colonial one), and Japan was, relatively speaking, a newcomer. Moreover, the Japanese were able to break the previous colonial pattern while maintaining a low political profile, whereas the Western powers had exercised economic domination through political control. Both the political and economic aspects of Japan's relationship with the five countries of the Association of Southeast Asian Nations (ASEAN), namely Indonesia, Malaysia, the Philippines, Singapore, and Thailand, will be considered in this chapter.

Economic Relations

The economic relationship is undoubtedly the most important. Certainly it is the most conspicuous and the most highly publicized, to the extent that it is sometimes asserted that Japan's interest in ASEAN is exclusively economic.

Trade

Trade is a major component of the economic relationship. Table 7.1 provides a summary of the amount involved. Trade with ASEAN accounts for approximately 13 percent of the value of Japan's total foreign trade, roughly 15 percent of its imports, and 10 percent of its exports. In recent years, Japan's imports from ASEAN have been increasing more rapidly than its exports, and the imports from ASEAN increased at a

TABLE 7.1
ASEAN's Trade with Japan, 1981 ($ million)

	Thailand	Singapore	Philippines	Indonesia	Malaysia	ASEAN
Total Exports	6,784	20,970	5,756	22,101	11,198	66,809
Total Imports	10,330	25,571	8,864	13,520	11,581	69,866
Exports to Japan	1,058 (15.5%)	1,938 (9.2%)	1,712 (29.8%)	13,263 (60.1%)	2,917 (26.1%)	20,888 (31.1%)
Imports from Japan	2,243 (21.7%)	4,454 (17.4%)	1,924 (21.7%)	4,115 (30.4%)	2,416 (20.8%)	15,152 (21.7%)

Source: International Monetary Fund, Direction of Trade Statistics, Yearbook, 1982.

more rapid rate than overall imports; however, this trend did not continue after 1980 with the downturn in world trade.

The relationship is more vital to ASEAN, for Japan is its most important trading partner, accounting for approximately 25 percent of its exports and imports, a figure that has remained virtually constant for the past decade.[1] With its powerful economy and worldwide trade interests, Japan's dependence on ASEAN is far less than that of the region on it. Calculating dependency as the value of exports in relation to gross national product (GNP), ASEAN's dependence on Japan is 8 percent, whereas Japan's dependence is 1 percent.[2]

The degree of dependency of the ASEAN countries varies. Table 7.1 shows that Indonesia is the most dependent on Japan, exporting more than half of its products to and importing one-third of its needs from Japan. Singapore is the least dependent, which is understandable since it is an international trading center.

Although ASEAN as a whole enjoys a favorable trade balance with Japan, there are significant variations among the individual members. The overall favorable balance in 1981, for example, was accounted for by the Indonesian surplus, which more than covered substantial deficits for the Philippines, Thailand, and Singapore. (The latter two regularly incur sizable trading deficits with Japan; Malaysia had come to enjoy a favorable balance until 1981. The Philippine balance varies considerably.) Indonesia's favorable balance, due largely to exports of mineral fuels and wood, is indicative of its economic importance to Japan globally as well as within the context of ASEAN. It has replaced Australia as Japan's third-largest trading partner and accounts for over one-half of ASEAN's total exports to Japan (63.5 percent in 1981).

Japan's trade relations with the ASEAN countries have not changed substantially since the 1960s. They are typical of relationships between developed and developing countries, in which the former supply manufactured goods and the latter provide primary products. The ASEAN countries have increasingly criticized this arrangement.

The importance of ASEAN to Japan is underscored by the fact that the region is Japan's major supplier for several raw materials: for example, natural rubber, tin, lumber, copper, bauxite, nickel, and wood. Less than 20 percent of Japan's crude oil comes from the region, but the percentage has been increasing steadily, as have imports of liquefied natural gas (LNG). Japan's major exports are manufactured products such as machinery, vehicles, metal products, textiles, chemicals, and plastics.

In the context of the North-South dialogue on trade, Japan finds itself in an embarrassing position. On the one hand, it wishes to secure good will that will encourage a stable supply of primary resources as well as access to the markets of the developing countries; on the other, its interests are those of a developed country. Moreover, its position on the issues raised is inevitably influenced by the Organization for Economic Cooperation and Development (OECD) partners with whom its economic ties are equally, if not more, important.

The primary producers in ASEAN strongly support a restructured international economic system in general and an integrated program for commodities in particular. Specifically, they want the developed countries, including Japan, to commit themselves to the establishment of various commodity stabilization schemes. They have proposed a plan for the stabilization of export earnings (STABEX) with Japan. The Japanese reaction has been cautious, but in the wake of Prime Minister Nakasone's 1983 tour of ASEAN there were indications that the government was ready to support the concept and to urge it upon the other developed countries.

Some of the less developed countries that are also producers of primary products have proposed the creation of cartels like the Organization of Petroleum Exporting Countries (OPEC) to strengthen their position vis-à-vis the developed nations. Although support for such an idea has been raised in ASEAN, these countries are more concerned with stability and orderliness in the trade of primary commodities. Instability in trade, whether of price or volume, disrupts their development programs by disturbing employment and the flow of income. During the Nakasone visit, for example, Indonesia sought and received a Japanese commitment to maintain purchase of Indonesian oil at 15 percent of its total oil imports. Thailand sought but apparently failed to receive a comparable type of commitment for its expected LNG exports.[3] What ASEAN members want from Japan (and the developed world) is support for their individual policies. In international organizations such as the United Nations Conference on Trade and Development (UNCTAD), they seek support for what is deemed a fairer system of international trade that will promote stability and fair prices.

Access to the markets of developed countries is another controversial issue. As a consequence of their failure to solve the recession-unemployment-inflation problem, many developed countries have resorted to protectionist measures. ASEAN countries, now well into the early stages of their industrialization programs, are pressing for expanded markets for manufactured goods. It is frustrating to find that the more processed the products are, the higher the barriers they find in developed countries.

The ASEAN countries want Japan to have greater empathy for their position on these trade issues. In particular, they are dissatisfied with the operation of the GSP (generalized system of preferences) scheme that covers agricultural and industrial products. First, for a number of products the tariff cuts offered are not very significant. Second, the coverage of products is still narrow and many export items of significance to ASEAN countries are excluded. Third, most schemes of the developed countries have safeguard mechanisms (for example, quotas and ceilings) that are often exercised to restrict imports from the less developed countries. Thus industrial products from ASEAN like footwear, textile garments, and certain rubber products are subject to quotas under the GSP scheme of Japan.[4]

In 1977 ASEAN jointly sought to negotiate with Japan and other OECD members the subjects of product coverage, depth of tariff cuts, and rules of origin. Only the Japanese response was encouraging. Japan agreed to include in its GSP scheme for ASEAN the concept of cumulation in the rules of origin. This means that Japan will treat all five ASEAN countries as a single entity. By so doing, imports from one ASEAN country that satisfy the rules of origin can be regarded as wholly originating in another ASEAN country.

Like the United States and the European Economic Community, ASEAN has sought to pressure Japan into opening its market to more manufactured goods. To date Japan's trade policies have been inclined to favor imports of raw materials. Thus, even though Malaysia's exports of crude rubber and sawlogs are allowed duty free into Japan, manufactured goods like footwear are subject to 10–30 percent tariffs or to other nontariff restrictions. In order to accelerate the development of the manufacturing sector, exporters of ASEAN manufactures require access to markets that are now heavily protected.

ASEAN countries appreciate that complete trade liberalization on the part of Japan would affect some of its less competitive industries. However, they argue that there is a case for phasing out such industries. In their view Japan should concentrate on high-skill and high-technology industries and leave the less sophisticated ones to the ASEAN countries. Some sort of industrial and technological complementarity needs to be developed parallel to the traditional international system of division of labor between producers of raw materials and manufactured goods. In the initial period some sacrifices and economic costs would inevitably be incurred by the structural changes. In the longer run, however, there would be mutual advantages in developing a new system of meshing the industrial sectors of Japan and ASEAN. Such a system would help the industrial development of ASEAN, with accelerated growth and development, this would lead to a stronger economic relationship and a larger volume of trade (especially in sophisticated capital inputs) between the two.

The Japanese perspective on these trade and development issues is, naturally, rather different. There are a number of reasons for this. In part, the difference is that between the developed and developing world, already noted. For example, in spite of frequent expressions of hope of serving as a bridge between North and South, Japan has shown little interest in reform of voting procedures for the World Bank and the International Monetary fund. Then, too, the Japanese feel they have already made more reductions in tariffs and trade restraints than most developed countries and that the problem is less that of access to the Japanese market than lack of knowledge about it and lack of initiative in developing it.

Two other factors to be remembered are domestic political pressures and relations with Japan's other major trading partners. The farmers marching on Tokyo with petitions for their Dietmen carry a message affecting ASEAN as well as U.S. beef and orange growers. The influence of sawmill operators, economically unproductive, perhaps, but a part of the Liberal-Democrats' rural base of support, has been credited with blocking increased imports of processed wood products from Indonesia.

The present emphasis in Japanese economic planning on the transformation of the industrial structure to one emphasizing knowledge- and technology-intensive industries complements ASEAN's goal. However, even though the Japanese have been more adept than most in adjusting their economic structure, such changes take time and the impact on ASEAN will be slower than desired. With the shipbuilding industry facing difficulties and with the Spinners Association filing dumping charges against the Republic of Korea (ROK), it is easy to imagine the obstacles to restructuring, especially in a time of slowed economic growth. It should also be noted that the development of industrial complementarity and the structural changes related thereto involve the newly industrializing countries (ROK, Taiwan, Hong Kong, Singapore) as well as ASEAN. They pose the most intense competition and, consequently, can be expected to figure more prominently in Japanese calculations.

Investment

In addition to trade, investment has become an increasingly important link in Japanese-ASEAN relations. As ASEAN's largest foreign investor, Japan now provides about one-third of its annual foreign investment. It is the leading foreign investor in Indonesia and Thailand, second in the Philippines and Malaysia, and fourth in Singapore. Although North America is the leading region in Japan's direct overseas investment (28 percent), Asia is a close second (27 percent), with ASEAN accounting for about 20 percent.

Although ASEAN will remain an important object of Japanese investment, current trends mitigate against any major increase in its share of the total. Traditionally Japanese overseas investment has emphasized natural-resource development rather than the manufacturing sector. Under pressure to reduce trade imbalances with its developed partners, the emphasis is now shifting. In fiscal 1982, for example, not only was there a decline in total direct overseas investment but an even sharper one in Asian resource development. On the other hand, investment in Europe and North America increased markedly.[5]

ASEAN countries need foreign investments in order to industrialize, and they seek investments through a variety of incentives, but their experience with Japanese investments has not been entirely satisfactory. Several criticisms have been leveled at them. It is suggested that the focus of investment is mostly in resource-oriented industries or in those that involve no significant transmission of technology and have low value added; that Japanese investments are in industries that are transferring the pollution problem to the ASEAN countries; and that some Japanese industrial investments are established solely for their promoters to enjoy the preferential privileges offered by the developed countries to the manufactured exports of less developed countries (which would be inconsistent with the original purpose of such preferential treatment, to promote industrial development of less developed countries). In sum, Japanese private investment, like foreign private investment generally, is accused of producing a new form of colonial exploitation with all of its attendant evils. In the Southeast Asian context, there is the additional criticism that local partners of Japanese ventures are drawn largely from the Chinese community, thus perpetuating the traditional Chinese grip on the local economy.

Aid

Aid is a third component in Japanese-ASEAN relations. Aid from Japan constitutes about 40 percent of the total aid ASEAN receives and a considerably larger percentage of official development assistance (ODA) received. Of the total foreign aid given by Japan, approximately 35 percent goes to ASEAN, with Indonesia receiving the lion's share. Although ASEAN will continue to be a major recipient of Japanese economic aid, the trends appear to be working against any sizable increase in percentage terms. For example, ODA, which received one of the few increases in the 1983 budget (7 percent), is seen by the Japanese government as directed, increasingly, to developing countries with the lowest per capita incomes. ASEAN countries are seen as moving into the category of recipients for whom loans, yen credits, and private investments are considered most appropriate. It is precisely these forms of aid, however, that have shown a decline since 1978.[6] In addition, as the international economic climate has worsened, there is increasing competition for these funds. The recently concluded $4-billion-aid package to ROK has led ASEAN to demand significantly larger amounts and to complain that Korea is receiving a disproportionately large amount. China has recently requested a yen-credit loan worth $6 billion. ASEAN will have to take its place in line, and even though that place will be a high-ranking one, the amounts will inevitably be viewed as disappointing.

The present state of the ASEAN Industrial Development Project, a major attempt at multilateral aid, has not increased Japanese enthusiasm for multilateral undertakings. Pressed by ASEAN to increase developmental assistance, Japan pledged $1 billion to help finance a major industrial project in each country. Designed to contribute to all-ASEAN, not purely national, development, the projects have been slow to materialize. Only the Indonesian one has reached the implementation stage and that only with additional Japanese aid to cover cost overruns. Singapore has dropped active participation, and other national projects are in varying stages of development.

Constraints on Relations with ASEAN

On the one hand, ASEAN sees Japan's involvement in ASEAN as a group as wanting; on the other hand, in Japan's perspective, ASEAN is slow, indecisive, and at times even confusing in its development. There is, for example, the ambivalent attitude of the individual ASEAN countries themselves toward ASEAN as a collective body. In public all the members extol the importance of ASEAN as a regional body. In private, they prefer bilateral relations with non-ASEAN countries. Important trade, aid, and investment relations are bilateral ones between outsiders and individual ASEAN countries rather than between outsiders and ASEAN as a regional body. This schizophrenic attitude clearly reflects the countries' weak commitment to ASEAN as an organization and the persistence of distrust among themselves. Such unresolved differences together with their intense competition for foreign investment have meant that each member still pursues nationalistic economic policies rather than regional ones. This is a source of friction among themselves and between themselves and outsiders. Although ASEAN has often criticized Japan and the other developed countries for not providing sufficient assistance to promote development, the group has yet to properly formulate a clear regional program for industrialization. With such uncertainties and constraints, it is difficult to expect countries like Japan to commit vast resources for the development of ASEAN.

It has often been remarked that Japanese-ASEAN relations are similar to U.S.-Japanese ones of twenty-five years ago. ASEAN, the weaker party, frequently feels its interests are slighted. Japan, the stronger party, is frequently annoyed at what appear to be exaggerated concerns and unreasonable demands of ASEAN. In spite of the points of friction, there is every reason to assume Japan's economic interest in the region will remain at a high level, especially in light of its continuing difficulties with other major trading partners and of the above-average projected growth rates for ASEAN.

A number of general constraints should be kept in mind, however. Some of the more obvious ones are: (1) diversification of sources and supply routes of resources, which retains a high priority in Japanese policy, with overconcentration on one region to be avoided; (2) the inevitable conflicts between economic interests of developed and developing countries on certain issues; (3) the importance of Japan's economic ties with its developed partners as well as with the newly industrializing countries; and (4) reservations in the Japanese business community about political stability and labor productivity and discipline in the region. In view of these constraints, congruence of interests is hardly to be expected. A satisfactory relationship will require compromise, and compromise involves a political component. For Japan to respond more fully to ASEAN interests is a political, not just an economic issue. The question is, does Japan have a clearly formulated political policy toward ASEAN?

Political Relations

Under pressure (particula. *v* from the United States) to play a more active role in Southeast Asia, Japan in the mid-1970s turned to ASEAN as a vehicle of policy. Support for ASEAN has won increased backing in both official and unofficial circles, and one can speak of an ASEAN lobby in Japan today. As already noted, however, ASEAN is not a united entity and precisely what a "support ASEAN" policy entails is not at all clear in many instances. A clearly formulated political policy toward ASEAN is still in the making, and the lack of one unquestionably has contributed to occasional misunderstanding and misapprehension about Japanese intentions. As in other regions, Japan has sought to emphasize its role in economic assistance and cooperation, about which it feels most confident. For domestic as well as international reasons, it has been reluctant to exercise political initiative.

In spite of the lack of a comprehensive political policy, however, circumstances have made it impossible to entirely avoid political decisions. Four issues can be used to illustrate this point: the Indochina problem; relations with China; Japanese defense policy and rearmament; and the Pacific Basin Community proposal.

Indochina

With the unification of Vietnam after 1975, the Japanese moved to expand economic contacts, partly on the political grounds that links with the noncommunist world might enable Vietnam to avoid falling completely under Soviet domination. This policy foundered on the strong ASEAN reaction to the Vietnamese invasion of Kampuchea; ASEAN demanded the complete withdrawal of forces and nonrecognition of the Vietnamese-backed Heng Samrin regime. Faced with a choice, Japan understandably backed ASEAN, a policy that has been pursued consistently and with growing political involvement. In response to ASEAN requests, the Japanese suspended the implementation of their aid program to Vietnam, and they have indicated to the Vietnamese it would not be resumed until a satisfactory political solution has been reached in Kampuchea. Going beyond the ASEAN policy of denying recognition to the Heng Samrin government, the Japanese have lobbied actively and effectively in the United Nations (UN) in support of the policy. They were active at the UN conference on Kampuchea in New York in 1981; Japan is now a member of the ad hoc committee appointed to try to reach a settlement. The extent of Japanese economic assistance to Thailand is regarded as, in part, a political gesture of support for the "front line" state in the ASEAN-Vietnamese confrontation.

Current Japanese policy continues to leave the initiative to ASEAN. Japan quietly supported the effort to create a coalition of the three anti-Vietnamese factions and has responded to the ASEAN desire to strengthen the two noncommunist groups (Son Sann and Sihanouk) by providing food and medical aid. Interviewed by the Thai press, senior Japanese officials were quoted as saying that "the Japanese government is determined to follow the ASEAN initiative and policy on the Kampuchean issue."[7]

During his Southeast Asia tour in 1983, Prime Minister Nakasone again assured ASEAN members that Japan would not unfreeze its aid to Vietnam until a satisfactory political settlement was reached. Moreover, the Japanese indicated a willingness to increase aid to Laos as one means that might contribute to breaking the deadlock.[8]

This stance would seem to place Japan in a position closer to that of Indonesia and Malaysia, which—because of their view of the threat from China—have been more inclined to compromise on the Kampuchean issue than have Thailand and Singapore (generally backed by the Philippines), who see the USSR as the major threat to security. To date, ASEAN unity on the issue has remained steadfast (some would argue that it has been the most important cement of the organization), and Japan has been spared a choice. Emphasis on economic contacts wherever possible and the continued appeal of "omnidirectional diplomacy" are added factors that would appear to move Japan closer to the Indonesian/Malaysian approach. Statements favoring a lifting of the aid freeze and ending the recognition of the Pol Pot government by some Liberal-Democratic party (LDP) Diet members indicate that there would be support for this approach within the governing party.[9] On the other hand, we should point out that Japanese perceptions of Soviet and Chinese roles in Asia are closer to those of Thailand and Singapore.

China

The so-called China Question has political implications for Japan's relations with ASEAN. ASEAN's concern is twofold: that Japan's economic asistance to China will mean a weakened commitment of ASEAN (less aid and less trade) and that a strengthened China will pose a greater threat to the region, especially in the form of aid to communist-directed insurgency movements. As noted, this apprehension is greatest in Indonesia and Malaysia, but even Prime Minister Lee Kwan Yew of Singapore, whose views on the subject are usually somewhat different, has publicly noted the ASEAN concern that a well-armed China may pose a greater problem for Southeast Asia than does the Soviet Union. Japan seeks to allay these fears by maintaining a mediating position. During Suzuki's ASEAN tour in 1981 and again during the visit of Indonesian president Suharto to Japan in October 1982 the theme was the same: China's modernization program poses no threat but rather serves as a stabilizing factor; moreover, Japan's economic assistance to China will not be at the expense of ASEAN; instead, an equitable balance will be kept. In a recent visit to Thailand, the director-general of the Self-Defense Agency stressed the point that, in the long run, Vietnam posed a greater threat to ASEAN than did China.[10]

It is unlikely that these differing perceptions of China's role in Asia will be entirely reconciled in the near future. Fear of Chinese subversion is not one of Tokyo's most salient problems, and, although the luster of the China market may have dimmed somewhat recently, Japan can hardly be expected to forgo the actual and potential advantages of expanded economic relations with China. The advantages of economic omnidirectionalism outweigh those of any specialized relationship with ASEAN that would restrict Japan's range of economic interests.

Japan's Defense Policy

The reaction in ASEAN countries to proposed increases in Japanese defense expenditures has varied according to country and to the issue immediately at stake. As long as discussion in Japan centered on the "1 percent issue," there was no great cry of alarm from ASEAN. During Suzuki's ASEAN trip, the prime minister of Singapore urged an increase in Japan's defense capabilities, pointing out that otherwise the military burden on the United States would increase, thereby reducing the latter's defense efforts in Southeast Asia. The foreign minister of Thailand indicated that a security role for Japan in the region would be welcomed. Indonesia's foreign minister noted that proposed budgetary increases in defense spending were being made in response to U.S. pressure, rather than the "free will" of the Japanese themselves. The president of the Philippines voiced no objections to expenditures "strictly for defense" and underlined a frequently-stressed ASEAN theme: Japan does not pose a threat as long as it is allied with the United States and the United States maintains a military presence in the region.[11]

On the other hand, the question of extending Japan's military capabilities to defend its sea approaches over a one-thousand-mile zone poses the problem in more concrete terms for ASEAN and has evoked a sharper, if still somewhat varied, response. Presidents Marcos of the Philippines and Suharto of Indonesia have been most vocal in expressing doubts. Marcos has publicly expressed his distrust of Japan and charged it with still harboring ideas of domination.[12] The issue was much on President Suharto's mind during his visit to the United States and Japan in 1982. To Japanese assurances that only areas north of Guam and the Philippines were covered and that the U.S. Seventh Fleet would assume responsibility beyond that zone (including the Straits of Malacca), Suharto, in effect, responded that sea-lane defenses might better be left to the countries concerned and that it should be a cooperative, not a one-sided, effort.[13] The official response in Singapore, often supportive of a Japanese role in regional security in the past, was rather muted. Prime Minister Lee Kwan Yew indicated there was no concern as long as Japan confined itself to a naval role in the western Pacific and the northern part of the China Sea; the foreign minister asserted there would be no problem as long as Japan did not develop nuclear weapons.[14] Malaysian officials, currently embarked on a "look eastward/emulate Japan" campaign, have not been openly critical.

Much of Prime Minister Nakasone's 1982 ASEAN visit was devoted to the effort to allay lingering doubts about Japan's defense policy;

indeed, the political aspects of the trip may be said to have outweighed economic ones. At each stop he stressed the points that sea-lane defense applied only to Japan itself, not to ASEAN waters; that Japan's defense effort was strictly limited; and that it would continue to be bound by nonnuclear principles and those of the peace constitution. Reports of the trip indicated he had a considerable measure of success.[15]

A major concern of ASEAN is not so much the immediate military threat from Japan as the fear of the withdrawal of the U.S. military commitment to the region. A militarily stronger Japan as an adjunct of U.S. power is one thing; a militarily strengthened Japan as a substitute or surrogate for U.S. power is quite another. There is also the fear that, however limited the scope of Japan's present intentions, a policy once embarked upon assumes its own momentum and leads to unforeseen consequences. ("Once it gets rolling, Japan will do with defense what it has with automobiles and semi-conductors."[16])

Another view, given some currency recently, is that Japan should provide the technology and economic assistance to enable ASEAN to build up its own defenses and thereby attend to its own security. In a variant of this approach, Japan is uged to contribute to upgrading ASEAN defenses as well as its own. What is important, in this view, is that the gap in military capabilities not be allowed to widen further; maintenance of an equilibrium is needed to reassure ASEAN.[17]

In summary, the reaction within ASEAN to an increase in Japan's defense program is lukewarm, but not stridently negative and by no means uniform. Both sides of the debate within Japan can find quotable material. Although the outcome of that debate will be determined largely by domestic politics and U.S. pressure and policies, not by ASEAN views, it is noteworthy that the prime minister apparently found it politically useful to secure official ASEAN backing for his policy.

Pacific Basin Community

International developments during the past decade have renewed the interest of some Japanese governmental and business circles in the concept of a Pacific Basin Community. Concern about the future U.S. commitment to Japan and to Asia, the energy crisis, the growth of protectionist policies, and the experience of the European Economic Community (EEC) have all served to make more appealing the idea of a regional grouping that would afford greater security in a world in which Japan seems increasingly vulnerable—politically and economically.

The late Prime Minister Masayoshi Ohira first took the initiative with the appointment of a private study group to report on the feasibility of the idea. Despite the fact that the group was private and consisted mainly of academics, representatives of the bureaucracy constituted one-third of the membership. The importance of the group was further attested to by the fact that its chairman, Saburo Okita, was foreign minister of the Ohira cabinet.

Although no formal proposals have been made by the Japanese government, the report of the study group has been used as a basis for discussions. The report suggested a loose regional grouping formed for economic and cultural purposes. Political and military matters were to be left out entirely. Membership was deliberately left vague to avoid political difficulties at the outset, though it was clear that countries with open economies would form the core of the community. The report emphasized the tentativeness of the group's suggestions and reiterated that continuing dialogues both at the official and private levels were necessary; it has been labeled as an "idea for the twenty-first century."

The idea has raised questions in the ASEAN countries. Officially expressed views have been cautious and noncommittal: What are the benefits? What are the drawbacks? What will it mean for ASEAN?

The unofficial reaction was more sharply critical and betrayed an underlying distrust of Japanese motives. Many saw it as an attempt to undermine and weaken ASEAN; some saw the plan as U.S.-inspired with Japan serving as frontman; there were questions about the role of Australia. (That the initial announcement of the plan had been made in Australia without prior consultation with ASEAN governments was an inauspicious launching from the viewpoint of ASEAN.)

ASEAN countries are also wary of being too closely identified with Japan and the United States in a grouping that might be contrary to the principle of neutrality as set forth in the Declaration of the Zone of Peace, Freedom, and Neutrality, which was designed to keep major power rivalries out of the region. Coupled with this is the fear that in the larger grouping the strength of ASEAN would be diluted and the members dominated by Japan and the United States.

Another reason for the skeptical response lies in the historical experience of the countries themselves. Even as a smaller group with more homogeneity and common interest, the association has taken a long time to achieve even the present level of understanding. Consequently, ASEAN members do not want their interests and energies to be diverted from ASEAN into the more problematic and heterogeneous Pacific grouping over which they would have no control.

*   *   *

If Japan can be said to have a political policy toward Southeast Asia, it might be labeled "Support ASEAN"—within the confines of overall foreign policy and without assuming any risk. It is a policy without detailed commitment and, hence, does not arouse domestic opposition. It enables Japan to play a supportive role without assuming the initiative; it dovetails with resource diplomacy, and it is congruent with the U.S. relationship, the first priority in foreign policy.

Economically, one can expect the asymmetrical nature of the relationship to continue. There are few alternatives to ASEAN's economic dependency on Japan, and given the time needed for further industrial development, a type of North-South relationship will persist. At the same time, the region continues to be an attractive one for Japanese trade and investment, and growing Japanese interest in encouraging offshore light industrial development fits in with local development plans. Conflicting interests, perspectives, and priorities will create friction (the Japanese will not be loved); ASEAN will seek to reduce its dependency; Japan's global interests will limit regional commitment; but mutual advantage will ensure close economic ties.

Notes

1. According to International Monetary Fund (IMF), *Direction of Trade Statistics, 1982* (Washington, D.C.: IMF, 1982), the figure is 26.1 percent.

2. Japan External Trade Organization, *White Paper on International Trade, Japan 1979* (Tokyo, 1979), p. 45.

3. *Japan Economic Journal (JEJ)*, 10 May 1983.

4. In May 1983, during Prime Minister Nakasone's tour of ASEAN, a 50 percent increase in import ceilings was announced. *Far Eastern Economic Review (FEER)* 19–25 May 1983.

5. *JEJ*, 14 June 1983.

6. See Akira Hiyoshi article in *Fainansu*, March 1982, as reproduced in *Joint Publications Research Service (JPRS), Japan Series*, 30 June 1982. Total aid disbursement for 1982 declined, making the stated goal of doubling ODA by 1985 virtually impossible to attain. Bilateral assistance increased slightly, but this increase was more than offset by a decline in multilateral aid. *JEJ*, 10 May, 14 June 1983.

7. *Nation Review*, Bangkok, 27 September 1982, as reproduced in *JPRS, South and Southeast Asia Series*, 18 October 1982.

8. *FEER*, 12 May 1983.

9. See statement by a member of the LDP Afro-Asian Study Group upon return of a delegation from visits to Hanoi and Phnom Penh. *Foreign Broadcast Information Series (FBIS)*, 11 September 1981.

10. *Nation Review*, 4 October 1982, as quoted in *FBIS*, 14 October 1982.

11. *FBIS*, 7, 13, 14 January 1981.

12. *FEER*, 22–28 October 1982.

13. *FBIS*, 22, 26 October 1982.

14. *FEER*, 22–28 October 1982.

15. *FEER*, 12–18, 19–25 May 1983. Also *JEJ*, 5 April, 10 May 1983. It might also be noted that the widely held view in ASEAN that Japan is interested only in economic matters is a counterweight to fear of Japanese rearmament. See article by Prakash Chandra in *Business Times*, 20 March 1982, as reproduced in *JPRS*, 13 May 1982.

16. *FEER*, 22–28 October 1982.

17. For these views and other official reactions, see Frances Lai Fung-wai, "Need for Rising Sun That Does Not Scorch," *Straits Times*, 23 October 1982; also Rodney Tasker, "A Conflict of Interests," *FEER*, 20–26 January 1983.

8

Japan and the Middle East

William R. Campbell

That Japan is dependent upon the Gulf states for practically all the oil it consumes is widely known. This chapter focuses upon less well known information to suggest some of the constraints on Japan's policy toward the Middle East. The following observations must be understood in terms of two facts: First, although Japan's manufacturing sector is second in size to that of the United States in the noncommunist world, it is more concentrated in oil and energy-intensive heavy and chemical industries than other industrial countries; and second, Japan is caught in the transition from such industry to the "knowledge-intensive" industry previewed and supported by the Ministry of International Trade and Industry (MITI) since 1971.

Japan's Dependence on Oil

Importance of the Middle East

A survey of the post–World War II history of Japan suggests that the character of its primary energy supply was the least determined of all the imperatives of development addressed throughout the 1950s and 1960s. Fateful choices by Japan's elites determined that oil would be its primary fuel and that this resource would come primarily from the Gulf.

By 1980, 87 percent of Japan's oil was supplied by Organization of Petroleum Exporting Countries (OPEC) nations. By comparison, the United States, West Germany, and Italy depended on OPEC crude for 30 percent, 76 percent, and 83 percent of their supplies respectively. The Middle East accounted for 73.2 percent of this total, the lion's share coming from Saudi Arabia, the United Arab Emirates (UAE), and Iran.[1] As can been seen from the data in Table 8.1, Japan's dependence upon Middle East crude oil has been profound.

The shift in the composition of Japan's primary energy supply is not apparent from the table. In 1978 petroleum accounted for 73 percent of Japan's primary energy supply, whereas in 1950, only 6.2 percent

TABLE 8.1
Origins of Japan's Crude Oil Imports (Thousands of Barrels Per Day)

	1960	%	1965	%	1970	%	1975	%	1977	%	1978	%	1979	%
Middle East	452	80.1	1338	89.0	2859	84.7	3541	78.2	3733	78.0	3645	78.3	3689	76.3
Saudi Arabia	110		292		490	14.4	1156	25.5	1465	30.6	1336	28.7	1372	28.4
Iran	23		326		1470	43.5	1122	24.8	820	17.1	785	16.8	479	16.0
UAE	---		8		156	4.6	418	9.2	538	11.2	481	10.3	489	10.1
Kuwait	218		356		287	8.5	387	8.5	376	7.8	372	8.0	442	9.1
Neutral Zone	29		248		349	10.3	232	5.1	170	3.5	232	5.0	313	6.4
Oman	---		---		97	3.0	129	2.8	169	3.5	168	3.6	191	3.9
Iraq	70		96		---	0	94	2.0	150	3.1	163	3.6	259	5.3
Qatar	2		12		4		3		45	.1	108	3.0	144	3.9
Pacific Basin	83	14.7	108	7.2	449	13.3	850	18.8	1024	21.4	994	21.3	1123	23.2
Indonesia	61		106		445		518		653		598		696	
Malaysia	---		---		---		23		70		93		111	
Brunei	22		2		4		149		163		152		164	
China	---		---		---		159		135		147		150	
Australia	---		---		---		1		3		4		2	
Other	29	5.2	57	3.8	68	2.0	137	3.0	31	0.6	18	0.4	22	0.5
Africa	---		---		46		131		24		10		13	
Venezuela	---		7		12		5		7		7		8	
U.S.S.R.	29		50		10		1		---		1		1	
TOTAL	564	100	1503	100	3375	100	4528	100	4788	100	4656	100	4834	100

Sources: Data for 1960 - Petroleum Association of Japan.
1965 - Tokyo Petroleum News, January 26, 1968.
1970, 1975 - Ministry of International Trade and Industry (MITI), quoted in
Japan Petroleum and Energy Yearbook: 1978.
1977, 1978, and 1979 - Japan Oil Statistics Today, December 1979.

had come from petroleum. Coal then made up 51.2 percent of its primary energy. By 1978, coal accounted for only 13.7 percent of Japan's primary energy supply. This reconfiguration of elements resulted from MITI's implementation of the Petroleum Industry Law of 1962. The law intensified the interactions between MITI oil administrators and oil-industry executives, especially those grouped in the Petroleum Association of Japan, an organization into which large numbers of MITI officials have retired.

As a result of MITI policies, whereas Japan had imported about 24 percent of its total energy requirement in 1955, by 1978, 84.7 percent of this supply was being imported.[2] About 66 percent of Japan's total energy supply came from crude, nearly 90 percent of which came from the Middle East. This shift in the composition of Japan's primary energy supply resulted from MITI's middle-term commitment to develop Japan's industrial infrastructure based on cheap oil. Japan's reliance on international oil companies and especially on Gulf oil was a consequence of Japan's "economic-adaptive" strategy, in which the state relied upon the market to secure oil, and of the decision of international oil concerns and the United States to supply the oil requirements of Europe and Japan from Gulf fields.

It is clear that oil has made the "Japanese miracle" possible. But one can understand oil's significance more fully by realizing that Japan is the world's largest consumer of electricity and that oil is the power source for 56.6 percent of the electricity generated in Japan.[3] Moreover, the Middle East absorbs an ever-larger amount of Japan's exports (at present about 12 percent), thereby materially aiding Japan to retrieve some of its petrodollars and to expand its economy so that the problems of income distribution can be solved with little or no political fallout.[4] Saudi Arabia is Japan's second-largest trading partner, following only the United States. Despite its acknowledged potential instability,[5] the Gulf is considered a very important export target. For example, Marubeni, one of Japan's largest trading companies, hopes soon to treble the extent of its Saudi activities; its plan calls for rapidly expanding activities throughout the Gulf.[6] The Japanese government provides insurance for such private companies against the loss of a substantial portion of their venture capital.

The importance of the Middle East for Japan's exports was also evidenced by Prime Minister Nakasone's aggravated desire to visit the Middle East, as expressed during the 1982 visit of King Hussein of Jordan to Japan. As Japan's energy diversification and conservation programs were taking hold and as its demand for oil was abating on account of the global recession, the importance of the Middle East as an export target for its obsolescent technology became increasingly evident to Japan.

The crucial questions seem to be whether Japan can reduce the rate of its dependence on Gulf oil, whether much of the oil that Japan will import through the 1980s and 1990s must continue to come from the Gulf, and what Japan's alternatives to oil are.

The Provisional Long-Term Energy Supply and Demand Outlook was prepared and announced in August 1979 by the Advisory Committee for Energy to the MITI. It showed that MITI had given priority to the development of nuclear energy, coal, and liquefied natural gas (LNG) as alternatives to oil. In addition, the Advisory Committee urged MITI to adopt energy-conservation strategies and to promote the search for diversified, stable supplies of oil. Even if the premises upon which the Advisory Committee based its recommendations were valid (which they are not), in 1990 Japan still would depend upon oil for 50 percent of its energy supply. About 60 percent of this oil would originate in the Gulf.

Search for Alternative Energies

On 28 November 1980, the cabinet approved MITI targets for oil-alternative energy supplies for 1990. To reduce its oil dependence to 50 percent by 1990, Japan must increase coal from 12.9 percent to 17.7 percent of primary energy, natural gas from about 4 percent to 10.2 percent, and nuclear power from 3.6 percent to 10.9 percent[7] and substitute knowledge-intensive for energy-intensive industry. Knowledge-intensive industry involves microchip manufacturing, social-systems industries, and industries based on new technologies such as carbon fibers and optoelectronics.

To meet the MITI nuclearization goal, Japan would have to add (in less than ten years, when the average lead time for light-water reactor construction is fifteen years) to its current installed capacity of about 15,000 megawatts (MW) an additional capacity to generate 37,000 MW at the astronomical cost of ¥10 trillion.[8] Only seven of the required units are under construction, with a combined capacity of about 5,600 MW. This suggests that the run-up in nuclear capacity is highly unlikely to meet MITI's optimistic expectations.

Japan must not only overcome the suspicion of nuclear power of an aging population in general and its siting in particular, it must also sort out the bureaucratic conflict over which nuclearization program to follow. Another conflict is that between MITI internationalists, who are pushing for the adoption of the most quickly available (typically U.S.) of the foreign technologies, and the Japan Nuclear Development Corporation (JNDC), which—partly as a consequence of the near disaster at Three Mile Island and the one at Japan Atomic Power Company's (JAPCO) Tsuruga plant in April 1981—insists upon promoting a comprehensive nuclear program based upon an indigenous technology. The JNDC also bridles at the prospect of Japan's continuing dependence upon foreign technologies and technicians. Furthermore, the members of JNDC aspire to the development of a high value-added export industry, such as could be predicated upon the nuclear technology that Japan presently is developing. Such a technology could be extremely attractive to Kuwait, the UAE, and Saudi Arabia, each of which has a relatively small power grid and relatively great need for a nonfossil fuel to fire the desalination plants.

It must be noted that because of safety concerns (largely directed at imported nuclear facilities), Japanese nuclear installations typically operate at very low load factors. Some hope has been expressed that this load factor can be increased by 20 percent.[9] If effected, 6 million kiloliters of oil a year could be saved, though this outcome is unlikely in light of the events of April 1981. As a consequence of safety considerations, Japan's nuclear facilities are down for long periods for routine inspection.[10] These factors substantially reduce the cost effectiveness that nuclear generating facilities promise.

Regarding the development of coal, Japan has somewhat better prospects. It is already the world's largest importer of coal. Its main fear is that the world coal market will be dominated by U.S. companies; possibly the same oil companies that previously diverted oil from Japan during the second oil crisis. This worry makes the linking to long-term supply agreements of overseas investments in the Soviet Union, China, and Australia to develop coal deposits especially interesting. The long-term availability of metallurgical-grade coal is crucial to Japan's steel industry.

"The main [economic] obstacle to the greater use of coal in Japan is not the availability of coal, but the acceptance of the costs and burdens—including those on the environment—of constructing coal-fired electricity generating plants."[11] Presently, the government offers subsidies partially to offset the cost differential between coal- and oil-fired installations, and it provides preferential loans for the construction of coal-fired generating stations. After 1985 authorities will allow no oil-fired stations to be built. Using these deadlines and the development of new technologies for burning coal (providing the prospect for yet another high value-added export), MITI is urging utilities, including the very powerful Tokyo Electric Company (TEPCO), to burn coal rather than LNG.[12]

LNG is an interesting primary energy source because Japan does not compete directly with either the United States or other importers for the fuel. Given its low thermal efficiency and the fact that the price of LNG is established by the price of crude, LNG is not cheap. But, as a TEPCO spokesman is reported to have said; "If we quantify the social costs, the inordinate delays, the remote and extra-large sites, and the ensuing transmission losses with which we have had to contend with nuclear power, then LNG is far less expensive. And in comparison to coal, the environmental problems are in an entirely different category."[13] Besides, LNG is available under twenty-year contracts and needs no sophisticated technology for burning. It is therefore a nearly ideal medium-term way (power plants last for about thirty years) to diversify energy sources. Importantly, relatively little of Japan's LNG comes from the Gulf. "TEPCO estimates that 37 percent of Japan's primary energy will be provided by electricity by 1995."[14] Something on the order of 15 percent of total electric generation will be based upon LNG.[15]

Global Context

We must place Japan's oil dependency within the context of the global availability of oil. To do this, it is imperative to understand that OPEC oil "constitutes the difference between total world demand for energy and the supply of energy from all non-OPEC sources."[16] In 1980, 70 percent of the world's petroleum reserves were controlled by OPEC. The organization accounted for 49 percent of world production; it controlled 80 percent of the oil in international trade.[17] Saudi Arabian oil represented 27.75 percent of OPEC oil in 1978 and 43.58 percent in 1981.[18] The initial increase in the Saudi share of OPEC oil was a result of the decline in Iran's oil production precipitated by the Islamic revolution. Later it was a result of the decline in both Iranian and Iraqi production consequent to the war between these two OPEC members. As Iranian and Iraqi production capacity was brought back on line in late 1981 and throughout 1982, the Saudi share of OPEC oil production dropped back toward about a one-third share.

OPEC oil is a residual because of the capacity of Saudi Arabia over a long period of time to produce without damage to its fields an amount of oil ranging from about 4 million barrels per day (bpd) to something over 11 million bpd.[19] "It is this ability to adjust production levels over such a broad range that gives Saudi Arabia its potential market power and makes producers and consumers of oil look to Riyadh and its oil policies with concern."[20]

Two factors limit Saudi flexibility. The multi-billion-dollar Jubail and Yanbu petrochemical complexes built for the Saudis by Japan require over 1 billion cubic feet of natural gas per day. This amount of natural gas must presently be produced in association with about 6 million bpd of oil.[21] Moreover, Saudi defense, foreign-aid, and development budgets for 1982-1983 suggested that about 8 million bpd of oil must be produced at a price of about $32 per barrel to provide adequate funds for these commitments.[22] These considerations seem to mean that, unless the Saudis are prepared to draw on their reserves, the lower limit for Saudi oil production is between 6 and 8 million bpd. The 8 million bpd figure is the softer of the two, since the Saudis could rely on income from pilgrims to Mecca, customs receipts, the export of natural-gas liquids, and the roughly $150 billion worth of overseas investments. Such income could have made up as much as 20 percent of the Saudi's $100 billion 1982-1983 budget. The Saudi situation has become more complicated as a result of oil prices hovering at about $29 per barrel and Saudi production at about 5 million bpd.

In 1978-1979 the power that Saudi Arabia enjoyed as a consequence of being a residual oil producer was brought home. As a result of Saudi actions, the contract price of OPEC oil went from an aveage 1978 price of $12.70 per barrel to $24 in December 1979. Until the end of 1978, when it rose to $19.19, the spot price of oil was very close to the contract price, suggesting market equilibrium. By December 1979, the spot price of oil was $41 per barrel, suggesting a market disequilibrium that was to lever the contract price of oil higher and higher over the next two years.

The cost of oil to Japan more than doubled. This was largely because, having perceived international oil companies to be diverting supplies, the Japanese aggressively entered the Rotterdam spot market, further driving up the spot price of oil. From the point of view of Japan, this action, plus direct deal and government-to-government contracts for oil, was necessitated because a reduction in energy supply would cause a contraction of industrial production and employment, compromise Japan's transition to a knowledge-intensive industrial infrastructure, and shrink its export markets. Because the Japanese elite, the Foreign Ministry more than MITI, is very sensitive about competing directly with the United States for markets, Japan is increasingly interested in trade with the communist bloc and trade in those goods where the targeted sector of a market is relatively free of U.S. and European Community (EC) interest.

Resource Diplomacy

Fully to appreciate the dependence of Japan on imported oil and the consequence for Japan of the increase in prices just related, it is useful to note the following. "Between 1950 and 1973, Japan's GNP grew at an average annual rate of 8.9 percent. . . . During that entire period the average delivered cost of Japan's imported crude from all sources was close to $2.00 per barrel."[23] In fact, on account of subsidized loans and other advantages that the internationals lavished upon Japanese refiners, "the real prices paid by Japan for its crude imports were even lower" than two dollars a barrel.[24] If we focus on the period 1960–1973, Japan's average annual growth rate was even higher at 10.5 percent. For the same period, the average annual growth rate for the United States was only 4.2 percent.[25]

Cheap energy gave Japan's firms a substantial competitive advantage over those of the United States, which had to pay higher prices for their energy because of oil imports quotas. The U.S. policy of providing cheap oil to displace coal in Europe and in Japan was coming home to roost, for during the late 1950s and the early 1960s U.S. dominance of the international political economy eroded.

As the competitive disadvantage of the United States was exacerbated by the burden of the Vietnam War, the dollar came under very heavy presure. The Bretton Woods international monetary regime collapsed, the collapse being capped when President Nixon, without consulting the Organization for Economic Cooperation and Development (OECD), took the United States off of the gold-exchange standard in 1971. The

Nixon administration's New Economic Policy precipitated an upward revaluation of the yen by 25 percent, thereby destabilizing the Japanese economy. The same year the administration reversed its China policy, again without prior consultation with Japan.

The gravity of the Nixon shocks was exacerbated by their context. After 1970, when the Libyan government had been able significantly to raise the price of oil by regulating the operations of Occidental Petroleum, it became apparent to Japan (especially to the "resource faction" lead by Soichi Matsune, chairman of Keidanren's energy committee; Sohei Nakayama, counselor to the Industrial Bank of Japan; and Hiroki Imazato, board chairman for a number of overseas petroleum development companies) that sooner rather than later OPEC countries would gain significant concessions from the international oil companies that had dominated the international oil regime. Early in 1971 the Gulf states, the prime source of Japan's oil, were able to raise the price of market crude against the firm opposition of the international oil companies.[26] Then Nixon's first energy message in 1971 made clear that the increasing demand for oil in advanced industrial states could outstrip supply.[27] Indeed, U.S. oil production peaked in 1970. After 1972, the United States was obliged to draw on world markets for additional oil. From 1970 to 1973, U.S. imports of crude rose 45 percent.[28] Finally, in late 1972, the international oil companies informed Japanese refiners not only of price increases but of supply cuts of up to 20 percent. At this juncture, the chairman of the Federation of Economic Organizations (Keidanren) opined that "the energy problem presented a threat to Japan's continuing economic livelihood."[29]

Caldwell's study of Japan's petroleum politics demonstrated that "when energy supply shortages are perceived as a threat to Japan's basic economic livelihood, business leaders may move ahead of some sections of the government, pushing for change even when such action runs counter to stated U.S. policy preferences."[30] The U.S. brief against which Japan finally would choose involved U.S. policy toward the Arab world, especially regarding the rights of the Palestinians. The need for Arab oil would put such a strain on the historical primacy of the U.S.-Japanese alliance, which had determined Japan's postwar foreign policy even under the leadership of the Liberal-Democratic party (LDP), that no less a figure than MITI Minister Nakasone would argue that energy had become as important as defense. With this declaration, MITI joined the business community of Japan in bringing increasing pressure on the Foreign Ministry, for which the primacy of the U.S.-Japan alliance remained key, to shift its point of view toward the "resource diplomacy" advocated by the *zaikai* (financial circles), Keidanren, and MITI.

Long-Term Strategies

If the LDP has one overriding goal, it is the survival of its coalition, which in turn depends upon the continued political stability of Japanese society. That stability depends largely upon the ability of the government to manage the consequences of two interrelated phenomena. First, Japan's population is aging rapidly. The expected annual population growth rate of 0.75 through the 1980s and 1990s "is based on increased longevity, not on the birthrate, which has already declined to the level of zero population growth."[31] Thus, the roughly 17–20 million persons who will be added to Japan's population by the year 2000 will make very substantial demands upon Japan's welfare structures. Second, Japan's employment system with its retirement age of around fifty-five soon must make room for better-educated younger workers who are presently either in high school, college, or university. More than "90 percent of those in the 15- to 18-year-old age bracket are in high school [and] nearly 40 percent of those between 18 and 22 are currently in colleges and universities."[32] It is this transition in the composition of the work force and of the population to which MITI's commitment to knowledge-intensive industry is directed. Not only will such an industrial policy reduce Japan's dependence upon oil as the major source of primary energy, it will address a pressing structural problem in Japanese society. But what about the present and the middle-term?

As Watanuki has argued, a rate of economic growth of 4 percent is too low to finance the transition that Japan must make in the next decade or two. According to Toyoaki Ikuta, a participant at the Tokyo summit that set a target for Japan's oil imports in 1985 of 6.3 to 6.9 million bpd, it might be very difficult for Japan to get the 6.3 million bpd stipulated in the previously cited Provisional Estimate of Long-Term Supply and Consumption.[33] His more realistic estimates suggest that "Japan's oil imports in 1985 and in 1990 might be at most 10 percent higher than the present level or might even remain at the present level."[34] Ikuta's estimate for oil imports is about 5.7 million bpd.[35] Given the generally unrealized promise of energy diversification, such levels of oil importation would sustain a growth rate of no more than 4 percent. Unfortunately, as Watanuki points out, even Ikuta's estimates for Japan's economic growth may be optimistic, because "Japan's economy depends a great deal on exports, and in view of the intensifying trade conflicts between Japan and the United States and Japan and the Western European countries, its ability to increase its exports in the future is somewhat doubtful."[36]

Japan is therefore faced with two imperatives. First, Japan must discover new markets that minimize confrontations with the United States and Western Europe. Second, if Japan is to realize the goal of 5.1 percent sustained annual growth envisioned in the New Economic and Social Seven Year Plan for 1979–1985, the government must secure a stable supply of 6.7–7.0 million bpd. The government had foreseen importing 6.3 million bpd; Ikuta believes that no more than 5.7 million bpd will be imported for the foreseeable future.

If Japan is to make the transition mentioned in the manner implied, the Gulf, especially Saudi Arabia, will loom increasingly large in Japan's resource diplomacy. Moreover, the direct deal and government-to-government contracting for oil have made Japan more, not less, dependent upon OPEC countries in general and Organization of Arab Petroleum Exporting Countries (OAPEC) countries in particular. Saudi Arabia's residual capacity can dominate the international oil regime, and Saudi Arabia and the Gulf oil-producing countries are especially important export targets. By 1980 only Saudi Arabia, Kuwait, and the UAE among the OPEC countries were running a current accounts surplus: These Gulf states are major targets for Japan's exports.

Policy Implications

Involvement with Middle Eastern Politics

Saudi Arabia and Kuwait were the earliest focuses of Japan's oil aspirations. In the late 1950s the nonoil Japanese financial interests (represented by Taro Yamashita), which had traditionally been engaged only in the downstream side of the oil industry, formed Arabian Oil in an effort to take advantage of an unofficial offer made by Saudi Arabia and Kuwait to representatives of the Japanese Foreign Ministry, Yamashita, and Ataru Kobayashi, head of the Japan Development Bank.[37] Within six months of the fruitful meeting held with the Saudis in February 1957, Yamashita was able to arrange financing for the project by involving important members of the Keidanren, electric companies, steel and financial concerns, and Japanese trading houses.[38] Intended to service heavy industry, Arabian Oil thus became Japan's first postwar national upstream oil project. "By 1964 Arabian Oil was supplying 20 percent of the oil consumed in Japan."[39]

This market share was the result of MITI's nationalists' organization of a quota system that forced Japan's oil refiners to purchase inherently unattractive high-sulfur oil produced by Arabian Oil. Yoshihasa Ojimi, the MITI official who actually arranged the quota system (the purpose of which was to reduce Japan's dependence on the international oil companies and to diversify sources of supply), presently is an official with Arabian Oil. According to Caldwell, although Arabian Oil has remained a MITI pet, its poor performance has made of it something of an embarrassment.[40] But this assumes that the primary mission of Arabian Oil remains upstream production.

Worth considering is the possibility that Arabian Oil constitutes the most important institutional link which Japan has with its second-largest trading partner. Indeed, the persons early associated with Arabian Oil seem to have played significant roles in the expansion of Japanese trade with the Middle East in general, the Gulf in particular, and Saudi Arabia specifically. Although Japan's imports from the Middle East doubled between 1971 and 1982, its exports to the region quadrupled.[41]

By 1979 Japan was more dependent upon exports to the Middle East than to the ASEAN countries, and the Middle East had nearly closed on the European Community as an important export target. Arguably, the Middle East is more important to Japan as a target for export growth than either the European Community or the United States because its markets are still growing. Equally important, this growing market is focused on products presently produced by Japan's heavy industry. This makes the Middle East markets essential to Japan as it negotiates the transition away from heavy industry toward knowledge-intensive industry. It makes Saudi Arabia uniquely important to Japan.

When Japan was obliged secretly to discover what were the minimum conditions that would qualify it as a friendly nation following the oil embargo in 1973, "the Foreign Ministry chose three business men who had experience in the Middle East, Foreign Ministry background, *and contacts with the Arabian Oil Company.*"[42] Tamura, who had been Japan's ambassador to Saudi Arabia and was then adviser to Arabian Oil, was able to meet with King Faisal himself. Morimoto, who had served in the Middle East, and Mizuno, son of the founder of Arabian Oil and its current president, met with petroleum and foreign-affairs experts not only in Saudi Arabia but also in Kuwait.

Interviews I conducted with relevant Saudi officials suggest that this was a momentous occasion for the Japanese, when Japan came clearly to realize the nature and the salience of the commitments of persons especially important in the determination of Saudi policy. In addition to King Faisal, the members of the mission met Kamal Adham, Faisal's brother-in-law and close adviser; two of Faisal's sons—Saud, who dominates the Supreme Petroleum Council and who became foreign minister in 1975, and Turki, who was intensely tutored by Adham and was to become head of Saudi intelligence in 1978; and Bandar, the son of Prince Sultan, the minister of defense who is second in line to succeed King Fahd to the monarchy.

This cohort holds the following values. First, they insist (minimally) on the return to the Arabs of all territory occupied by Israel in 1967, including East Jerusalem. In addition, they are strongly interested in a resolution of the Galilee conundrum favorable to the resident Arab population, which according to the secret, racist Koenig Memorandum of 1976 was to be "thinned out." It is in part Israel's Galilee policy that so engages Saudi interest in events in Lebanon. Second, this group is committed to the creation of a Palestinian homeland, preferably in association with Jordan. (The cohort was outraged when they learned that Anwar Sadat had entertained Menachem Begin's secret proposal in late 1977 that, in return for a Palestinian "entity" running south along the Mediterranean from Lebanon's border, Sadat would acquiesce in Israel's annexation of the West Bank and Gaza.) Third, members of this group are fully prepared to effectively link Saudi oil policy to a favorable resolution of their foreign-policy initiatives. Fourth, they believe that any oil pumped beyond what Saudi Arabia requires to meet its development objectives should win political concessions from the OECD in general and from the United States in particular. Fifth, the cohort is increasingly suspicious of military cooperation with the United States. Recently, Saudi Arabia moved to break the exclusivity of this relationship by making a $4 billion arms purchase from France. King Fahd has openly speculated about Soviet arms purchases. U.S. policy toward the Lebanon crisis has exacerbated this trend.

A sixth characteristic of the group is that it generally favors normalization of relations with the Soviet Union. One reason it has not moved further toward the realization of this goal is that formalization of relations with the Soviets is a potential threat to the United States and Japan. Seventh, the group's members are certain that great powers have no friends: Their salient commitments are to their national interests. For the time being, the oil weapon seems the best way to keep the United States interested in the fate of Saudi Arabia and its monarchy. Since the Soviet Union is practically independent of the need for foreign oil, the Saudis must establish leverage indirectly through Eastern Europe, whose need for oil the Soviets are hard pressed to service. Eighth, the group believes that oil is a wasting asset, even in the ground. It must be used to secure modernization. However, this group of individuals is especially interested in uncoupling modernization and Westernization. They are interested in Japan as a model of successful uncoupling, and as a result they are especially supportive of Nakasone's recent nationalist and traditionalist initiatives. Indeed, the group displays a keen interest in having Japan (as well as France and Germany) more fully engaged in Saudi Arabia's future. In part to service this end the group has urged that Saudi Arabia, and other members of the Gulf Cooperation Council, make very substantial deposits in Japanese and West European banks.

Finally, but most importantly, this group does not believe that the United States ever will put the required pressure on Israel to force it to settle the outstanding problems in Gaza and the West Bank, regarding their Palestinian populations, nor do they believe that Israel ever can be induced to treat its Muslim Arab (or indeed its Jewish Arab) citizens equitably until the United States comes to see its global strategic interests served only by a favorable resolution of these questions. With Israel every day creating settlements in Gaza and the West Bank, this conclusion is pregnant with implictions. Indeed, some analysts argue (correctly, I think) that Prince Sultan's initiatives on behalf of a resolution of the crisis in Lebanon were predicated on the assumption that the Geneva talks would collapse, exposing the true colors of the United States. Since the failure of these talks and the announcement of the U.S.-Israel strategic accord, the semiofficial press in Saudi Arabia and throughout the Gulf has subjected the United States to unprecedented criticism. Crown Prince Abdallah has orchestrated this assault. On this account, he has never been more popular.

King Fahd and Crown Prince Abdallah both sustain value complexes similar to that described above. The line of succession through the 1980s and 1990s—from Fahd to Abdallah to Sultan—is set. Moreover, the junior princes—Saud, Turki, and Bandar—are the candidates most likely to succeed to the monarchy when their generation comes into its own. For the Japanese, this line of succession suggests that the values discussed will continue to influence Saudi policy well into the twenty-first century. Japan must be prepared to accommodate these facts.

Institutions for Energy Security

The Tamura meetings occurred within a specifiable context. We have seen what that context was from the Saudi side. It is now appropriate to rehearse the important features of the Japanese context. By 1973, Japan was fully engaged in trying to negotiate the early stages of its transition from heavy to knowledge-intensive industry. Its elite was fully cognizant of the failure of "independent" oil development and of the importance of the Gulf states to the political and economic future of the LDP and of Japan. Here we need to focus on the creation of the institution most crucial for the successful negotiation of Japan's resource diplomacy, the Committe for Energy Policy Promotion.

Sohei Nakayama, chairman of the Resources Subcommittee of the Economic Advisory Committee to MITI, became convinced—as a result of the disappointing and potentially dangerous experience of Japanese political and business leaders in attempting to address Iran's requests in the late 1960s and early 1970s for Japanese participation in its development projects—that "Japanese companies could no longer simply plan for their own expansion but should also be willing to cooperate more fully in large-scale projects planned by producer governments."[43] He felt that a high-level coordination organization was required to provide MITI the assets to guide Japanese firms in their foreign initiatives. Nakayama set up the Committee for Energy Policy Promotion for this purpose in mid-September 1973, a matter of weeks before the oil embargo.

Nakayama was also instrumental in setting up the Japanese–Saudi Arabia Cooperation Organization, "which was to direct its efforts toward Middle East producer nations."[44] Ataru Kobayashi, then chairman of Arabian Oil, was chosen to direct the organization. At this time oil imports from Saudi Arabia accounted for only 17 percent of Japan's total imports, but they were expected to increase. Iran's share of total Japanese imports was 37 percent.[45] The stage was set for "the first open break with American foreign policy in post-war diplomatic history that Japan dared to make."[46] For even before the oil embargo it had become apparent to figures important in Japanese society that a fundamental transformation in Japan's foreign policy was (perhaps fatefully) long overdue. It must also have become apparent to those power brokers that Japan's future lay with the Arab states of the Gulf, not with Iran, if Iran should pursue policies inimical to the interests of these states, which soon came to be the case.

To appreciate fully the impact of Iran's actions on the Gulf states, it is necessary to understand that to the Arabs there exists an entente among the United States, Israel, and Iran. In the months preceding the October War, the United States and the shah of Iran were supporting Iraqi Kurds in their rebellion against the central government. The price extracted for halting this support was a territorial settlement, involving the Shatt al-Arab, favorable to Iran. Also during this time, the shah occupied several small islands belonging to Saudi Arabia in the Gulf, further adding to the losses suffered by the Saudis as a result of Israeli occupations. These events seemed to the Arabs to be occurring with the blessing of the United States, especially since by virtue of Nixon's Guam Declaration Iran had become a regional superpower.

To be sure, the implication of the 1969 Nixon Doctrine was that both Iran and Saudi Arabia were to be made regional superpowers by means of U.S. largess and training. But it was clear from the beginning that Iran was to receive preferential treatment, arguably on account of its geostrategic location and its more favorable structural features.[47] That Iran should become *primus inter pares* was perturbing to the Arabs in general and to Saudi Arabia in particular. Their perturbation was exacerbated by actions that reaffirmed Iran's historical claim to Bahrain and drew Iran into closer association with Israel. Saudi animosity toward Iran reached a fever pitch when the shah's closest Arab friend, Anwar Sadat, went to Jerusalem, and Iran finally guaranteed to supply Israel with the oil that it would lose as a result of returning the Sinai to Egypt.

In 1977 the Senate Committee on Energy and Natural Resources, chaired by Henry Jackson, published a staff report. Noting the special relationship between Iran and the United States, the report's authors asserted: "If Iran is called upon to intervene in the internal affairs of any Gulf state, it must be recognized in advance by the United States that this is the role for which Iran is being primed and blame cannot be assigned for Iran's carrying out an implied assignment."[48] Ominously, the report spelled out the bottom line for the U.S. policy in the Gulf that was preferred by the interests Jackson represented: "As Iran's oil reserves peak and decline, across the Gulf will be Saudi Arabia with plentiful oil reserves, enormous wealth and little to spend it on in terms of native population as seen from Iran."[49]

"Scoop" Jackson was part of the influential Pahlavi lobby as well as of the closely allied pro-Israeli lobby. These forces were in turn closely associated with members and sympathizers of the Committee on the Present Danger. The salient commitments of these groups were the prosecution of the East-West conflict and the paramount importance of Western Europe to the preservation of the American way of life. It has been suggested that the shah finally was compromised in official perceptions by virtue of the activities of the Saudis and elements of the Japan lobbies, which were able successfully (accurately) to portray the shah as a dying megalomaniac whose policies would certainly destabilize the situation in the Gulf to such an extent as to invite great-power confrontation.

The points of this rehearsal of information are twofold. First, if the Japanese intelligence network is as good as it is reputed to be, it should have been clear to the Japanese early in the 1970s, before the oil crisis, that their future lay with the Arabs. Second, well before the Islamic revolution in Iran, the Japanese should have begun to reduce their dependence upon Iranian oil. In the form of Arabian Oil, the Committee for Energy Policy Promotion, and the Japan–Saudi Arabia Cooperation Organization's close contact with the Saudi Supreme Petroleum Council, there were in place institutions that could effectively mediate a shift in Japan's resource diplomacy. As the data in Table 8.1 illustrated, beginning in 1970 Japan began to concentrate its Middle East oil dependency on the Arab states of the Gulf generally and on Saudi Arabia in particular. Nevertheless, Japan maintains in Iran a multi-billion-dollar investment in the form of a petrochemical plant. This plant is very important to the present regime in Iran. There is evidence that the Saudis (and the Iraqis who threaten to bomb the installation) are using the plant as a means of pressuring the Japanese into making an effort to moderate the Iraq-Iran conflict.

Other institutions, such as the Japan Oil Development Company (JODCO), an important consortium established in February 1973, made significant contributions to Japan's Arab adventure. But the initiatives and policy shifts that were recommended or supported by JODCO do not differ from those of, say, Arabian Oil. Indeed, Hiroki Imazato, chairman of Onessen Petroleum and member of the Standing Committee of the Committee for Energy Policy Promotion, became JODCO's first president.

JODCO's success in oil exploration and development have been less than inspiring. Its large deficits prompted a reorganization of the company in 1976 but not its dissolution. Here, too, it is worth suggesting that (at best) part of the reason for the continued existence of JODCO has to do with the lines of access its Middle East operations provides to nonoil business and financial interests. Its close links with the leadership of the LDP make JODCO an important politico-economic asset for the increasingly beleaguered party, the survival of which depends heavily on export-driven economic growth.

Shifts in Japan's Foreign Policy

To state the obvious, Japan has very strong incentives for mounting a foreign policy with which OAPEC countries can live. Practically, this means that Japan's foreign policy must be pro-Arab/Palestinian and must be prodevelopment. Moreover, the interests of Japan and (at least) the more conservative OAPEC states coincide in their determination to preserve the integrity of the international political economy. It is this commitment that gives the foreign policies of these countries their managerialist bent, quite independent of any constitutional or infra-structural limitation on the militarization of their foreign policies.[50] The seriousness with which these countries take interdependence may be appreciated by noticing that Japan's foreign-aid programs to non-oil-producing Third World countries have increased threefold and by recognizing Saudi Arabia's self-consciously increased dependence upon Japan. After noting that the Middle East currently accounted for 20 percent of Japan's exports, *The Arab World Weekly* went on to remark that the Middle East visits of Foreign Minister Sunao Sonoda and Prime Minister Takeo Fukuda were motivated by Japan's hope "to develop interdependence to balance Japan's dependence on the Middle East for oil. . . . By fostering interdependence Japan hopes to guarantee its oil supplies whatever happens in the Middle East, develop its export business in that region, and foster economic and political stability so as to ensure that the oil and export trade is undisturbed."[51] Further, Saudi Arabia (often in cooperation with Kuwait and the UAE) is willing to threaten potential price radicals with an increase in production sufficient to eliminate whatever price leverage such radicals might nominally enjoy.[52] The stability of the international political economy is essential to Japan's survival.

As Japan assumes in fact the position to which it is entitled by virtue of its economic power, it may begin effectively to use its role in international organizations to second the efforts of OAPEC. As matters stand, Saudi Arabia and Japan rank seventh and sixth, respectively, in contributions to the International Monetary Fund (IMF). And, as the second-largest shareholder in the World Bank, Japan's voting power on the executive board is soon to be substantially increased. The effectiveness of this increased voting power could be greater than one might expect, since the Reagan administration has announced that the United States, which has about 20 percent of the voting power on the board, will hold its contribution to the International Development Agency (IDA) to $750 million annually for the next three years.

Japan, on the other hand, since 1970 has undertaken two "aid doubling" programs. The first was a success, but the current program, which began in 1981, is unlikely to meet its target on account of the weakness of the yen in relation to the dollar. Japan ranks fourth among major industrial nations in terms of overseas development assistance. If this effort continues, it will nicely complement the efforts of OAPEC countries to aid non-oil-producing developing countries. By 1980, OPEC aid to such countries accounted for 38 percent of all official aid funding.[53] OAPEC supplied about 80 percent of this aid. At least in part, Japan's efforts to aid non-oil-producing developing countries is a response to a direct proposal made by Saudi Arabia to Foreign Minister Sonoda on his visit to Riyadh in January 1978.[54] Such cooperation as emerges between Japan and OAPEC will almost certainly be destined to uncouple international development assistance from the East-West conflict—to the likely displeasure of the United States.

Also provoking forces in the United States committed to the prosecution of the East-West conflict was the role Japan was reputed to have played in what came to be known as the Andrew Young affair. When the Trilateralists were in power in the United States under President Carter, it is reported to me that the Japanese made available to United Nations (UN) Ambassador Young assets that enabled him more effectively to play his part in the delicate negotiations taking place among the United States, the Saudis (Crown Prince Fahd coming to the United States in May 1977 for this purpose), and the Palestinian Liberation Organization (PLO) to establish the conditions under which the United States would begin *official* talks with PLO representatives. This initiative was cut short, much to the dismay of the Saudis, when Sadat made his surprise visit to Jerusalem.

Much earlier, during the secret meeting to establish the minimum conditions for Japan's being declared a friendly nation so that it might escape the further scourge of the oil embargo, Morimoto had made it clear that even a strongly pro-Arab/Palestinian statement ". . . would merely buy Japan an admission ticket. In the future, Japan would have to take more concrete steps, including posture cooperation in development projects."[55] In the event, Japan paid for oil by making a statement more radical even than that offered by the European Community. The statement called for Israeli withdrawal from *all* territory occupied in the 1967 war. This was a very strong gloss on the meaning of UN Resolution 242 that called only for Israel's withdrawal from territories occupied in 1967. Second, the statement urged more strongly "recognition and respect for the *legitimate rights of the Palestinian* peoples."[56] Most importantly, the Japanese left open the prospect of revising their policy toward Israel. Japan's embassy is still in Tel Aviv.

As a result of current events in Lebanon, Japan is once again speaking of the possibility of a revision in its policy toward Israel and has taken another step along this road. In March 1983, Foreign Minister Shintaro Abe took the extraordinary step of inviting the chief of the Tokyo office of the PLO to the emperor's birthday party. Later in March, he stated that "the Japanese government would maintain close contacts with the organization which, in his view, represents the Palestinian people and thus should be permitted to participate in Middle East peace negotiations."[57]

There seems to exist in Japan very broad political support for the pro-Arab/Palestinian initiatives that the successful prosecution of "resource diplomacy" require. Former Foreign Minister Toshio Kimura has, since the first oil crisis, headed a suprapartisan organization within the Japanese Diet to pursue friendlier relations between the Japanese and the Palestinians. Interestingly, one member organization of the coalition, the Democratic Socialist party, which has close ties with Israel's Histadrut, has not opposed either Japan's or Kimura's initiatives. Significantly, Kimura headed a delegation of the coalition to Beirut for talks with the PLO in December 1980. Kimura and his delegation left from Paris, where they attended the first general meeting of the Japan-French club,[58] which seeks to improve relations between the EC and Japan. This club is in part a response to Foreign Minister Masayoshi Ito's 1980 initiatives to tighten relations between Japan and the EC. In fact, Ito proposed to German Foreign Minister Hans-Dietrich Genscher that German and Japanese ambassadors in the Third World should step up their mutual contacts and exchange information so as better to coordinate Tokyo-Bonn relations with Japan's relations with the EC.[59]

The point to be made is this. Japan has or is putting into place institutions and assets that can service the new look in Japanese domestic and foreign policy that Prime Minister Yasuhiro Nakasone represents. Nakasone is on record as asserting that it is time for Japan to become a "big political power."[60] The constituency that he and the LDP must carry in order to accomplish this is primarily the youth. Japanese youth are drifting rightward, and they resent the way Japan is "ignored politically by other industrial countries whose economics have faltered while Japan's has amassed 10 percent of the world's trade and total gross national product."[61] We have seen that this constituency must be brought into the Japanese economy in the 1980s and 1990s, while those reaching fifty-five years of age or over are retired. This transition depends upon Japan's access to Arab oil and Arab markets. The objective conditions for a Japanese-Arab symbiosis exist. To follow its prompting could provide an additional satisfaction for the Nakasone constituency, a satisfaction that would come from challenging the design of the great power that imposed the postwar constitution upon them.

Notes

1. Committee for Energy Policy Promotion (Japan), *Japan and the Oil Problem* (Tokyo, October 1981), p. 6. Hereafter cited as CEPP.

2. United Nations, *World Energy Supplies, 1973–1978* (New York: United Nations, n.d.), p. 60.

3. CEPP, p. 9.

4. Japan Institute for Social and Economic Affairs, *Japan 1982: An International Comparison* (Tokyo, 1983), p. 26.

5. Japan's *1981 Diplomatic Yearbook* (p. 20) calls the Middle East the most explosive region of the world. Nonetheless, Foreign Minister Yoshio Sakurauchi recognized the Middle East not only as "an important oil producing area" but also as "a strategic key to East and West." *Foreign Broadcast information Service (FBIS)*, 29 January 1982, speech to 96th Diet on 25 January.

6. *Middle East Economic Digest*, 1982, p. 23.

7. *Atoms in Japan* (Tokyo), December 1980, pp. 6–7.

8. Ibid. Ironically, Japan's energy czars who through the Oil Law of 1962 caused Japan's dependence and vulnerability, hoped for nuclear power to provide "a long-term buffer against the harsh reality of growing vulnerability." Martha Caldwell, *Petroleum Politics in Japan: State and Industry in a Changing Policy Context* (Ann Arbor, Mich.: University Microfilms International, 1981), p. 147.

9. *Atoms in Japan*, March 1980, p. 5.

10. Richard P. Suttmeier, "The Japanese Nuclear Power Option: Technological Promise and Social Limitations," in Ronald A. Morse (ed.), *The Politics of Japan's Energy Strategy* (Berkeley: University of California Press, 1981), p. 116.

11. Yujiro Eguchi, "Japanese Energy Policy," *International Affairs* (Spring 1980), p. 266.

12. Roger W. Gale, "Tokyo Electric Power Company: Its Role in Shaping Japan's Coal and LNG Policy," in Morse, *The Politics of Japan's Energy Strategy*.

13. Ibid., p. 100.

14. Ibid., p. 96.

15. Ibid., p. 100. By the year 2000 Japan still will rely upon oil for about 75 percent of its total energy. Herbert I. Goodman, "Japan and the World Energy Problem," in Daniel I. Okimoto (ed.), *Japan's Economy: Coping with Change in the International Environment* (Boulder, Colo.: Westview Press, 1982), p. 24.

16. Goodman, "Japan and the World Energy Problem," p. 25.

17. Ibid.

18. William B. Quandt, *Saudi Arabia's Oil Policy* (Washington, D.C.: The Brookings Institution, 1982), p. 15.

19. Saudi Arabia could develop a capacity to pump about 16 million bpd. For reasons bearing on Gulf politics, it has chosen not to go forward with such development.

20. Quandt, *Saudi Arabia's Oil Policy*, p. 4.

21. John A. Shaw and David E. Long, *Saudi Arabian Modernization: The Impact of Change on Stability* (New York: Praeger, 1982), p. 20.

22. Edmond O'Sullivan, "Saudi Budget Shifts Emphasis from Infrastructure to Human Resources," *Middle East Economic Digest*, 1982, pp. 16–18.

23. Goodman, "Japan and the World Energy Problem," p. 47.

24. Ibid., p. 54.

25. "Economic Report of the President Transmitted to the Congress," January 1981, p. 353.

26. John M. Blair, *The Control of Oil* (New York: Pantheon Books, 1976), pp. 220–230.

27. Robert Engler, *The Brotherhood of Oil* (Chicago: University of Chicago Press, 1977), p. 95. Moreover, at this time the United States and Japan were vigorously competing for low-sulphur Indonesian oil.

28. U.S. Department of Energy, Energy Information Administration, *Annual Report to Congress*, 1980, vol. 2, p. 49.

29. Caldwell, *Petroleum Politics in Japan*, p. 141.

30. Ibid., p. 165.

31. Joji Watanuki, "Japanese Society and the Limits of Growth," in Daniel Yergin and Marlin Hillenbrand (eds.), *Global Insecurity* (New York: Penguin Books, 1982), p. 188.

32. Ibid.

33. Cited in ibid., p. 185.

34. Ibid., p. 186.

35. Ibid.

36. Ibid., p. 187.

37. Caldwell, *Petroleum Politics in Japan*, p. 85.

38. Ibid., p. 86.

39. Ibid., p. 87.

40. Ibid., p. 124.

41. Japan Institute for Social and Economic Affairs, *Japan 1982: An International Comparison* (Tokyo, 1982), p. 26.

42. Caldwell, *Petroleum Politics in Japan*, p. 203. Italics added.

43. Ibid., p. 174.

44. Ibid., p. 156.

45. A member of an Iranian delegation to Japan in the early 1970s has informed me that Japan's Foreign Ministry officials were much more favorably disposed to cooperate with Iran than with the Arabs. Indeed, Iran's position in the Iran-Iraq conflict was favored.

46. Yoshi Tusurmi, "Japan," *Daedalus* (Fall 1975), p. 124.

47. Former director of the Central Intelligence Agency (CIA) and then ambassador to Iran, Richard Helms, pointed to a map on the wall of his Tehran office and remarked: "Iran is, in political terms, the real center of the world." *Christian Science Monitor*, 13 September 1978, p. 12.

48. *Access to Oil—The United States Relationship with Saudi Arabia and Iran*, Staff Study, Senate Committee on Energy and Natural Resources (Washington, D.C.: Government Printing Office, December 1977), p. 111. Cf. Hans Tofte, former head of CIA covert operations, letter to the editor, *New York Times*, 20 December 1978, p. A26.

49. "Access to Oil," p. 84. See also the statement of General George Brown, chairman of the Joint Chiefs of Staff: "The military programs the Shah has coming, it just makes you wonder whether he doesn't someday have visions of the Persian Empire." *The Guardian*, 20 October 1976, p. 11.

50. Walter Arnold noted the conditions for the resurgence in Japan of economic nationalism in "Japanese Economic Nationalism: Protectionism Versus Internationalism," *Canadian Review of Studies in Nationalism* 10, no. 2. (Fall 1983). It is worth suggesting that the developments that I am describing will help to blur the distinction between internationalists and nationalists.

51. *Arab World Weekly*, 22 September 1979, p. 3.

52. See Steven A. Schneider, *The Oil Price Revolution* (Baltimore: Johns Hopkins University Press, 1983); Edith Penrose, "OPEC's Importance in the World Oil Industry," *International Affairs* (January 1979); and David J. Teece, "OPEC Behavior: An Alternative View," in James M. Griffin and David J. Teece (eds.), *OPEC Behavior and World Oil Prices* (London: George Allen and Unwin, 1982). OAPEC has increasingly internationalized its aid on account of the inability of OAPEC countries presently to effectively manage the organization's aid commitment. The internationalization of this aid has the consequence of making OAPEC countries deeply interested in the rules and operation of international development agencies. See David Blake and Robert S. Walters, *The Politics of Global Economic Relations* (Englewood Cliffs, N.J.: Prentice-Hall, 1983); and Philippe D'Arvisenet, "Desequilibre des paiements et problèmes de financement au lendemain du deuxieme choc petrolier," *Revue d'Economie Politique* (September-October 1981).

53. D'Arvisent, "Desequilibre des paiments," p. 691.

54. *FBIS*, Arabian Peninsula, 19 January 1978, C5, *KYODO*.

55. Caldwell, *Petroleum Politics in Japan*, p. 204.

56. Ibid., italics added.

57. *FBIS*, Japan, 31 March 1983, C2, *KYODO*.

58. *FBIS*, Japan, 8 December 1980, C3, *KYODO*.

59. *FBIS*, Japan, 24 September 1980, C3, *KYODO*.

60. *New York Times,* 17 August 1983, A4.

61. Ibid.

9
Japan and Africa: Beyond the Fragile Partnership

Hideo Oda
Kazuyoshi Aoki

Japanese Passivity and African Expectations Prior to the 1973 Oil Crisis

Until the first oil crisis after the Yom Kippur War in 1973, Japan-Africa relations had been chiefly in the trading field and depended not on governmental initiatives but on private ones. As the Japanese government had a strong interest in neighboring Asian countries and in the Western countries, the African continent had received little consideration at the governmental level from the 1960s until the oil crisis. However, unencumbered by the shadow of a colonial past, Japan has been striving to improve relations with African countries. The major relationship is, of course, still in the field of trade.

Although the continent regularly constituted only a small percentage of Japan's overall world market, the trade relationship has been constantly increasing both in exports and imports. Total Japanese exports rose almost fourfold, from $603 million in 1965 to $2.3 billion in 1973. Also, imports from Africa rose more than fivefold in the same period, from $192 million in 1965 to $1 billion in 1973. Such an increase in trade meant that Japan was becoming an important trading partner with Africa during this period. There were, however, a few problems in this trading relationship.

First, the trading pattern had a typically vertical structure, in which Japan exported industrial manufactures and imported raw materials. For example, in 1973, Japan exported industrial manufactures such as metal goods, textiles, synthetic fiber, and machinery and imported items such as fiber, iron ore, crude oil, and foods. Second, Japanese trade with Africa was regularly unbalanced, with exports running usually at twice the level of imports. Third, trading partners in Africa were limited to countries that had natural resources necessary for Japan. The principal aim of Japan's trade was to import raw materials because of the scarcity of natural resources in Japan itself. Whether an African country had

153

natural resources or not was a decisive factor in Japanese trade with that country. Therefore, Japan tended to trade with such countries regardless of their domestic political problems or of whether a great deal of international criticism was directed against them.

The most pronounced case in point was the Republic of South Africa. Black African countries had turned their attack against the apartheid regime after their independence because of their insistence upon the overall liberation of Africa from colonialism and racial discrimination.[1] In addition to establishing the Liberation Committee of the Organization of African Unity (OAU) and supporting the liberation groups in southern Africa through the committee, they introduced many resolutions in the United Nations calling for sanctions against South Africa. But the Japanese government preserved an attitude of indifference toward these resolutions. Moreover, as the Japanese were given the position of "honorary whites" by the South African government, Japanese trade materially increased to the extent that South Africa ranked first among Japan's African trading partners. The main reason for trading with South Africa seems to be the availability of many important resources not obtainable elsewhere and of a better market for Japanese goods than in other countries. Japan has given priority to economic self-interest over African political aspiration toward the "liberation of Africa." Such a Japanese attitude has basically continued from the 1960s to the present day and has excited considerable criticism from African countries. These features of the trading patterns have given the impression that Japan has looked upon Africa merely as a supplier of natural resources in an export market.

Such a Japanese attitude was also revealed in its aid to Africa. Japan's official development assistance (ODA) to Africa closely followed its trade pattern.[2] First, Japanese aid to Africa had been restricted in the 1960s by the priority given to Asia, and it has done little to offset the continent's unfavorable trade balance. Second, the pattern of ODA allocation has been consistent with the Japanese practice of focusing its aid efforts on significant economic partners, particularly suppliers of raw materials. That is, the distribution has been heavily concentrated on a handful of favored countries, such as Kenya, Madagascar, Niger, Sudan, Tanzania, Zaire, and Zambia. This pattern has not really changed from the 1960s to the present day, and those countries together have received over four-fifths of Japan's total aid to Africa from 1960 to 1982. Third, little aid was given to the least developed countries, particularly the francophone states of West Africa (with some exceptions). We think that in part this reflected language difficulties and the closed nature of the francophone community. Fourth, aid has often been provided for infrastructural projects whose aim has been to facilitate the export of primary products— the so-called tied aid that linked aid to the promotion of internal industries. Such aid affected Japan's reputation in the developing countries.

As mentioned earlier, Japanese aid was given in line with Japanese national interest rather than in response to the demands and the situation of recipients, in spite of the expectations of African countries. It seemed that Africa entertained great expectations of Japan's economy and advanced technology on the grounds that Japan had achieved a remarkable development from a war-torn land and that the Japanese were a colored race as were the Africans. These expectations, in part, appeared from the visits of many African leaders to Japan: Emperor Haile Selassie of Ethiopia (November 1956 and May 1970), President Mobutu Sese Seko of Zaire (April 1971), and President Ahmad Ahidjo of Cameroon (April 1973) all came to Japan. But political leaders of Japan did not visit Africa during this period and in general Japan's response was passive, with a few exceptions such as yen loans and technology transfer to countries such as Nigeria, Ghana, Kenya, Uganda, Tanzania, Ethiopia, Madagascar, and Zaire.

In conclusion, the Japanese-African relations were of minor significance in Japan's foreign relations in the period. Japan had the policy of separating economics from politics in relation to Africa, and its policy had shown remarkable success in terms of expansion of trade.

After the Oil Crisis: Changeover in Japan's Policy

The oil strategy worked out by the Arab oil-producing countries during the fourth Arab-Israeli war had a great impact on Japan. Oil is often called the lifeblood of Japanese economy, since it is the primary source of more than 70 percent of Japan's energy, and nearly 100 percent of the oil Japan uses domestically (about 280 million kiloliters a year) is imported. The threat of Arab oil sanctions and the fourfold increase in the oil price came as a great shock, and the government, industries, and consumers in general reacted excessively to this shock.[3] The prices of a wide variety of items rose by 26 percent, and the period became known as one of "price madness." There were also scandalous examples of firms attempting to profit from this golden opportunity by buying up and hoarding certain commodities. Diplomatically, Japan, like other advanced countries, was compelled to condemn Israel's failure to withdraw from the territories that it occupied in 1967. In addition to this diplomatic action, the oil crisis reordered the framework of Japanese foreign policy in three respects. First, the weakness of the United States in the face of Arab threats showed that it was totally unable to protect Japan in its hour of need. Second, the Middle East, which had never formed a large element of concern in Japanese foreign policy, now became of dramatic importance and demanded far more attention. Finally, the oil crisis underlined with savage clarity how dependent Japan was upon distant and uncontrollable supplies of essential raw materials. It is now important for Japan to disperse its sources of supply and secure them by active policies of aid, investment, and diplomacy.

As a result of these factors, Japan's heightened consciousness regarding raw materials, particularly energy resources, became dramatically clear in the mid-1970s. Diversification of Japanese diplomatic efforts became a prime problem facing the government, though Japanese foreign relations remained predicated upon a close relationship with the United States. In January 1974, Prime Minister Kakuei Tanaka visited five countries of the Association of Southeast Asian Nations (ASEAN) where Japanese economic penetration had created hostile public opinion. He tried to deepen the economic cooperation and friendships between Japan and ASEAN countries through Japanese economic aid and sympathetic behavior toward Southeast Asia. In the same year, a series of high-ranking emissaries went to Iran, North Africa, Arabia, and the Levant, promising help with an entire series of development projects. Japan not only became involved in major economic cooperations in the Middle East but also sought to deepen understanding and to try to strengthen links with the Arab world.

In addition to the growing importance of the Middle East to Japan, Latin America and Australia have assumed a new significance for Tokyo's policymakers. Prime Ministers Tanaka and Masayoshi Ohira both visited Latin America in pursuit of oil and other raw materials, and Japan has entered into economic cooperation agreements with Brazil. In all these areas, there have been objections to Japanese economic influence. But, as in relation with Europe, these have been balanced by the proponents of open commerce and economic freedom who have seen great value in developing trade with Japan. Japan's efforts to diversify its diplomacy were an expression of a sense of crisis prevalent among the Japanese in the mid-1970s, and the policy of diversifying foreign relations seemed to attain success to some degree.

As a result of this policy, it seemed apparent that Japan's attitude toward Africa gradually changed from negative to positive. As a first sign, on June 5, 1974, Japan made a public announcement of the suspension of sports, cultural, and educational interchanges between Japan and South Africa. That day was one week before the eleventh summit conference of the OAU that adopted a condemnatory resolution about the relationship between South Africa and the Western countries. Although such a resolution has seldom been effective, it did come to exert direct pressure upon Western countries who were more sensitive to the demands of developing countries after the oil crisis. In relation to the public announcement, Japan started to make an examination of possible restrictions on trade with South Africa. Moreover, Japan awarded diplomatic recognition to Guinea Bissau on August 1, 1974. Previously, when a resolution advocating a welcome to the independence of Guinea Bissau and a censure on Portugal's illegal possession and aggression was adopted by an overwhelming ninety-three to seven vote (with thirty abstentions) in the 28th General Assembly of the United Nations (UN) in November 1973, Japan had abstained from voting. Therefore, Japan's recognition itself marked a turning point in foreign relations with Africa.

This recognition also was the first one among the Western countries, which generally opposed the recognition of Guinea Bissau, and it seemed an indication that Japan was taking a more pro-African position.

However, a more notable event was that the then foreign minister, Toshio Kimura, made an official visit to Ghana, Nigeria, Zaire, Tanzania, and Egypt from 31 October to 9 November 1974. His visit to Africa was the first ever by a Japanese foreign minister, and it opened up a new vista in relationships between Japan and Africa. After talks with the political leaders in the five countries, he then confirmed that Japan should stand firmly for anticolonialism, antiracism, and support to national liberation movements in southern Africa and that Japan should also deepen economic cooperation with Africa.[4] As he had already confirmed Japan's commitment to Africa in a speech before the General Assembly of the UN in September 1974, his visits were welcomed by African countries as a manifestation of positive Japanese diplomacy toward Africa.

On the one hand, we can discover in these developments in 1974 a reflection of a changeover in Japan's foreign policy toward Africa. On the other hand, we may say that these developments were forced on Japan by a desperate need to secure raw materials, rather than being decided on the basis of a proper understanding of political and economical aspiration in Africa in general, and in particular, of racism in Rhodesia and South Africa. Japan's African policies would seem to be easily influenced by the fluctuations of the world's raw materials market. Indeed, when Japan successfully weathered the first oil crisis of 1973, and the Japanese economy satisfactorily recovered from the triple dilemma of inflation, recession, and balance-of-payments deficits by the end of 1975 (relative to the economies of other countries), Japan's African diplomacy fell into inactivity. For example, as compared with many visits of African government functionaries to Japan, no person of ministerial rank made an official visit to Africa for a number of years after Kimura's visit in 1974. Finally, in July 1979, Sunao Sonoda made a visit as foreign minister to Nigeria, Ivory Coast, Senegal, Tanzania, and Kenya.[5] At that time, he expressed the desire to promote mutual understanding and cooperative relationships between Japan and these countries. But again it might be said that the principal cause of his visit was the desire to secure raw materials, because Japan faced the onset of the second oil crisis in 1979 and was keen to move away from the dependence on Middle East oil and gas. Moreover, Japan has consistently increased the trade between Japan and South Africa while still formally insisting on antiracism and antiapartheid in Africa. This is an indication that Japan has given priority to economic demands over political commitments. It can be said, therefore, that Japan's African diplomacy continues in the customary pattern, although it became more positive after the first oil crisis, both in the political and economical fields.

TABLE 9.1
Japan's Official Development Assistance to Africa (South of the Sahara) ($ million)

	Grant					
	Gratis Cooperation	Technology Cooperation	Subtotal	Loan	Total	Share (%)
1974	2.8	8.1	10.92	25.31	36.23	4.1
1975	2.19	8.84	11.03	47.79	58.82	6.9
1976	---	11.75	11.75	34.18	45.93	6.1
1977	9.52	14.89	24.41	31.84	56.25	6.3
1978	18.25	23.45	41.70	63.79	105.49	6.9
1979	46.25	26.70	72.95	113.77	186.72	9.7
1980	54.43	31.93	86.36	136.55	222.91	11.4
1981	83.48	40.29	123.77	86.76	210.53	9.3
1982	88.06	40.70	128.76	139.47	268.23	11.3

Source: Ministry of Foreign Affairs, Diplomacy Blue Book, 1975–1983.

Aid

Against this background of a changeover in Japan's diplomacy, relations with Africa have shown progressive development in many aspects after the mid-1970s. First, we should examine the state of Japanese aid to Africa. Table 9.1 indicates Japan's ODA to Africa (south of the Sahara) and Africa's share of total Japanese ODA from 1974 through 1982, which has shown a net increase during the period. There appear to be two turning points in the Japanese aid. Needless to say, the first was the oil crisis in 1973. Japanese aid doubled from $19.89 million in 1973 to $36.23 million in 1974. The second turning point seems to have been the visit of Prime Minister Takeo Fukuda to six southeast Asian countries in August 1977. At that time, he reiterated the Fukuda doctrine of close peaceful relations between Japan and ASEAN states and promised an increase in Japanese aid, a program of cultural exchanges, and frequent consultations with ASEAN leaders. Although his promises were directed at the ASEAN countries, they were also carried out in other regions. He expressed the so-called all-around diplomacy (Zen-Hoi Gaiko) that aimed to deepen the interchanges with all countries and to establish mutually trustful relationships with them regardless of the difference of political conviction and country size.

Alongside the Fukuda doctrine declared in August 1975, the Committee on Foreign Economic Cooperation had already presented a report entitled *On the Promotion of Future Economic Cooperation,* at the request of the government.[6] In the report, the committee advocated the establishment of an idea of economic cooperation and an increase in grant aid. Since then, the Japanese government has given more importance to economic aid in the country's diplomacy. This basic policy manifested itself at the meeting of the Conference of International Economic Cooperation and the Ministerial Conference of the Organization for Economic Cooperation and Development (OECD) in December 1977. It was at this juncture that Japan embarked on a five-year program to double its ODA. As a result, Japan's total development assistance increased by 55 percent in 1977, by 19 percent in 1979, and by 16 percent in 1980. By the end of the 1980 fiscal year, Japanese aid was more than double the total given in 1977, and the ratio of aid to gross national product (GNP) increased from 0.23 percent in 1978 to 0.32 percent in 1980.

In this framework, Japan's ODA to Africa also rose almost twofold from 1977 to 1978 (Table 9.1). Although its share of the total has been unlikely to increase, Japan's ODA to Africa persistently increased in absolute terms from 1978 until a falloff in 1981. The principal cause of this falloff can be found in Japan's huge budget deficit, in the decline in the yen rate compared to the U.S. dollar, and in the increasing indebtedness of many African countries.[7]

Some important points should be considered in connection with Japan's aid to Africa. First, although Africa's share of Japanese ODA rose from 2 percent in 1970 to 11.3 percent in 1982, Africa received only 5 percent of the total Japanese overseas aid from 1960 to 1982. This is because Japan's aid has been directed primarily toward the developing countries of Asia, which together received 70.5 percent during that period. Accordingly, Africa's share has been very small, and this trend is unlikely to change in the near future because of Japan's declaration that the pattern of ODA allocation is thought to be "appropriate." We may say that such an allocation, in part, gives a good indication of priorities in Japan's foreign relations: Africa seems to be of minor importance to Japan. Second, as already mentioned, the distribution of Japanese aid in Africa has been heavily concentrate on a handful of favored countries. For example, leading recipients in 1982 were Tanzania ($50 million) and Zaire ($43 million), followed by Madagascar ($26 million), Zambia ($23 million), Kenya ($19 million), Mauritania ($18 million), and Sierra Leone ($10 million). Moreover, these seven countries together received over four-fifths of the total Japanese aid to Africa from 1960 to 1981. This pattern is consistent with the Japanese practice of focusing its aid efforts on significant economic partners, particularly suppliers of raw materials. Third, little aid has been given to the least developed countries. African countries constitute the majority of the group of least developed countries in the world, and they surely have a claim to receive more aid from Japan. Japan concurred with the pledge

TABLE 9.2
Japanese Trade with Africa (South of the Sahara) ($ million)

	Exports	Imports
1973	2,305 (6.2)	1,067 (2.8)
1974	4,384 (7.9)	2,260 (3.6)
1975	4,707 (8.4)	1,900 (3.3)
1976	4,899 (7.3)	1,694 (2.6)
1977	5,281 (6.6)	1,816 (2.6)
1978	4,682 (4.8)	1,970 (2.5)
1979	3,756 (3.6)	2,829 (2.6)
1980	6,215 (4.8)	3,371 (2.4)
1981	7,444 (4.9)	3,358 (2.3)
1982	5,822 (4.2)	3,450 (2.6)

Note: The figures in parentheses give the percentage of Africa's
        share of total Japanese trade.

Source: Ministry of Foreign Affairs, Diplomacy Blue Book, 1978,
        1982, 1983.

to either double aid to the least developed countries or to guarantee them annual aid flows amounting to at least 0.15 percent of its GNP called for at the Paris Conference on the least developed countries in September 1981.[8] Although Japan has also shown its commitment to Africa by taking up full membership in the African development bank, Japan has not yet fulfilled the pledge to double aid.

Because of these problems, Japanese aid policies are under continual review.[9] Needless to say, Japan's experience with Africa is still in its infancy when compared to Asia, where Japan has long experience. We believe that Japan will have to decide the aid policies after careful consideration, because aid will constitute a large part of Japan-Africa relations.

Trade

Trade plays another large part in Japan-Africa relations. Japanese trade with Africa has increased notably since the first oil crisis (see Table 9.2). Total Japanese exports to Africa rose from $2.307 billion in 1973 to $4.384 billion in 1974 and $7.444 billion in 1981. However, in 1982 they fell to $5.822 billion. Japanese imports from Africa followed a similar pattern. They rose from $1.067 billion in 1973 to $2.260 billion in 1974 and $3.371 billion in 1980. They increased notably after 1978, although they fell to $3.358 billion in 1981. This drop was caused by various factors. One was the falling price and demand for oil. Nigeria and the north African countries, which together make up the bulk of trade between Japan and Africa, have been hard hit. Another factor was the worldwide recession, which bit deeply into Japanese trade with Africa.

On the whole, however, Japanese trade with Africa has steadily increased, no matter how small a share the continent constituted. We believe this trend will not change in the near future. Today, the continent represents a regular 5 percent of Japan's world market. But given the scarcity of natural resources in Japan itself, it is apparent that Africa, with its many important raw materials such as copper, cobalt, asbestos, oil, cocoa, and coffee, is and will continue to be important for Japan. From the time of the oil crisis and Japan's heightened consciousness regarding raw materials, Japan's interest in Africa has increased, because Japan would like to diversify the sources of raw materials. In February 1978, the Japanese government sent an economic mission to Senegal, Ivory Coast, Tanzania, and Nigeria. The mission, led by Fumihiko Khono, who was the chairman of the Committee on Africa of the Federation of Economic Organizations (Keidanren), had friendly discussions with the leaders of the four countries and exchanged opinions on economic cooperation and Africa's economic problems. This was a manifestation that Japan's business circles showed an active interest in Africa under the auspices of the government. Such business practice was coincident with mounting demands for a comprehensive national-security policy in Japan after the oil crisis.

Many Japanese came to realize that economic survival for Japan, which is dependent upon the importation of many resources, was as important as political security. Japan had not paid close attention to this until the oil crisis and now had to establish a comprehensive national-security policy that could cope effectively with any international threats. As a result of this demand, in December 1980 the Suzuki administration created the Comprehensive National Security Council, composed of the prime minister and nine ministers.[10] From such a standpoint, it appeared that the Japanese government and Japan's business circles were giving attention to the relations with Africa, particularly the trading ones. In fact, Japan had much to be pleased about in its economic relations with Africa and has gained access to the vital raw materials that were sought.

The many problems in Japanese trade with Africa nevertheless will be a serious source of friction between Japan and Africa in the near future.[11] One problem is a substantial surplus in Japan's trade with the continent. Although the Japanese government continues to increase its levels of aid to Africa, this aid does little to offset the continent's unfavorable trade balance. To date, economic friction that has developed concerning large Japanese trade surpluses has not become a troublesome political issue. From the African perspective, though, there is little reason to view the present relationship with pleasure. On the positive side, Japan provides a growing market for raw materials and is a competitive supplier of advanced technology and of high-quality consumer goods. However, if Japan does little to assist African countries to export to its market, other than to provide the raw materials that Japan so desperately needs, and if Africa does not also receive a share of Japanese aid sufficient to offset the trade deficit, African leaders will exert growing pressure on Japan to rectify this situation in future years.

Another problem is the Japanese trade pattern. As raw materials and fuels account for close to 70 percent of all Japanese imports, metals (both in ore form and refined) and mineral fuels constitute half of the Japanese purchases from Africa. On the other hand, capital goods in general play an increasing part in Japan's sales to Africa. Iron and steel account for around 15 percent of all sales; motor vehicles, particularly trucks, a similar proportion; telecommunications and other electrical capital goods contribute perhaps a further 8 percent. Textiles, which made up one-third of Japan's exports to the continent twenty years ago, are now reduced to a 5 percent share, behind consumer electrical items. The so-called vertical trading is encountering criticism from the Third World in general. It may also excite considerable criticism among African countries. Although virtually all African countries are accustomed to trade with Japan, the main trading partners are limited to those that have raw materials and can purchase Japanese goods (Table 9.3). And they are influenced strongly by Japan's economic recession.

The final problem is the Japanese trade with South Africa. Despite African and UN criticism of Japan, South Africa is Japan's principal trading partner on the continent. Japan's exports to South Africa rose from $979 million (20 percent of the total exports to Africa) in 1978 to $1.655 billion (30 percent) in 1982, and the imports rose from $1.042 billion (52 percent of the total imports from Africa) in 1978 to $1.840 billion (53 percent) in 1982. The main reasons for such a substantial increase in the trade are that South Africa has many important raw materials that Japan cannot obtain from other sources and is the most active market for Japanese capital goods in Africa. As Table 9.4 indicates, Japan's import dependence on South African minerals is very high. Accordingly, it would be difficult for Japan to cut off trade with South Africa in the near future. However, after the independence of Portuguese Africa in the mid-1970s and particularly the independence of Zimbabwe in April 1980, black African countries have intensified criticism both of South Africa, which rigidly adheres to apartheid systems, and also of those countries that have been intimately related with South Africa and have purchased minerals from Namibia, which is under South Africa's illegal control. Accordingly, Japan will not escape criticism on the score of the policy of separating economics from politics. It seems natural that, as the Japanese-African relationship deepens, Africa's expectations of Japan will increase, and Japan will have to respond to these expectations if it wants relations to develop positively.

TABLE 9.3
Japanese Trade with African Countries ($ million)

	EXPORTS					IMPORTS				
	1978	1979	1980	1981	1982	1978	1979	1980	1981	1982
Angola	36	30	83	83	52	6	60	103	28	2
Benin	9	23	22	29	27	6	6	4	4	3
Botswana	0.1	1	0.4	1	1	0.2	0.5	0.6	0.4	0.4
Burundi	8	10	10	13	13	—	3	5	3	2
Cameroon	47	38	74	76	71	28	38	44	39	38
Central Africa Rep.	3	4	3	2	5	2	5	10	8	7
Chad	2	0.2	0.1	0.1	—	13	11	7	9	0.7
Congo	5	6	17	25	23	8	8	14	17	11
Djibouti	17	17	24	26	25	—	—	—	—	0.0
Ethiopia	51	51	63	66	57	21	28	29	31	32
Gabon	15	17	44	51	46	6	13	20	8	11
Gambia	2	3	5	3	6	—	—	—	—	—
Ghana	41	33	28	33	23	105	112	123	120	77
Guinea	2	2	3	4	4	2	0.1	—	—	0.1
Ivory Coast	145	76	122	87	74	56	66	46	51	49
Kenya	149	127	189	143	113	16	24	17	13	9
Liberia	1,646	931	1,416	1,690	1,009	191	425	338	312	166
Madagascar	29	52	37	15	23	24	37	58	47	41
Malawi	29	30	21	15	14	2	2	4	11	12
Mali	7	5	7	7	5	4	7	9	10	4
Mauritania	7	4	3	13	9	20	26	29	52	57
Mauritius	25	24	32	19	16	2	0.1	0.1	0.1	0.1

TABLE 9.3 (Cont.)

Mozambique	31	10	35	15	18	44	38	19	27	22
Niger	23	19	20	17	16	--	--	0.1	2	1
Nigeria	953	807	1,494	2,159	1,209	8	42	120	340	8
Rwanda	17	18	29	28	23	7	6	2	1	2
Senegal	8	15	9	10	15	12	11	15	15	14
Seychelles	3	4	4	4	4	0.1	0.2	0.2	0.1	0.8
Sierra Leone	23	14	36	16	21	0.2	0.6	1	2	0.8
Somalia	2	3	5	6	3	2	0.9	--	0.1	--
South Africa	979	993	1,800	2,222	1,655	1,042	1,299	1,741	1,728	1,840
Swaziland	3	6	6	6	4	24	28	21	8	9
Tanzania	110	72	113	93	91	12	29	23	19	18
Togo	13	16	25	27	26	1	2	0.9	3	2
Uganda	15	8	17	10	9	35	52	37	15	24
Upper Volta	5	6	10	19	9	4	4	17	12	11
Zaire	24	26	45	80	52	84	116	134	72	60
Zambia	26	41	55	52	51	168	294	297	273	227
Zimbabwe	0.1	0.1	29	70	55	--	--	31	49	45
Algeria	729	346	452	473	677	38	58	451	701	525
Egypt	400	397	644	795	661	83	95	142	208	167
Libya	354	547	526	1,063	285	16	101	358	351	46
Morocco	66	37	44	69	81	48	70	85	103	107
Sudan	84	76	68	101	77	58	53	56	57	45
Tunisia	16	72	67	94	67	1	0.5	1	0.9	1

Source: Ministry of Foreign Affairs, <u>Diplomacy Blue Book</u>, 1983.

TABLE 9.4
Advanced Countries' Dependence on South Africa in Raw Materials
Imports (%)

	Japan	United States	United Kingdom	West Germany	France
Platinum	41	25	37	--	22
Vanadium	100	62	60	50	31
Chromite	41	91	30	29	17
Manganite	48	9	43	52	40
Nickel	20	--	--	11	14

Note: Japan's figures were for 1978, others for 1975.

Source: Japan's Foreign Trade Monthly, and Africa Confidential,
January 17, 1979.

Investment

Finally, we would like to examine the present state of Japanese investment that has given rise to Africa's expectations. Most analysts agree that the investment will be a key factor in Japanese-African relations. From April 1951 to March 1982, Japan had invested over $2.0 billion in 720 different ventures in sub-Saharan Africa. This amount represents just 4.4 percent of total Japanese direct investment overseas in the period. It is small compared with 29 percent in Asia, 27.1 percent in North America, 16.2 percent in Latin America, 11.6 percent in Europe, 6.5 percent in Oceania, and 5.2 percent in the Middle East.[12]

The African continent receives far less Japanese investment than most other regions, for various reasons. Japan's investment capital outflow was directed chiefly toward mine development in neighboring Southeast Asia and establishment of a commercial-sector bridgehead in the United States. Africa is viewed in Japan as a bad risk. Furthermore, Japan has had no long-standing historical relationship with Africa, and the Japanese firms know little about Africa. In our view, Japanese investment in Africa will not sizably increase in the near future.

Even so, it is apparent that Japan's investment pattern in Africa is now changing on the basis of partnership with African interests. Originally, roughly half of all the Japanese investment in Africa was concentrated in ship leasing and similar maritime enterprises in Liberia, which received $791 million of the total in 346 ventures. But the impact of the oil crisis brought about a recognition that Japan's economic security demanded development of stable sources of raw materials and progressive internationalization of Japan's once insular business outlook. As a result, the Japanese involvement has broadened over the years from mining and vehicle assembly to local manufacturing in which African countries want more participation by Japan. Today, other leading recipients apart from Liberia are Zaire ($244 million, 45 ventures), Nigeria ($153 million, 74 ventures), Niger ($73 million), and Zambia ($45 million).[13] Generally speaking, those ventures already on the continent are performing well and are much appreciated by the Africans. African countries are eager for more Japanese investment, but Japanese firms, which prefer to manufacture in Japan and export rather than invest in overseas production facilities, are still generally negative about investing in Africa.

Prospects for the Near Future

In conclusion, Japan has developed relations with Africa since the mid-1970s. This development was presumably caused by Japan's ardent demand for raw materials in Africa after the first oil crisis. Accordingly, its interest seems to be confined to the fields of economic cooperation, trade, and investment. Moreover, Africa's shares of these are relatively minor as compared with other regions, and such a trend does not appear likely to change in the near future. However, the Japan-Africa relationship is deepening, and Africa's expectations of Japan will continue to increase remarkably. Japan will thus have to address these expectations regardless of Africa's position in Japan's foreign relations. In that sense, the 1980s will be a very important period for the future of the Japan-Africa relationship.

In recent years, many government figures of African countries have visited Japan. These include President Kenneth Kaunda of Zambia (September 1980), Prime Minister Robert Mugabe of Zimbabwe (May 1981), President Julius Nyerere of Tanzania (March 1981), President Daniel arap Moi of Kenya (April 1982), and President Hosni Mubarak of Egypt (April 1983). This is an indication that African countries have increased their expectations of Japan. In contrast, very few high officials of Japan have made an official visit to Africa except for Toshio Kimura in 1974 and Sunao Sonoda in 1979 (both as foreign minister). Moreover, although Japan had diplomatic relations with fifty-one African countries, in 1983 there were only twenty-two Japanese embassies in Africa compared to twenty-three African embassies in Japan. These facts show that Africa's position in Japan's foreign relations is still relatively minor. Needless to say, if Japan wishes to enforce a comprehensive national-security policy, it has to encourage more friendly relations with Africa as well as other regions and to deal with the associated issues carefully and effectively.

The first issue is that of promoting personal and cultural exchanges between Japan and Africa. As mentioned above, few of Japan's leading figures have visited Africa, in vivid contrast to the visits of African leaders to Japan. Also, the number of Japanese residents in Africa is

7,457 persons, which represents only 2 percent of total Japanese residents abroad at present.[14] Promotion of personnel exchange is vital in order to broaden mutual understandings.

The second issue concerns increased Japanese aid to Africa. Japan is now the world's fourth-largest donor of overseas development assistance. But Japan's contributions appear insufficient in the context of Japan's overall prosperity; this is particularly the case for Africa, where Japan contributes only 6.5 percent of total African bilateral aid receipts from OECD donors. Today, most of black Africa needs resources for economic development and wants more Japanese aid. Consequently, if Japan wants to improve relations with Africa, it should increase aid to Africa, pay attention to the need of African countries, diversify aid channels, and help with aid to establish human rights in African countries.

The third issue is the formulation of the principle of give-and-take in Japanese trade with Africa. Large Japanese foreign-trade surpluses have stirred considerable criticism among the trading partners and have given rise to economic frictions. Japan should make every effort to reduce these economic frictions in Japan-Africa relations.

The fourth issue is that of Namibia and the apartheid of South Africa. These will be the touchstones by which to test Japan's African policy. A great deal of criticism has been directed against South Africa and the Western countries that have developed relations with it even after the independence of Zimbabwe. Japan will not escape this criticism and should cooperate with the "contact group" (United States, United Kingdom, Canada, France, West Germany) and the front-line states (Zambia, Tanzania, Mozambique, Botswana, Angola, Zimbabwe) toward a settlement of the Namibian issue in the form of majority rule. Also, it is desirable that Japanese firms that operate in South Africa lay down a code of practice, such as the so-called Sullivan Code and the European Community Code, and work toward the upgrading of blacks and other nonwhites in all levels of employment. Given the paucity of natural resources in Japan, it is difficult to break relations with South Africa. Accordingly, Japan has to strive to remove all racial discriminations in South Africa and give a full explanation of its position to the African countries. Japan's present policy of separating economics from politics will not be tolerated by the African countries for much longer.

Japan needs to tackle these problems effectively if it wishes to develop a sound and fruitful relationship with the whole continent.

Notes

1. Hideo Oda, *Politics and Ideologies in Contemporary Africa* (enlarged ed., Japanese) (Tokyo: Keio Tsushin Co., 1975), Chap. 8.

2. Kazuyoshi Aoki, "Japan's Asia-Africa Policies in the Postwar Era" (Japanese), *Gekkan Rekishi Kyoiku* 5, no. 1 (January 1983), pp. 58–59.

3. Takayoshi Hamano, "The Japanese Economy in the 1980s," in Rei Shiratori, ed., *Japan in the 1980s* (Tokyo: Kodansha International, 1982), p. 135.

4. On Kimura's visit to African states, see the interview in *Gekkan Africa* 15, no. 2 (February 1975), pp. 6–11, 31; and *Asia* 11, no. 2 (February 1976), pp. 74–87.

5. See, for example, "Mr. Sonoda's Speech at the Cabinet Meeting," *Gekkan Kokusai Mondai Shiryo*, no. 8 (August 1979), pp. 129–130.

6. Kazuyoshi Aoki, "Japan's Asia-Africa Policies," p. 54; and Ministry of Foreign Affairs (Japan), *Diplomatic Blue Book*, 1976.

7. *Africa Economic Digest*, 10 December 1982, p. 12.

8. John Ravenhill, "Japanese Aid to Africa," *New African*, May 1983, p. 41.

9. Study Group of Policy Toward African Market, Ministry of International Trade and Industry, "Proposal on African Policies," *Gekkan Africa* 15, no. 4 (April 1975), pp. 11–19.

10. Kazuyoshi Aoki, "The Changes of International Environment and Domestic Politics," in K. Uchida, R. Shiratori, and N. Tomita, eds., *Hoshu Kaiki* (Tokyo: Shin Hyohron, 1981), p.218.

11. Hideo Oda, "Current African Situations and the Problems of Japan's Foreign Policy," *Kohmei* 159 (July 1975), pp. 88–94.

12. David Morris, "Japanese Investment in Africa," *New African*, May 1983, p. 39; and *Africa Economic Digest*, 10 December 1982, p. 13.

13. *Africa Economic Digest*, 10 December 1982, p. 13.

14. Ministry of Foreign Affairs (Japan), *Diplomatic Blue Book*, 1983, p. 624.

10
Japan and Korea

Edward A. Olsen

Colonial Legacy

Historical Background

Japan's economic relations with contemporary Korea are heavily marked by its colonial legacy. For that matter, all aspects of Japan-Korea ties are burdened by that legacy. Japan's precolonial relations with Korea are ancient indeed, reaching back to an era when both were students of Chinese culture. In that learning process Korea absorbed Sinic attributes over a longer period of time, more quickly, and more pervasively than Japan, becoming an intermediary for the Sinicization of Japan. Despite Korea's heritage as an older brother within the Chinese culture family, Japan periodically expressed its ingratitude by showing aggressive intentions toward Korea. Not until the late nineteenth century, however, was Japan able to assemble the wherewithal to contemplate carrying out any such ambitions. Intent on building a strong state based on contemporary Western imperialist models and cognizant of its own internal liabilities, Japan decided it needed zones of influence and/or colonies.

By that point Korea was floundering after emerging from its Hermit Kingdom phase, searching for a way to make itself viable in an era of tremendous change in Asia. At various times groups within Korea looked to China, Russia, Japan, and the West for aid, comfort, and advice. Tokyo took advantage of Korea's uncertainty and its material weakness to impose itself on the Korean people, ostensibly as a rescuing agent saving that country from its own ineptness. In reality, Tokyo had ulterior motives based on its imperialist goals. Korea was the first major step in Japan's attempt to conquer Asia.

The core of Japan's motives at the time was a set of classic geopolitical doctrines evolved from the work done by the German theorist Karl Haushofer, who ironically received major insights into such issues while stationed in Japan with the German diplomatic mission.[1] These ideas focused on the need of a densely populated nation with a resource base that cannot meet its demands to expand into areas that can support them (lebensraum). That, mixed with doses of imperial manifest destiny, noblesse oblige, and Japanese racism, produced a potent set of drives behind Tokyo's expansionism.

In Korea the Japanese established an agenda for change. As apologists for Japan are prone to point out, Tokyo did introduce a host of modern techniques and achieved considerable material advances. Korea became, as a part of Japan, almost as up-to-date as Japan itself in certain sectors of the economy. However, it cannot be emphasized too strongly that none of what Japan did in Korea was for the benefit of Koreans or their country. Japan used Korea for Japanese purposes. Despite the infrastructure created in Korea, the impact on Korea was to drain that country to serve the needs of Japan. Japanese, not Koreans, made the profits, developed the skills, and took the credit. In return Koreans lost their freedom, wealth, pride, and—most important—their identity as a sovereign nation. The Japanese engaged in cultural genocide in Korea, trying to remake the Koreans into second-class Japanese.

Though the Japanese experienced considerable material success, they had virtually no success at converting the Koreans. A few Koreans sided with Japanese goals and prospered accordingly, but the majority of Koreans chafed under colonial rule. Anti-Japanese activists tried by any means available to rid their country of the hated Japanese. When Japan's defeat in World War II brought an end to the colonial era, Koreans were profoundly glad to see the Japanese leave. The Koreans, intent on having as little to do with Japan as possible, intended at the first opportunity to pay the Japanese back for what they inflicted on Korea.

U.S. Policy Toward Japan and Korea

In the first decade of the postwar era Japan and Korea had very little to do with each other. Occupied Japan had no real say in its foreign relations. It was forced to accept what the Americans provided, but—on balance—was pleased with the benefits that accrued from U.S. benevolence. Cold war pressures combined with the realization that even a prostrate and defeated Japan had more potential than the free countries of Asia made it evident to U.S. decision makers where the United States' priorities had to lie. The United States made its interests in rebuilding Japan the cornerstone of its postwar Asia policy, saw that policy succeed far beyond initial expectations, and by the 1980s found itself in the position of trying to bring its former enemy into an economic and strategic partnership.[2]

Midway in the first postwar decade the Korean War broke out. In contrast to U.S. preoccupation with occupying Japan and getting it back on its feet, Washington—after having assumed authority in the southern half of Korea and having been instrumental in establishing the Republic of Korea (ROK)—maintained only lukewarm interest in Korea. It was very much a backwater, ignored as much as possible by Washington. In that respect the famous Dean Acheson statement excluding Korea from the U.S. defensive perimeter was accurate except for one oversight. In order to deny Japan to the spread of communism, the U.S. occupiers had to view the threat emanating from Korea in terms prewar Japanese geopoliticians would understand. Korea and Japan were a package deal strategically, and the United States did what was required in Korea to give Japan the breathing room it needed.

Koreans were amply perturbed by the attention Japan received from 1945 to 1950 and by the casualness with which the United States treated Korea. They felt they were being slighted and that Americans were being distracted by the Japanese. The United States did make some economic and military efforts to get the fledgling ROK on its feet, but they were halfhearted and poorly conceived. The United States had no important long-term goals for Korea as it did for Japan. Korea was a basket case after the Japanese were expelled, and South Korea, in particular, was a sorry specimen. Overpopulated, underskilled, poorly led, poverty ridden, corrupt, and embittered, the ROK offered the United States little reason to be optimistic about that country's future or to proclaim the existence of any vital national interests in it. On balance, however, Koreans benefited greatly by their proximity to Japan. If they had not been so close to such a valuable target, it is problematic whether the United States would have drawn the line against global communist aggression in Korea. In short, South Korea was rescued by the United States from North Korean aggression less because of what the ROK per se meant to Washington than because of what Korean security meant to a vulnerable Japan.

Quite clearly, Japan benefited almost as much as South Korea did militarily from the U.S. decision to prevent communist aggression from engulfing Northeast Asia. Japan was absolutely unable to defend itself; in lieu of fighting for its own interests, Japan happily stayed on the sidelines as its U.S. mentor not only fought the war but channeled a great deal of war-generated business in occupied Japan's direction. Japan was nearby, was capable of doing the repair and supply tasks required, and could use all the economic stimulation available. By the end of the war many millions of dollars of such business had been diverted to Japan, giving that country's economy a tremendous shot in the arm precisely when it was needed. Arguably, the Korean War was as important to reviving Japan's economy as World War II was in bringing the United States out of the Great Depression. Japan emerged from the Korean War an independent country once more; its economy was on fairly solid footing, and it possessed in the United States a strong protector that asked for nothing in return other than that Japan be peaceful and prosper sufficiently to eliminate the prospect of communist subversion or attack.

Korea, on the other hand, was in worse condition than it had been after the colonialists were ousted. Both North and South Korea were devastated by three years of war. In terms of destruction of what had existed prior to 1950, North Korea suffered more damage because it had more to start with, but both countries were in dire straits economically and shattered materially. The contrast with Japan's reborn prosperity and peace could not have been stronger nor more grating on the sensibilities of either set of Koreans. Once again Japan had benefited from Korea's misfortunes. It was like rubbing salt into the wounds of war.

Post–Korean War Developments

In the twelve years between the end of the Korean War and the normalization of Japan-ROK relations in 1965 the economic gap between Japan and the two Koreas grew still larger. Bolstered by the continued presence of a U.S. security shield that required Japan to spend very little on its own defense and gave the Japanese both a sense of security and access to virtually all the markets encompassed by Pax Americana, Tokyo was able to guide Japan toward new heights economically. This was the era that saw Japan regain and surpass the momentum that had been sidetracked by World War II. Japan was on the fast track economically, able to focus on export-led growth without having to worry about providing the political or strategic wherewithal that made it possible. Moreover, Tokyo was favored by the presence of capable leadership.

In sharp contrast, the two Koreas were burdened with extraordinarily heavy defense burdens as they coped with each other. The funds and labor expended for defense, while necessary, were distinct liabilities economically. Moreover, their respective leaders were not oriented toward economic priorities, focusing their energies instead on strategic and political matters. In North Korea the Kim Il-sung regime single-mindedly pursued its self-imposed mandate of creating a state strong enough to accomplish its aborted agenda in the south. Taking full advantage of its dictatorial powers, the lingering skills of the older North Korean generation who had industrial experience from the colonial period, and North Korea's better natural resource base, Pyongyang was able to get its economy moving again by the late 1950s. However, its preoccupation with rigid communist central planning and Kim Il-sung's autarkical fetish caused North Korea's economy to slip into a rut by the early 1960s. This process was exacerbated by the emergent Sino-Soviet conflict that put North Korea under intense strain.

Despite its problems, for much of the time from 1953 to 1965 North Korea managed to hold its own in comparison to South Korea. Throughout the Syngman Rhee years Seoul could not get its act together economically. Rhee, an unreconstructed Confucian elitist whose life and career were centered on political factionalism, was out of his element when it came to administering a pragmatically functioning economy. He preferred to leave details to his underlings and their U.S. advisers. Unfortunately, the underlings were not all well qualified, and many shared with their leader a disdain for grubby real-world work. Moreover, the U.S. advisers tended to be pessimistic about South Korea's prospects and locked into the common wisdom inherited from the colonial blueprint for Korea's economy, which held that southern Korea's natural advantages dictated that it would remain primarily agricultural. The huge influx of refugees from the north that led to South Korea's overpopulation also reinforced this phenomenon. In any event, by the time Rhee was ousted in mid-1960, South Korea was stagnating economically. When the Park Chung-hee regime seized power nine months later the prospects for an economic turnaround looked bleak indeed; the new team had no experience in economic matters and their coup had shaken the already low levels of confidence on the part of foreign business people.

At first the Park government floundered about. In retrospect its main advantages were its authoritarian ability to instill discipline in what had been a rather disorganized society prone to fractious infighting, its skills in managing a large organization (the army) using modern techniques, and—ironically—its relative ignorance of what South Korea's limitations were. The latter quality tended to free the government from the blinders of Japanese-cum-American ideas of what was appropriate for southern Korea. Furthermore, Seoul at that point was not well disposed to listen docilely to the United States, in light of Washington's blatant unhappiness with the way Park seized power and set back democracy. In any event South Korea after 1961 entered into a period of trial-and-error economics, settling in a rather short time upon a revised version of the Japanese blueprint. This time, however, Park and his followers—all of whom were raised and educated in the colonial era—decided to try to do for the ROK what Japan had done for itself.

This process got rolling slowly in South Korea because the South Korean technocrats were feeling their way. What they needed was money, advice, and customers. Americans provided some of each, but not enough to be decisive. The big change in South Korea's fortunes occurred after 1965. That year was doubly important for South Korea: It marked the political normalization of relations with Tokyo, which opened the way for major Japanese trade and investment in the ROK, and it approximated the major expansion in the Vietnam War, which provided the ROK economy with the same sort of shot in the arm Japan had received from the Korean War. As a result of this fortuitous conflux of events and South Korea's receptivity to foreign economic opportunities, the ROK's economy rapidly slipped into high gear in the late 1960s.

Japan's Economic Inroads into Korea

North Korea, on the other hand, started to discover that its economic engine could not pull it out of the rut the Kim regime had steered into. In the late 1960s, while South Korea was looking outward for economic opportunities, North Korea became increasingly rigid in its pursuit of economic autarky (*juche*) aimed at making Pyongyang so self-reliant that it would be invulnerable to foreign economic, political, or military pressures. The main area of success was in Pyongyang's efforts to build a strong military machine. In its own terms, North Korea was a success story. And, in terms of its standing versus most other communist states, Pyongyang had reason to think of itself as successful. However, the first stages of what would become a yawning gap between North and South Korea's economic standing appeared by the late 1960s.[3]

No country was more aware of what was taking shape in the two Koreas than Japan, for it—more than any other outside power—was responsible for South Korean successes. One must hasten to underline that the South Korean people and their leaders were fundamentally responsible for those successes. Without their hard work and sacrifice none of what often is referred to as the Korean "economic miracle" could have happened. Moreover, the United States played an important role as a provider of funds and markets for South Korean economic expansionism. Certainly, South Koreans prefer to credit the United States with their successes if they are going to praise any outsiders. In fact, praising Americans is common and politically astute because the United States is very important as the key guarantor of the physical security the ROK needs to maintain its prosperity. However, the reality of the situation cannot be denied. Within a few years after normalization Japanese economic inroads into the South Korean economy had made Japan the ROK's most important trade partner, source of investment, and increasingly explicit development model.

The reasons for this are not difficult to discern. Though South Koreans probably would have preferred the United States to come first in all these categories, Americans were not as forthcoming, available, generous, or pragmatic as the Japanese. Americans had geopolitical ideas about the ROK and slighted its economic potentials. It took a long time for U.S. leaders to recognize that the ROK was changing before their eyes, and the U.S. public has not yet adjusted to that fact.[4] While U.S. business people were fumbling the opportunity or, more commonly, ignorant of its existence and while the U.S. government was preoccupied with its strategic concerns in Korea, the Japanese hit the ground running economically and happily left geopolitical matters to the Americans.

Having no desire to play a military role in Korea and being very wary of getting entangled in Korean politics, the Japanese entered South Korea under what had become their standard doctrine during the 1960s: *seikei bunri* (separate economics and politics). Or, at any rate, they wanted to appear that way. In fact, from the outset of the normalization talks through their successful if arduous conclusion and the subsequent bilateral expansion of commercial relations, the Japanese had become enmeshed in South Korean politics. Though both sides avowed a desire to minimize political considerations, the resumption of bilateral relations was highly emotional and politicized.

The Japanese paid a price for their reentry into Korean affairs in terms of meeting South Korean demands for reparations for past Japanese sins. Though South Korean dissidents protested the reparations as a sellout, they became an important source of capital for South Korean economic growth, as were the funds Japanese business people poured into Korea to take advantage of cheap labor, lenient tax provisions, a nearby location, and lax environmental regulations. Moreover, some Japanese will tell one in private that they paid another sort of price to enter Korea: gifts or bribes, depending on one's interpretation. Underlying the Japanese ability to penetrate South Korea's burgeoning economy so swiftly and thoroughly was the love-hate relationship between Koreans and Japanese in which Koreans, many of whom could speak Japanese and thrive in a Japanese cultural milieu, envied—and wanted to emulate—what Japan had accomplished. This was very true of some key officials in the Park years.

A major difficulty with that relationship was that the ease with which the Japanese moved back into South Korea stimulated a great deal of antipathy toward the "ugly Japanese," real or imagined. Certainly much of it was, and is, real. The Japanese often act arrogantly in Korea, throw their weight and money around, and are prone to treating Koreans like objects rather than equals. On the other hand, South Koreans visibly have a chip on the shoulder when it comes to Japanese. They seem to delight in pushing the Japanese as far as they can get away with. Many Koreans resent the profits Japan has made in Korea, view Japanese motivations with suspicion of economic imperialism, and hate to be seen as adjuncts to either a Japanese or a U.S.-Japanese economic system (precisely what North Korea accuses them of being). Moreover, many South Koreans mirror the private Japanese views that they had to bribe Japanese (mostly through kickbacks) to get Japan involved in the Korean economy. Given this obstreperous tendency to tweak Japanese noses when possible, some Koreans get rather blatant in their "we paid for it, we've got a right to be pushy" attitude.

At the same time that Japan was rushing into closer economic cooperation with South Korea, Tokyo did its best to be evenhanded toward the north. In a rare example of Japanese trade following Japan's political interests into an unattractive situation, very rudimentary Japanese trade relations were begun with North Korea. There was from the beginning a basic problem with this evenhanded tactic: North Korea did not have much to offer Japan. The contrast with South Korea's appeal to the Japanese could not have been more marked. North Korea was comparatively backward, unproductive, inflexible, ideological, inept, penurious, and—worst of all—even more suspicious of Japan than South Korea. That Japan persisted in its politicized trade efforts with North Korea was a sign of the domestic pressures on Tokyo to be impartial.

Strategic Implications of Korea for Japan's Foreign Policy

Two Koreas

Though Japan's conservative political and economic eiites have a great deal of sympathy for South Korea's position and share considerable

TABLE 10.1
South and North Korean GNP and Per Capita GNP

	GNP ($ 100 Million)		Per Capita GNP ($)	
	South Korea	North Korea	South Korea	North Korea
1967	42.7	23.9	142	186
1968	52.3	25.7	169	194
1969	66.3	27.6	210	203
1970	78.3	29.7	243	213
1971	91.5	34.7	278	243
1972	102.5	40.8	306	279
1973	131.5	47.8	386	319
1974	181.3	55.8	523	363
1975	202.3	64.0	573	406
1976	274.2	77.2	765	478
1977	351.7	83.2	965	502
1978	473.5	91.9	1,279	541
1979	597.4	125.1	1,597	719
1980	574.0	---	1,532	---

Source: Korean Overseas Information Service, Statistical Data on Korea, 1982.

mutual empathy with the elites in Seoul, they are not free to follow their instincts. There exists in Japan a sizable body of pro-Pyongyang ethnic Korean residents—about half of the 600,000 Korean minority population. They do not have a direct say in Japanese decisions, but they can get disruptive. Moreover, and more important, they are supported by a variety of Japanese who either favor Pyongyang for ideological reasons or are strongly opposed to South Korea for a number of reasons. Some abhor Seoul's leaders because they see in them clones of Japan's prewar militarists. Some dislike Japan's involvement in U.S. support for the ROK, seeing it as a trap that will lead Japan into war. Others simply hate Koreans of any stripe and want no more to do with Seoul than with Pyongyang. In any event, to mollify such pressures, Tokyo is compelled to tilt toward Pyongyang now and them.

During the 1970s Japan's proclivity toward South Korea was accentuated by the phenomenal growth of the ROK economy as it became the "new Japan" with the most potential to reach the big leagues. Using almost any indicator, South Korea during the 1970s outdistanced its northern rival. The data in Table 10.1 indicate the scope of this spread.

The basis of South Korea's rapid expansion was its emulation of Japan's export-led growth model. However, it was not simply a matter of copying the contemporary model. Instead, learning from Japan's

TABLE 10.2
South and North Korean Trade ($ million)

	South Korea			North Korea		
	Exports	Imports	Total	Exports	Imports	Total
1970	835.2	1,984.0	2,819.2	366.0	439.0	805.0
1971	1,067.6	2,394.3	3,461.9	310.0	690.0	1,000.0
1972	1,624.1	2,522.0	4,146.1	360.0	630.0	990.0
1973	3,225.0	4,240.3	7,465.3	510.0	750.0	1,260.0
1974	4,460.4	6,851.8	11,312.2	770.0	1,200.0	1,970.0
1975	5,081.0	7,274.4	12,355.4	690.0	930.0	1,620.0
1976	7,715.3	8,773.6	16,488.9	620.0	800.0	1,420.0
1977	10,046.5	10,810.5	20,857.0	690.0	700.0	1,460.0
1978	12,710.6	14,971.9	27,682.5	950.0	960.0	1,910.0
1979	15,055.5	20,338.6	35,394.1	1,150.0	1,160.0	2,310.0
1980	17,505.0	22,292.0	39,797.0	1,500.0	1,600.0	3,100.0

Source: Korean Overseas Information Service, Statistical Data on Korea, 1982.

history of adaptation to foreign examples, South Korea melded some elements of prewar Japan's military-led and highly disciplined model with some elements of postwar Japan's export-oriented, technocratic, government-advised, innovative and flexible, and U.S.-dependent growth model. All this was overlaid on a U.S.-influenced framework, greatly accelerated, and made to function in a compressed time span. Because it worked, South Korea's export-led economic growth skyrocketed while North Korea's economy stayed on a relatively low plane, as witnessed by the trade data in Table 10.2.

By the 1980s there was no doubt on Tokyo's part about where its interests lay. They were unequivocally in South Korea rather than North Korea. Table 10.3 shows the comparative figures. In terms of Japan's global trade the two Koreas show a comparable disparity in ranking, with North Korea of minimal economic importance to Japan. As the data in Table 10.3 illustrate, despite a recession-induced slump South Korea's economic importance to Japan is on the increase and is today intrinsically important to Tokyo, unlike North Korea.

For the two Koreas the situation is even more impressive. To South Korea, Japan ranked either first or second as its trade partner, depending on the year and the indicator, as Tables 10.4 and 10.5 illustrate. For North Korea, too, Japan ranks first in its trade with noncommunist states.[5] The real significance of these data is that, because South Korea's economy is both much larger and far more trade oriented than North

TABLE 10.3
Japan's Trade with North vs. South Korea ($ million)

	South Korea		North Korea	
	Exports	Imports	Exports	Imports
1975	2,246	1,307	181	65
1976	2,828	1,919	96	72
1977	4,113	2,160	126	67
1978	6,056	2,630	185	108
1979	6,201	3,358	281	151
1980	5,393	3,040	376	181
1981	5,640	3,395	290	140

Source: International Monetary Fund, Direction of Trade 1982.

Korea's, these ratios demonstrate a degree of importance to Japan that goes well beyond percentages.

Japan's Dilemma

As Japan looks to the future of its Korean relations, it faces a dilemma. Tokyo quite clearly prefers to deal with Seoul on economic issues rather than with Pyongyang. The latter's economy offers Japan very little, and its leaders are politically obdurate and economically inept. It is one of Japan's poorest prospects. Yet Tokyo continues to woo North Korea, usually in a low-key fashion.[6] Furthermore, South Korea increasingly is becoming to Japan what Japan has become for the United States—too much of a good thing. Yet Japan continues to pursue South Korea economically and in broader political terms.[7] Why?

The answer to this says a great deal about contemporary Japan's overall relations with both Koreas. Tokyo knows that it has a tremendous stake in keeping Korea the proverbial "land of the morning *calm;* in other words, it is crucial to Japan's well-being that Korea not become a source of instability. Tokyo also knows that Washington means it when it says the United States will keep its strategic commitments to the ROK, but Japan must do all it can to keep the status quo on an even keel. I include myself among a minority of U.S. critics of Japanese defense policy who argue that Japan must assume some responsibility for Korean security because it is so vital to Japan, the United States cannot bear such burdens indefinitely, and Japan can readily afford the costs.[8] To foreclose that possibility, to help keep U.S. commitments intact, and to bolster the ROK's ability to make a persuasive argument that it is sufficiently important to the United States that Americans should assign a high intrinsic value to South Korean security, Japan goes out of its

TABLE 10.4
South Korea's Major Export Markets (%)

	Total	United States	Japan	Hongkong	Taiwan	Indonesia	United Kingdom	West Germany	Others
1962	100.0	21.9	42.9	8.6	2.6	---	2.9	0.4	20.7
1967	100.0	42.9	26.5	4.7	1.0	0.4	2.5	1.6	20.4
1972	100.0	46.7	25.1	4.5	1.0	1.3	1.8	3.2	16.4
1977	100.0	31.0	21.4	3.4	1.0	0.7	3.0	4.8	34.7
1978	100.0	31.9	20.7	3.0	1.1	0.8	3.1	5.2	34.2
1979	100.0	29.1	22.3	3.5	1.1	1.3	3.6	5.6	33.5
1980	100.0	26.3	17.4	4.7	1.2	2.1	3.3	5.0	40.0

<u>Source</u>: Korean Overseas Information Service, <u>Statistical Data on Korea</u>.

TABLE 10.5
South Korea's Major Import Markets (%)

	Total	United States	Japan	Hongkong	Taiwan	Indonesia	United Kingdom	West Germany	Others
1962	100.0	52.2	25.9	0.1	1.7	---	1.5	4.6	14.0
1967	100.0	30.6	44.5	1.2	2.7	0.1	0.5	3.1	18.3
1972	100.0	25.7	40.9	1.4	1.9	2.5	2.9	2.7	22.0
1977	100.0	22.6	36.3	0.3	1.0	2.3	1.4	3.2	32.9
1978	100.0	20.3	40.0	0.3	1.0	2.7	1.4	3.3	31.0
1979	100.0	22.6	32.7	0.4	1.0	2.9	2.5	4.1	33.8
1980	100.0	21.9	26.3	0.4	1.4	2.2	1.4	2.9	43.5

Source: Korean Overseas Information Service, Statistical Data on Korea.

way to do what it can to see that South Korea remains economically sound and strategically strong.

In doing so Tokyo violates much that normally would be considered common sense economically. Whereas South Korea once was so far behind Japan that Tokyo need have no concern that it could ever catch up, this is starting to change. Motives driving the South Koreans urge them to play catch-up with Japan as diligently as Japan did with the West.[9] Japan still does not have much reason for concern, because South Korea is very unlikely to bridge the gap. However, it does not go down well among many Japanese for Tokyo to help facilitate a burgeoning rival's strengths. This is particularly true among those Japanese who harbor generalized anti-Korean feelings or specifically anti-Seoul emotions for any of the reasons cited previously. However, Tokyo has no more choice in the matter of what it can do to keep the ROK viable politically, credible militarily, or prosperous economically than the United States does about assuring the well-being of Japan.

Meanings of the Status Quo in Korea

There are a number of interesting parallels in U.S.-Japanese versus Japan-ROK relations. In both instances there is a mentor-student pattern in which the student is seen by the teacher as too proficient. Both display love-hate attitudes of envy-resentment, respect-suspicion, affinity-superiority, and knowledge-ignorance. But most important is the strategic similarity. The United States cannot permit Japan to be weakened or intimidated to the point where it becomes vulnerable to Soviet pressures and helps tip the geopolitical balance against U.S. interests. Similarly, Japan cannot afford to see the ROK succumb to North Korean aggression. In this regard, however, the parallel is not exact.

Unlike the United States, which cannot stand by while Japan shifts to the other camp under any circumstances, be they peaceful or violent, Tokyo probably could tolerate the "loss" of South Korea or North Korea if either occurred peacefully. That is, if the two Koreas were to be unified peacefully—either under Seoul, Pyongyang, or some joint arrangement, Tokyo might be able to tolerate it. Officially, of course, Japan is a strong advocate of such a reunification. That is the ostensible purpose behind Tokyo's evenhanded diplomacy that so aggravates Seoul.[10] Nevertheless there are substantial reasons to doubt that Tokyo means what it says. Were Korea to be peacefully reunified the resultant state, regardless of its political coloring, could rather easily become a threat to Japanese interests. Such a Korea would have a combined population of about fifty-five million, would combine the productivity of the south with the indigenous resources of the north, would possess armed forces in excess of one million, and would share a common antipathy toward Japan. Under such circumstances it is not unreasonable for Tokyo to worry that a strong Korea might try to exact on Japan a vengeance that the Korean people would relish. Though it is not an orthodox assessment, it seems quite likely that Japan is not anxious to see a peacefully unified Korea, because it would severely damage Tokyo's existing leverage over the two Koreas and pose new threats.[11]

Even less desirable is the prospect of one Korea conquering the other, because it would involve a war in Japan's backyard. Regardless of who might win or of whether it would produce another stalemate, reviving the status quo, the act of war is what concerns Japan. That concern is not with war per se. True, the Japanese do not like war anymore and prefer to leave such nastiness and expense to their U.S. surrogates for as long as the United States is willing to foot the bill, assuming that Americans will bear the brunt of defending South Korea so that the communist threat does not get too near Japan. What does concern the Japanese is that Americans would be fighting the war partly from Japan, and it could spread to Japan rather easily. The trouble with this concern is that it is devilishly difficult to explain to Americans or South Koreans, who already suspect Japan is shirking its responsibilities for its own security as expressed on the Korean flank.

Still more difficult to handle is the nightmare that stalks Japanese scenarios of a Korean war gone wrong. Should the north win, it would mean an aggressive communist regime on Japan's doorstep, the failure of the United States to carry the day in Korea (which would raise severe questions about Washington's commitment to Japan), and—worst of all—a flood of ex-South Koreans streaming into Japan seeking refuge. The latter would be intrinsically unwelcome and would enormously complicate Tokyo's postwar relations with the successor Korean regime.

Another dilemma in all this results from the frailties of the status quo. Should war break out again in Korea, there is some possibility—perhaps a strong probability—that tactical nuclear weapons would be used to throw back the North Korean aggressors. Militarily this might make sense, but it is psychologically abhorrent to the Japanese people, which makes it a controversial issue for Tokyo. Japan's leaders prefer to say nothing about the prospect and act like the proverbial head-in-sand ostrich, hoping the problem will go away while they ignore it. If Tokyo persists in this do-nothing manner, very reminiscent of its feigned ignorance over U.S. nuclear weapons activities in the vicinity of Japan, Japan will have to face the consequences. Those consequences could—at best—be a local nuclear war on Japan's border, fallout spreading eastward with the prevailing winds onto Japan, and the possibility that adverse Japanese public opinion would jeopardize the U.S. nuclear umbrella over Japan.

From this brief outline of what could await Japan if the status quo in Korea were shattered by war, it is clear why Tokyo is so enamored by that status quo. As things stand, Japan seems to have the best of all possible worlds in Korea: The peninsula is divided, and the Americans are looking after Tokyo's strategic interests with minimal complaint. To maintain this state of affairs Tokyo does its utmost to keep South Korea and North Korea from each other's throats, to help the Koreas maintain parity in their status vis-à-vis each other, and to encourage Washington to stay the course.

Toward that end, Tokyo is compelled to override domestic grousing about its strong ties with Seoul, accept with equanimity the pushiness of South Korean leaders who demand a lot and complain even more, and make an effort to accommodate as best it can Pyongyang's testiness and suspicions. Domestic and/or South Korean problems can be coped with much easier than can North Korea. A combination of time, logic, and persuasion usually suffice with the former. But North Korea poses an especially serious problem because its leadership is cantankerously paranoid, its socioeconomic system offers so little to make Japan's evenhandedness appear credible on the nonpartisan grounds on which Tokyo tries to base it, and one of Pyongyang's accusations hits a nerve.

Korea and Japan's Defense Policy

North Korea regularly and vociferously charges that Japan is in collusion with the United States and the ROK against it. Pyongyang sees all sorts of evidence that such a plan is well advanced.[12] As I retorted to a U.S. analyst who charged the United States with giving Japan an ultimatum of rearm or else, "If only it were true."[13] The sort of strategic system that North Korea says is about to be born between the United States, Japan, and South Korea is very much what is needed by those three countries. Some Americans think this way, as do a growing number of South Koreans who grudgingly accept the idea as a way to keep the United States committed a bit longer than might otherwise be the case. However, Japan is not at all enamored of the notion and does everything it can to nip it in the bud. The latter actions include Tokyo's emphasis on keeping the U.S.-Japanese and U.S.-ROK strategic networks as separate as possible, linked primarily by the United States at the fulcrum; its stress on the domestic impossibility of selling a triangular scheme; and its periodic actions that accentuate South Korean doubts about the wisdom of the whole concept. As long as Tokyo and Seoul think they can delay or prevent truly close trilateral strategic arrangements, they will do so. Clearly, it is up to Washington to press the case for such an arrangement.

Should the United States push that line, as is likely, Japan will find itself even more closely linked to South Korean security and the North Korean threat to Northeast Asia peace and stability than it is today. Though prevailing wisdom holds that Japan cannot do or afford to do anything militarily for Korean security, it is patently wrong. Japan's defense budget for 1980–1981 was approximately three times that of the ROK. Even when North Korea's defense expenses are combined with South Korea's, Japan's still is about twice the amount.[14] Were Japan to up its budget to only half the percentage of gross national product (GNP) figures common to South Korea or the United States as part of an across-the-board increase in burden sharing, Tokyo would have ample funds to supplement what both Washington and Seoul are spending on Japanese regional defense interests.

Specific figures must remain hypothetical and subject to negotiations, but an expenditure of 3–4 percent of GNP on defense-related matters by Japan would give Tokyo enough money to do precisely what it is doing now, with another $24–36 billion left over. Whether such money would be used for armaments, military aid, or economic aid that would free other sources of South Korean funds for military purposes also is a matter to be negotiated. Clearly, however, much could be done with Japanese money to shore up the ROK's existing weaknesses in conventional armaments.[15] In light of Tokyo's self-interest in preserving regional peace, keeping Korea calm, deterring a nuclear war in its neighborhood, and tempering U.S. pressures, the possibility of strategic cooperation between the United States, Japan, and South Korea must be seen as much more credible than conventional wisdom would suggest.

Geopolitics of Japan-Korea Relations

Based on what has been said, it is evident that Japan's economic relations with Korea now and in the future are not part of Tokyo's ordinary foreign economic policy. Normally the most pragmatic, apolitical, and benign people in their foreign economic affairs, the Japanese are very different when it comes to Korea. Politics and strategy impinge directly on Japanese perceptions of Korea, motivating their economic actions in important ways. Arguably, only vis-à-vis the United States and the Middle East does Japan also allow politics to play such a determining role. However, even in those important instances, Tokyo knows that what seems to be so important today may be altered by time and circumstances into a decidedly less crucial factor. That is especially true of oil-based Middle Eastern factors.

None of this is true about Japan's interests in the fate of Korea. The proximity of Korea makes everything that happens there very important to Japan, a condition that cannot be fundamentally altered by time or circumstances. Thus, though Japanese may talk as if Korea is simply one of many foreign economic concerns and a relatively secondary one at that, in fact Tokyo's relations with North and South Korea—or any unified succesor—constitute a special case. That status puts Korea in a different category from the themes addressed in this book, that Japan's foreign relations have been overshadowed by the problems of integrating its domestic economy into the world market. Even on what seem to be narrowly economic grounds, Japan-Korea relations involve much broader issues that cut to the heart of Japan's existence and prosperity. Any such economic issues must be incorporated by Tokyo into its geopolitical posture and be made strategic in the broadest, as well as the narrowest, usage of the concept. Because of this relationship Japan will be compelled to do things to and for Korea that are out of step with its ordinarily low-profile posture. So, regardless of how unhappy the Japanese people may be today or in the future about the necessity of coping with the various problems Korea poses for Japan, Tokyo has no choice other than to be concerned and take appropriate actions.

Notes

1. Andreas Dorpalen, *The World of General Haushofer* (New York: Farrar & Rinehart, 1942), pp. 7–38; and Hans W. Weigert, *Generals and Geographers: The Twilight of Geopolitics* (New York: Oxford University Press, 1942), pp. 176–191.

2. Ronald A. Morse and I addressed the failures experienced by the United States in this process in "Japan's Bureaucratic Edge," *Foreign Policy,* Fall 1983.

3. I addressed the evolution of the North and South Korean political economies in a number of articles and book chapters upon which the preceding assessments were based. They include "Korea, Inc.: The Political Impact of Park Chung-hee's Economic Miracle," *Orbis,* Spring 1980; "The Political Implications of Resource Scarcity on the Korean Peninsula," *Korean Observer,* Winter 1981; "The United States' Korea Policy: Offering Pyongyang an Economic Carrot," *Journal of Northeast Asian Affairs,* Fall 1982; "The Two Koreas," in James E. Katz, ed., *Arms Production and Trade in Developing Countries* (Lexington, Mass.: Lexington Books, 1984); "The United States, Japan, and North Korea," in Yong S. Yim, ed., *The Politics of Adversary Relations in East Asia* (College Park: University of Maryland Press, 1984); and "The Societal Role of the ROK Armed Forces," in E. A. Olsen and S. Jurika, eds., *The Armed Forces in Contemporary Asian Societies* (Durham, N.C.: Duke University Press, 1984).

4. This problem was addressed by me in "Korea's Image in U.S. a Mish M*A*S*H," *Asian Wall Street Journal,* 2/21/83.

5. *International Monetary Fund 1982 Direction of Trade,* pp. 290–291.

6. For examples of a higher-profile effort to influence North Korea, see *Asahi Shimbun,* 5/18/83, p. 2 (for coverage of Foreign Minister Shintaro Abe's first-ever contact with a Democratic People's Republic of Korea [DPRK] official) and the *Mainichi Shimbun,* 7/20/83, p. 3 (for coverage of a Diet delegation visit to North Korea that raised the prospect of some sort of more official Japan-DPRK contacts). See also *Foreign Broadcast Information Services* (*FBIS*), 4, 7/11/83, pp. C2–3.

7. For representative coverage of Prime Minister Nakasone's political and economic overtures toward Seoul and his development of some rapport with President Chun, see *Christian Science Monitor* 1/7/83, p. 8; *Time* 1/24/83, p. 53; and *FBIS,* 4, 5/26/83, p. C3 and 6/6/83, p. C1, E1.

8. See, inter alia, "Nichi-bei-kan sogo anpo taisei o nozomu," *Chuo Koron,* February 1983, pp. 152–159; and "The United States, Japan, and North Korea."

9. I addressed this manifest destiny of South Korea in "South Korea: A Case Study," presented at a Georgetown CSIS/Los Alamos Laboratory conference, 9/13/83.

10. For a typical critical analysis of one such episode, Foreign Minister Abe's attempt to broach unification as an opening wedge in Japan-DPRK official diplomatic contacts, see *Chungang Ilbo,* 5/19/83, p. 2.

11. These points were explored by me more thoroughly in "The American and Japanese Stake in Korean Unification," *Journal of East Asian Affairs,* Spring/Summer 1983.

12. For examples of such analysis, including an alleged text of a memorandum creating a triangular military alliance, see *FBIS,* 4, 9/8/82, pp. D3–4; 4/25/83, pp. D1–10; 5/25/83, pp. D8–9.

13. "Enticing Japan," invited response to the February 1983 article by David Morrison "Rearm or Else: America's Ultimatum to Japan," *Inquiry,* April 1983, p. 8.

14. *Military Balance 1982–1983* (London: International Institute of Strategic Studies, 1982), p. 124–125.

15. For an analysis of those weaknesses, see William L. Scully, "The Korean Peninsula Military Balance," *Backgrounder* (n.p.): Asian Studies Center, The Heritage Foundation, 7/11/83).

11
Japan and Taiwan: Community of Economic Interest Held Together by Paradiplomacy

Walter Arnold

This chapter sets out to explain why and how Japan and Taiwan have been able to maintain and expand effective and viable economic ties over the last decade in the absence of any formal diplomatic or political relations. It is contended that the motivational basis ensuring continuous economic exchange and cooperation is economic complementarity, hence mutual interest. The tacit understanding of the conditions governing the informal Taiwanese-Japanese arrangement of 1972 has successfully regulated economic and cultural relations and the exchange of persons since the break of diplomatic relations. In this chapter I argue that Japanese-Taiwanese economic ties have maintained their viability for two major reasons. The first is the paradiplomatic effort of various semipublic organizations on both sides that are bound together by a community of economic interests. Second, both Taiwan and Japan seem to have successfully transcended the obvious international political risks and impediments to their relationship by pursing a policy of *seikei bunri*, or separation of politics from economics. The following discussion will focus on the institutional arrangements and environment of Japanese-Taiwanese economic ties in general and will shed light on some of the major problems afflicting this important relationship over the past decade.

Institutional Arrangements After 1972

In the wake of the 1971 rapprochement between the United States and the People's Republic of China (PRC) latent pro-PRC forces in Japan's Liberal-Democratic party (LDP) and big business intensified the pressures to reassess Japan's relations with Taipei and Beijing. Yet Prime Minister Eisaku Sato, a longtime ardent supporter of Taiwan, remained a formidable impediment to normalization of relations with the PRC. The stalemate was resolved when Kakuei Tanaka, a strong advocate of Japanese recognition of the PRC, succeeded Sato as prime minister in

July 1972, and Sino-Japanese relations were quickly normalized; diplomatic relations with Taiwan were broken off. In a swift political move the PRC acquiesced in Japan's pursuit of its profitable trade with Taiwan. Beijing indicated that it would tolerate an informal arrangement for the continuation of this important economic relationship.

As early as December 1972 the new *modus operandi* was functional with the formation of the Koryu Kyokai, or the Interchange Association, on the Japanese side, and the Ya Tung Kuan Hsi Hsieh Hui, or East Asian Relations Association (EARA), on Taiwan's. The Interchange Association opened up offices in Taipei and Kaoshiung; the East Asian Relations Association set up offices in Tokyo, Osaka, and Fukuoka.[1] Staffed by seasoned foreign-service veterans, the offices of both organizations assumed the tasks of consulates and defined their mission as promoting the development of trade and technological and cultural relations.[2] Both organizations have close ties with their respective governments and economic communities and thus have been capable of functioning effectively as paradiplomatic links between Japan and Taiwan.

Since 1973 the East Asian Relations Association and the Interchange Association have held several high-level economic and trade conferences. The most recent one was on December 12, 1983, in Tokyo, and trade relations and technical cooperation between Japan and Taiwan were discussed.[3] Over the past decade the paradiplomatic efforts of these two associations have been supplemented by the activities of various private organizations formed to promote ties between Taiwan and Japan. The Industrial, Spiritual, and Cultural Association has figured prominently in the advancement of technical training and exchanges between Taiwan and Japan. Similarly, the Sino-Japanese Cultural and Economic Association acts as intermediary for scholarships from the Japanese Association for Overseas Technical Scholarships, which offers advanced industrial and technical training in Japan.[4]

Japanese Economic Interests in Taiwan

With deferred payments, equipment, and capital investment amounting to over $125 million in 1972, most of the approximately four hundred Japanese companies present in Taiwan at the time of the break in diplomatic relations were reluctant to abandon Taiwan as an investment and marketplace however little new investment was committed or placed on order in 1972. Although almost all Japanese companies decided to remain in Taiwan, some set up "dummy companies" to disguise their name and operations because they were fearful of eventual reprisals from the People's Republic of China. These fears turned out to be unfounded. By the end of 1973, Japanese private investment in Taiwan had increased to $135 million with an additional $330 million in private and government-guaranteed loans.

Japanese trade and investment in Taiwan have long constituted the basis for shared economic interest and economic complementarity and have played an important role in Taiwan's economic and industrial development. During the early 1960s Taiwan began to offer an attractive package to foreign investors consisting of tax holidays, exemptions, government guarantees, subsidies, and loans for foreign investors, in addition to cheap labor and a relatively liberal policy for repatriation of profits. Moreover, in the course of Taiwan's basic structural transformation from a raw-materials producer to a producer of capital-intensive industrial goods in the late 1960s, it had turned primarily to Japanese industrial and financial circles for deferred-payment credits and technical assistance in order to obtain the requisite technology, equipment, and investment.[5] In the late 1960s Japanese investment was concentrated mainly in textiles, electronic and electrical appliances, metals, and machinery equipment and contributed substantially to the development of Taiwan's processing industries.[6] During the 1970s Japanese investment shifted to steel, heavy machinery, shipbuilding, chemicals, and refineries and in the early 1980s to heavy trucks and automobiles. Japanese investment in Taiwan, which from 1966 to 1972 accounted for 21 percent of Japan's total foreign investment, jumped to 30 percent during the period from 1973 to 1979.[7]

Japanese foreign investment and trade seem to have played a critical role in Taiwan's industrial advancement. On the other hand, it must also be recognized that Taiwan has functioned as a most important receptacle for dated Japanese technological and industrial processes; in fact, over the past decade, Taiwan has become a major outlet for Japan's declining industries.

Against the backdrop of an ever-expanding and ubiquitous presence in Taiwan of Japanese firms, enterprises, trading companies, and commercial and financial institutions, it seems reasonable to suggest that Japanese-Taiwanese economic interdependence has increased over the past ten years. Indeed, bilateral trade between Japan and Taiwan quintupled from $1.514 billion in 1972 to $8 billion in 1983.[8] However, it would be misleading to suggest that Taiwan has become an exclusive Japanese economic domain. To the contrary, foreign-trade statistics for 1983 listed the United States as Taiwan's major partner with $17 billion in two-way trade, and Japan a distant second with $8 billion, out of a total of $45 billion.[9] Japan's preponderant position in Taiwan's economy and share in foreign trade must be explained mainly in terms of an aggregate of factors ranging from geographic proximity and relative cultural affinity to Japan's role as most efficient producer and major intermediary of technology to Asia.

Notwithstanding the phenomenal growth of Japan's informal trade with Taiwan and the basic economic complementarity between the two, the Japan-Taiwan relationship has encountered several critical economic challenges in the course of the past decade. Two issue areas have been of particular significance: the civil aviation dispute of 1974–1975 and, more important, Taiwan's chronic balance-of-trade deficit with Japan. In the absence of any formal diplomatic relations, both issue areas had to be dealt with through informal arrangements and a paradiplomatic effort on both sides.

The Civil Aviation Dispute

The civil aviation dispute began as a political incident in 1973 and was finally resolved in 1975 on the basis of economic considerations. It marked the first critical test for the arrangement governing the relationship between Taiwan and Japan in the post-derecognition era.

During the 1973 negotiations for a PRC-Japan Civil Aviation Agreement, Japan attempted to retain existing, profitable air links with Taiwan. The People's Republic of China, however, raised stern objections concerning Taiwan's use of *China* (in ideographic compound form) and demanded that the name China Airlines had to be changed; Taiwan flatly refused to comply.[10] Under pressure from the People's Republic of China, but also lured by the potential of the China market, Japan suspended the flights of its national carrier, JAL (Japan Airlines), to Taiwan and on April 20, 1974, signed a Civil Aviation Agreement with the People's Republic of China. Taiwan retaliated by severing its air links with Japan. As it turned out, Taiwan could ill afford the lapse of flights to Japan for long, because short-term economic costs were simply too high. Flights were resumed fourteen months after the suspension. Not only had China Airlines incurred substantial monetary losses, but equally important, Taiwan's overall economic relationship with Japan appeared to be in jeopardy because of the lack of this important communication and transportation link.[11]

The civil aviation dispute attests to the salience of economic considerations underlying Taiwan's relations with Japan. Moreover, by disassociating political considerations from functional economic concerns, Taiwan displayed a willingness to pragmatically accommodate to realities. Finally, the civil aviation dispute clearly evidences that Japan was effectively practicing *seikei bunri* and that the separation of politics from economics has become one of the salient features governing Japan-Taiwan relations.

There are indications that Japan's pragmatic separation of politics from economics has been strongly conducive to maximizing economic benefits from its relationship with Taiwan while minimizing political frictions over Taiwan with the People's Republic of China. Taiwan's own version of separating politics from economics proved to be an effective approach to its foreign economic relations after most nations had severed their diplomatic ties in the early 1970s. Such a separation permitted Taiwan to maintain old economic ties and to search for new ones without being impeded by the lack of formal diplomatic recognition.[12]

Adhering to the principle of separating politics from economics in their relationship, both Taiwan and Japan have successfully refrained from utilizing foreign trade as a means for political purposes. Instead, the separation has undergirded Japanese-Taiwanese economic ties and brought economic benefits to both sides.

Trade Structure and Problems from 1972
to the Early 1980s

Perhaps the single most important structural feature affecting Taiwan's economic relations with Japan (and the world) has been the high degree of Taiwan's foreign-trade dependence in its developmental effort. The share of imports and exports combined in Taiwan's gross national product (GNP) has fluctuated around 95 percent over the past decade, with Japanese imports growing at an annual rate of about 24 percent. The growth rate of Taiwanese exports to Japan has increased from 16 percent in the early 1970s to 32 percent at the end of the 1970s.[13]

Although frequently understated, the role of the Taiwanese economy in Japan's trade has been important over the past several decades, particularly for Japan's medium- and small-size enterprises. Japan's continuous granting of most-favored-nation status to Taiwan may be seen as an implicit indication that Japan recognizes Taiwan as one of its more important markets and trading partners in Asia.

With the informal Taiwan-Japan arrangement solidly in place by early 1973, the two-way trade has continued to expand ever since. However, given the fact of two economies at entirely different stages of development, Japanese-Taiwanese trade has tended to be structurally uneven as far as composition, volume, and monetary value are concerned. Taiwan's exports to Japan over the past decade consisted mainly of low-value agricultural and fishery products, minerals, sundry items, textiles, light industrial goods, and—more recently—chemicals and chemical products. Japan, on the other hand, has been exporting primarily basic metals, machinery, electrical equipment, transportation equipment, and other manufactured goods to Taiwan.[14]

The argument can be made that Japan is little dependent on Taiwan, since Japan can easily replace most Taiwanese imports with substitutes from other countries in East Asia. On the other hand, Taiwan depends to a considerable extent on Japan for its supply of metals, machinery, and consumer goods. In fact, with the shift in Taiwan's production and consumption patterns during the 1970s and early 1980s, its dependence on Japan has been increased further. The great structural transformation of Taiwan's economy, increasing wealth, and disposable income seem to have reinforced Taiwan's role as major importer of Japanese machinery, finished industrial products, and consumer goods.

A glance at the statistics in Table 11.1 reveals that over the past decade the Taiwan-Japan two-way trade has increased in volume and monetary terms and that Taiwan's relative economic dependence on Japan has not been diminished. This is clearly manifest in the chronic trade deficits that rose from $670 million in 1972 to $3.108 billion in 1983. As pointed out earlier, the causes of Taiwan's trade deficits are essentially structural in nature: Taiwan exports mainly raw materials and low value-added goods and products that tend to fetch lower prices than the high value-added goods and products Japan exports to Taiwan.

TABLE 11.1
Japan's Trade with Taiwan, 1965–1983 ($ million)

Year	Total Trade	Imports	Exports	Balance
1965	375	157	218	+61
1966	402	147	255	+108
1967	465	137	328	+191
1968	623	151	472	+321
1969	787	181	606	+425
1970	951	251	700	+449
1971	1,210	285	925	+640
1972	1,514	422	1,092	+670
1973	2,537	892	1,645	+753
1974	2,962	954	2,008	+1,054
1975	2,631	811	1,820	+1,009
1976	3,475	1,192	2,283	+1,091
1977	3,842	1,289	2,553	+1,264
1978	5,335	1,750	3,585	+1,835
1979	6,843	2,476	4,367	+1,891
1980	7,439	2,293	5,146	+2,853
1981	8,400	2,500	5,900	+3,400
1982	7,200	2,400	4,800	+2,400
1983	8,064	2,478	5,586	+3,108

Sources: For 1965–1980, The Europa Yearbook, 1982
            For 1981, Free China Weekly, March 14, 1982, p.1.
            For 1982–1983, Central News Agency, January 24, 1984.

The important empirical and analytical task that remains is to explain why Taiwan has acquiesced in view of the perennial Japanese trade surplus of the past decade and also to explain the course of action taken by Taipei. Among the multitude of explanations two major caveats come immediately to the fore. For one, the expansion of Japan's trade surplus in 1972 coincided with the break in diplomatic relations. As a result, Taiwan's authorities have been left in a very vulnerable political position vis-à-vis Japan. Operating through the EARA, Taiwan has attempted to present its trade-related grievances and concerns to the appropriate Japanese authorities. However, in view of a decade of ever-increasing trade deficits and tensions, it appears that the informal Taiwan-Japan trade arrangement and the EARA did not prove sufficiently effective instruments to remedy the trade problem or even to reverse the basic trend. Comparing Taiwan's situation with some of Japan's other major trading partners, the European Economic Community (EEC) and the United States, for example, one easily discerns that Taiwan does not enjoy the benefit of any special institutional arrangement designed to "smooth" its trade relations with Japan. There can be no doubt that the absence of formal diplomatic relations has greatly contributed to the asymmetrical development in trade since 1972 and that there is little room left for Taiwan to maneuver in its present relationship with Japan. Finally, the very tentative nature of the Taiwan-Japan ties represents a most formidable nontariff barrier in this complex arrangement in which, arguably, Japan has capitalized on Taiwan's weakness.

A second important caveat has been Taiwan's dependence on Japan as a major source for economic and technological imports. During its worldwide export offensive in the latter half of the 1970s, Taiwan's export efforts and success greatly depended on a secure and stable supply of semifinished goods from Japan as well as their timely delivery.[15]

Cognizant of the apparent politico-economic vulnerability and constraints surrounding its relations with Japan, Taiwan's authorities over the past decade have devoted their major resources and political attention to the promotion and diversification of exports and imports. In spite of Taipei's diversification attempts, Japanese trade with Taiwan grew at a constant 24 percent per year during the 1970s.[16] Imports from Western Europe and the United States have tended to be more expensive in terms of price and time; according to one report, Japanese machinery and equipment is often at least 30 percent cheaper than its competition because of lower export prices, freight, and insurance.[17] A few illustrative examples of Taiwan's attempts to respond to Japan's chronic trade surplus are the "Buy American" campaign Taiwan began in 1973, fearful of growing too dependent on Japanese imports,[18] and the exclusion a year later of Japanese bidders on major shipbuilding, electrification, and petrochemical projects, at a time when the deficit with Japan approached the psychologically important $1 billion mark.[19] What was the result? There was little tangible improvement: Japan's 1975 trade surplus dropped only $45 million to $1.009 billion. Taiwan's trade deficit with Japan rose again in 1976 and has risen every year since then, with the exception of 1982-1983. Although over the years Taiwan has shown increasing concern and occasionally manifested displeasure with the asymmetrical development of its trade with Japan, Taiwan refrained from taking draconian measures. However, this all changed when Taiwan's economic miracle hit the snag of the 1980–1982 recession.

Quasi Trade War in 1982

By the close of the 1970s Taiwan's authorities had become increasingly concerned about a combination of worldwide stagflation and protectionism in overseas markets, all factors which had begun to impair further rapid growth of Taiwan's export economy. These factors brought into sharp focus the problems underlying Taiwan's economic ties with Japan. Most prominent and most critical in this respect was the declining value of the Japanese yen; the direct impact and potential threat of the decline began to pose formidable policy problems for Taipei. For one, the "cheap" yen had added yet another competitive edge to Japanese products on the Taiwanese market and led to increased imports, thus further exacerbating the already strained balance-of-trade situation. More importantly still, the Japanese export boom of 1980 induced by the "cheap" yen meant that many Taiwanese products were clashing head on in their quest for market share at the global level.[20]

As a result of this increased worldwide competition for market shares, and partially also because of a declining competitive advantage in specific areas (soaring labor costs and lower productivity gains), Taiwanese firms and authorities showed great determination to preserve and defend existing market shares in order to maintain the critical export momentum. In short, Taiwan of the early 1980s was no longer willing to acquiesce in Japanese trade supremacy. And when the Taiwan-Japan two-way trade of $8.5 billion resulted in a staggering $3.45 billion deficit problem for Taiwan in 1981, the time had come for Taipei to treat the trade deficit as a most serious politico-economic issue.

In early 1982 Taiwan demonstrated increasing determination to reduce the $3.4 billion trade deficit with Japan. The deputy director general of Taiwan's Board of Foreign Trade warned: "We want Japan to realize that this kind of imbalance is intolerable. Japan must take positive steps to buy more from this country."[21] And in a surprise move in mid-February the Board of Foreign Trade unilaterally banned the import of more than fifteen hundred consumer items from Japan for an indefinite time, and heavy trucks and diesel engines for one year.[22] Such forceful action took an unsuspecting Tokyo by surprise; it also touched off an intracabinet squabble in Taipei because the decision was taken by Economics Minister Chao Yao-tung without consulting Finance Minister Hsu Li-teh or Premier Y. S. Sun.[23] Taiwan's authorities, however, were quick to point out that this retaliatory action was to be understood primarily as a warning, and the import ban itself would have little economic impact, with an estimated total value of $160–200 million, about 5 percent of Taiwan's 1981 trade deficit with Japan. Moreover, Taipei insisted that the import ban was not a protectionist measure in support of any local industries and entrepreneurs but rather a means to bring Japan to the negotiation table.[24]

In view of the past record, little could be expected from such negotiations, since for almost a decade both Taiwan and Japan had been meeting on a private and semiofficial basis to discuss ways and means to reduce Taiwan's trade deficit. Moreover, in 1979 the Taiwan-Japan Trade Balance Committee was established to promote Taiwanese exports to Japan and to reduce the trade deficit by $500 million each year. This notwithstanding, Taiwan's trade deficit with Japan continued to increase year by year.

On March 4, 1982, Japan's Interchange Association office in Taipei issued a four-point note on the ban of Japanese imports; it threatened countermeasures, including cancellation of Taiwan's preferential tariff and trade status.[25] Taipei trade circles were quick to point to the negligible impact of Japan's preferential tariffs on Taiwan's imports, arguing that nontariff barriers constituted the greatest impediment for the access of Taiwanese products to the Japanese market. On March 12 Taipei instructed the East Asian Relations Association to conduct negotiations with Hiroshi Hitomi, the director of Japan's Interchange Association office in Taipei, in search for a more equitable solution for the chronic trade-deficit problem. Subsequently director Hitomi returned to Tokyo for consultations with the Interchange Association's head office and government officials in Tokyo.[26]

In spite of Japan's threat to cancel tariff privileges, Taipei demonstrated its genuine determination to solve the trade-deficit issue. In April Taipei banned the import of heavy-duty tractors, and subsequently it rejected an application from Fujitsu, Japan's largest computer producer, to set up an assembly plant for computerized machine-tool devices.[27] In August Taipei devalued the Taiwanese dollar in the hope to make its exports to Japan more competitive. By and large, the defiant stand against Japan by the Board of Foreign Trade and other Taiwan authorities found considerable support (and applause) in business circles. Nevertheless, it was widely acknowledged in Taipei that the bulk of Taiwan's imports was provided by Japan (28 percent in 1981); since these Japanese imports consisted mainly of capital goods and semifinished industrial products, all vital for Taiwan's export industries, they could not simply be stopped without inflicting serious damage to the national economy.

And yet, although Japan had signaled warnings to Taipei about possible consequences of this import ban, Tokyo could ill afford to get embroiled in a trade war with Taiwan. For one, a two-front trade war with the EEC countries and North America loomed large. Moreover, in 1981 Japan's trade with Taiwan netted a record surplus of $3.4 billion. In fact, in 1982 Taiwan took on renewed significance as a marketplace for many Japanese enterprises because of the worldwide protectionist policies of Europe and North America and because of the disappointments and financial losses suffered by many Japanese firms in the China market. It is not surprising then that Japan's economically motivated pragmatism prevailed and Tokyo gradually softened its stance vis-à-vis Taipei's incessant calls for more equal trade relations. As a result, a major trade and tariff war between Taiwan and Japan was successfully warded off.

Toward a New Economic Relationship

In the spring of 1982 Taiwan's export community, in cooperation with the Taiwan-Japan Trade Balance Committee and under the leadership of the China External Trade Development Council (CETDC), which declared 1982 as "Export to Japan Promotion Year,"[28] began to draw up wide-ranging plans to promote exports to Japan. However, as Taiwanese business and industry began the vigorous export drive to close the Japan trade gap, leading economists urged caution. They argued that such an export offensive was not sufficient to narrow the trade deficit, but that instead more Japanese investment and technical assistance were needed to upgrade Taiwan's industrial structure, which had earlier been diagnosed as the major cause of Taiwan's chronic trade deficit with Japan.[29]

These arguments notwithstanding, Taiwan's foreign-trade authorities and export industries combined their efforts and pushed quite hard to crack open the Japanese market for a greater variety and larger quantity of Taiwanese products. During 1982 and 1983 the CETDC liaison office in Tokyo, with the explicit approval of the Ministry of Economic Affairs in Taipei, was in the forefront of various Taiwanese export promotion efforts in Japan. The CETDC has sponsored and organized numerous trade shows and fairs in Tokyo and Osaka. Moreover, several specialized fairs and business seminars were organized to promote a wide range of goods from Taiwan, including toys, minerals, sporting goods, machinery, hardware, bicycles, furniture, leather goods, textiles, electrical appliances and machinery, livestock, and fishery products.[30] And finally, large Japanese retailers were invited to Taiwan to attend export exhibitions. In 1982 alone the CETDC arranged for two groups of Japanese buyers to come to Taiwan on buying missions in the spring and summer, after which Taipei eased the ban on the import of 842 items of Japanese products in August 1982.[31]

The trade deficit was also the major issue of discussion during the 7th Sino-Japanese Trade Conference held in Taipei, October 28–29, 1982. Forty participants discussed trade, investment, and technological cooperation, and Japanese delegates indicated their support for the improvement of Taiwan's industrial structure. Moreover, the Japanese agreed to send yet another purchasing mission to Taiwan and to assist Taiwan's trade missions in Japan. From November 4 to 16, 1982, the East Asian Relations Association and the Japanese Interchange Association jointly sponsored a series of investment and technical-cooperation seminars in Tokyo, Nagoya, Osaka, and Fukuoka. These seminars, primarily intended to induce further Japanese capital investment and technical cooperation, were led by Taiwan's vice economic minister Wu Mei-tsing, who headed a large trade mission consisting of officials from the Industrial Development and Investment Center, the Investment Commission, the Industrial Development Bureau, and the Export Processing Zone Administration. While in Japan the trade mission held extensive talks with Japanese industrial circles.[32]

The November 22, 1982, announcement that Taipei would lift the ban on 689 Japanese consumer items was a clear indication that Taipei had made some progress in its relentless drive to narrow its trade deficit with Japan. Taipei authorities made it clear that this gesture was a demonstration of Taiwan's sincerity in improving its trade ties with Japan. Further, it became clear that Taipei expected reciprocity from the Japanese government.[33]

A new phase in the Taiwan-Japan economic relationship was ushered in with the December 23, 1982, announcement that Taiwan's authorities had chosen Japan's largest auto maker, Toyota Motor Corporation, as a partner in a $550 million joint venture to produce compact cars in Taiwan.[34] A spokesman said that Toyota will have a 45 percent stake in the joint venture, and China Steel Corporation, a public enterprise, will hold 25 percent. The remaining 30 percent will be held by nine Taiwanese companies, including Formosa Plastic Corporation, Taiwan Cement Corporation, and Sampo Corporation and Tatung Corporation, both electrical-appliance makers. The plant is expected to begin operation in 1986 and will have a capacity to produce 300,000 cars by 1993, with half of the output earmarked for export.[35]

Negotiations over the joint venture had been continuing for two years and at one time Nissan Motor Company was the front-runner. Taipei authorities selected Toyota rather than Nissan because Toyota has its own worldwide sales network; that will make it easier for the joint venture company to export and sell half of its output abroad.[36] Taiwan's domestic auto makers vehemently opposed the joint venture and complained that the China Steel–Toyota joint venture posed a major threat to their very existence. It has been pointed out repeatedly that Taiwan's domestic market is of insufficient size to absorb any additional increase in capacity. On the other hand, Taiwan's technocrats, based in the Ministry of Economic Affairs under the able leadership of Minister Chao Yao-tung, viewed the joint venture with Toyota as an excellent opportunity to upgrade Taiwan's deficient industrial structure, since Toyota has apparently agreed to work closely with Taiwan's parts makers in order to upgrade their technology and product quality.[37]

Although the China Steel–Toyota joint venture was bogged down by further, protracted negotiations that postponed a final agreement until December 26, 1983, its demonstration effect and impact on Taiwan-Japan economic relations were immediate and considerable. During 1983 several large Japanese industrial enterprises and financial institutions showed active interest in exploring Taiwan as a market and investment place. For example, Japan's Long-Term Credit Bank, operating through its Hong Kong Subsidiary, participated in a syndicated loan to China Steel. The loan was put together by four major Japanese banks in consort with the China Steel–Toyota joint venture. Wary of negative reactions from the People's Republic of China, many Japanese banks have stayed away from Taiwan for the past decade.[38] In July 1983, Hino and Isuzu, two major Japanese truck manufacturers, submitted formal investment proposals for a joint venture with Huatung Automotive Company, a Taiwanese manufacturer of heavy trucks.[39]

Perhaps the best received overture of Japan's interest in closing its trade gap with Taiwan, besides China Steel's joint venture with Toyota, has been the well-publicized success of the Japanese trade mission that visited Taiwan from September 5 to 13, 1983. Led by Hiroshi Anzai, chairman of Tokyo Gas, the mission consisted of some 230 members representing general trading companies, special trading companies, department stores, and manufacturing firms. This was the largest Japanese buying mission that had ever come to Taiwan, and its goal was to redress the trade imbalance with Taiwan with estimated purchases of some $600–700 million worth of Taiwanese products.[40]

During a banquet in honor of the Japanese buying mission, Economics Minister Chao Yao-tung called on Japan to assist Taiwan to upgrade its industrial structure and to pump more investment into Taiwan. This goal, according to Chao, can be achieved through greater technical cooperation and through increased investments from Japanese firms in Taiwan. Success of this program would narrow the ever-widening trade gap between Taiwan and Japan, Chao said. The other way to narrow the trade gap would be for Japan to increase its import of Taiwanese products. Chao went further in saying that it was his hope that Japan would positively promote trade, investment, and transfer of technology instead of just passively buying products from Taiwan.[41]

When at the end of its purchasing activities the Japanese buying mission publicly announced that it had placed orders in the amount of some $1.13 billion, Taipei's authorities were obviously pleased and lauded the mission's purchases and orders as a sign of Japanese sincerity in improving its trade imbalance with Taiwan. However, Japan closed 1983 with a $3.108 billion trade surplus with Taiwan. Even so, in view of Taiwan's overall trade surplus of some $5 billion and Japan's recent efforts to close the trade gap, it is likely that in the near future Taiwan will pursue the trade-deficit issue less vigorously than during the past.

As for the immediate future, the Japanese seem to have credibly demonstrated their willingness to narrow the gap in their two-way trade with Taiwan. However, it is very unlikely that Taiwan's trade deficits with Japan will remain on a downward trend for very long. To the contrary, Taiwan's policy of upgrading its industrial structure will necessitate even greater imports of sophisticated Japanese capital goods and technology, all of which will lead to new increases in the trade deficit. It is almost inevitable that the present disparity of the industrial structures in the two economies will lead to further trade imbalances until Taiwan manages to "catch up" economically and technologically. Meanwhile, the latent danger of renewed trade and tariff conflicts looms large.

Notes

1. *Asahi Shimbun*, December 27, 1972.
2. Ibid.
3. *Chung Yang Rih Pao (CYRP)*, December 12, 1983.
4. Gene T. Hsia, "Prospects for a New Sino-Japanese Relationship," *China Quarterly*, no. 60, pp. 720–749.

5. Tzong-shian Yu, "The Development of Relations Between the Republic of China and Japan Since 1972," *Asian Survey* 21, no. 6 (June 1981), pp. 633–638.

6. Ibid.

7. Ibid.

8. Central News Agency (*CNA*), January 8–11, 1984.

9. Ibid.

10. *Far Eastern Economic Review* (*FEER*), January 7, 1974, p. 12.

11. Since then China Airlines has been using Haneda, Toyoko's old international airport.

12. In 1983, for example, Taiwan had economic ties with all advanced industrial states, a great many Third World nations, and also socialist states, including the PRC.

13. S.W.Y. Kuo, G. Ranis, and J.C.H. Fei, *The Taiwan Success Story: Rapid Growth with Improved Distribution in the Republic of China, 1952–1979* (Boulder, Colo.: Westview Press, 1981), pp. 24–25.

14. *Japan Statistical Yearbook 1982,* Statistics Bureau, Prime Minister's Office, pp. 291–292, 304.

15. Geographic proximity represents one of Japan's edges in its economic ties with Taiwan.

16. Kuo, Ranis, and Fei, *The Taiwan Success Story*, pp. 21–27.

17. *FEER*, March 5, 1982, p. 66.

18. *Business Week*, October 12, 1983, p. 40.

19. See Thomas J. Bellows, "Taiwan's Foreign Policy in the 1970s: A Case Study of Adaptation and Viability," *Asian Survey* 16, no. 7, p. 604.

20. *FEER*, December 22, 1983, p. 22.

21. *Business Week*, April 19, 1982, p. 48.

22. *CYRP*, February 14, 1982, p. 1.

23. *FEER Yearbook 1983*, p. 261.

24. *Business Week*, April 19, 1982, p. 48.

25. *CYRP*, March 5, 1982, p. 1.

26. *CYRP*, March 14, 1982, p. 1.

27. *Business Week*, April 19, 1982.

28. *CYRP*, March 12, p. 1.

29. *FEER*, December 22, 1983, pp. 21–26.

30. *CYRP*, March 13, 1982, p. 2.

31. *CYRP*, August 8, 1982, p. 1.

32. *Taiwan Industrial Panorama* 10, no. 11, November 1982, pp. 1–2.

33. *CYRP*, December 24, 1982.

34. Ibid.

35. *Asian Wallstreet Journal Weekly*, July 4, 1983.

36. *CYRP*, December 26, 1982, p. 1.

37. *Asian Wallstreet Journal Weekly*, July 25, 1983, p. 17.

38. *Wall Street Journal*, April 13, 1983, p. 30.

39. *CNA*, August 1, 1983.

40. Ibid., September 1983, no. 4, p. 1.

41. Ibid., pp. 3–4.

12
Japan and Latin America

Akio Hosono

In the last twenty years economic relations between Latin America and Japan have changed substantially. This chapter has the following purposes: (1) to review the basic aspects of these changes, (2) to analyze the main causes for such changes; and (3) to discuss the possible lines of action to promote desirable economic relationships and cooperation between Latin America and Japan. I prepared this chapter on the basis of different studies and discussions in forums concerned with the mutual relationship.[1]

The Expansion and Diversification of Mutual Economic Relations

Trade Expansion and Diversification

Trade between Latin America and Japan expanded steadily in the 1960s and well into the 1970s while exhibiting marked tendencies toward greater diversification. It is noteworthy that the mutual economic interchange was not marred by any serious setbacks during this extended period of time. Japanese exports to Latin American countries increased from about US$304 million in 1960 and US$1.187 billion in 1970 to US$10.516 billion in 1981, recording an average annual rate of increase of 18.4 percent.[2] This growth figure was slightly smaller than for total Japanese exports in the same period; taking the 1970s alone, however, the rate of growth of Japanese exports to Latin America surpassed that of total exports. (See Table 12.1.) Meanwhile, Japanese imports from the Latin American countries grew from US$311 million in 1960 to US$6.669 billion in 1981, with an annual growth rate of about 15.7 percent.[3]

Japanese exports to Latin America accounted for an increasing share of total exports in the 1970s, going from 6 percent in the second half of the 1960s to 6.9 percent in 1981. But Latin America's share in total Japanese imports started to decline after the global oil crisis, primarily as a result of drastic increases in oil imports from areas other than Latin

TABLE 12.1
Trends in Total Japanese Trade and Trade with Latin America

				(millions of dollars)
	Total Exports	Exports to Latin America	Total Imports	Imports from Latin America
1960	4,055	304	4,491	311
1965	8,452	488	8,169	707
1970	19,318	1,187	18,881	1,373
1975	55,753	4,765	57,863	2,524
1976	67,225	5,013	64,799	2,465
1977	80,495	6,292	70,809	3,065
1978	97,543	6,621	79,343	3,047
1979	103,032	6,555	110,672	4,517
1980	129,807	8,917	140,528	5,700
1981	152,030	10,516	143,290	6,669
Average yearly increase (%) 1960-1981	18.8	18.4	17.9	15.7

Source: Ministry of Finance, Gaikoku Boeki Gaikyo (The Summary Report on Trade of Japan) 1982.

America. Latin America accounted for 4.6 percent of the Japanese import market in 1981. (In contrast, Japanese imports from the Middle East, which had accounted for 15.4 percent of total imports in the three-year period before the oil crisis, leaped to 28.3 percent during the three-years after the crisis. The Middle East now claims more than 30 percent of total Japanese imports.)

The Japanese share in total exports from Latin America showed similar increases from the levels in the 1960s. The Japanese market, which had accounted for 3.2 percent of Latin American exports in the first half of the 1960s, increased its share to nearly 4 percent in the second half of the 1970s. Meanwhile, imports from Japan increased their share of total Latin American imports from 3.5 percent to approximately 8 percent.

It should be noted that as the growth rate of Japanese exports to Latin America has been higher than that of its imports from the region, the trade deficit of Latin America with respect to Japan has increased considerably, especially during the 1970s. The deficit in 1981 amounted to approximately $3.9 billion. Nevertheless, we should remember that about 53 percent of the deficit is credited to Panama and that its imports from Japan consist mainly of ships with flags of convenience. In other words, a large part of the Japanese exports to Panama cannot actually be considered exports to that country. Furthermore, we should take into account a certain quantity of exports by some Latin American countries to Japan that is not registered as such, because it is exported through third countries on account of such problems as inadequate port facilities.

It is also important to mention that the trade deficit of Latin America vis-à-vis Japan occurred in the 1970s. In the 1960s Latin America had a favorable balance against Japan. The turning point was marked in the beginning of the 1970s, and the region's trade deficit intensified after the oil crisis. As is mentioned later, important changes should have occurred in the structure of mutual trade in the first half of the 1970s (see Table 12.1).

Analyzed by country, the most important for Japan as an export market is apparently Panama, which occupied 21 percent of the total Japanese exports to Latin America in 1981 (but as mentioned before, the high percentage of this country is due to a special factor). Mexico and Brazil constituted the second and third markets for Japan, having 16.2 and 13.0 percent of total exports respectively. They were followed by Andean countries such as Venezuela, Chile, and Colombia, as well as Argentina (see Table 12.2).

On the other hand, the important exporters to Japan are Brazil (which provides 23.7 percent of all Japanese imports from Latin America) and Mexico (21.6 percent), followed by Andean countries such as Venezuela, Peru, Chile, and Ecuador, as well as Argentina (Table 12.2).

Keeping pace with the expansion in trading volumes, the composition of exported products from both Latin America and Japan became markedly more diverse. In Japanese exports to Latin America, the most visible change was the increased share of machinery in the 1970s, growing from 43.8 percent in 1960 and 49.54 percent in 1970 to 74.0 percent in 1981 (see Table 12.3). In Latin American exports to Japan, the recent increases in petroleum exports from Mexico, Ecuador, and Peru are common knowledge. Another fact worthy of special mention is the growth in manufactured exports to Japan; these products, which had accounted for a mere 3.6 percent of total Latin American exports to Japan in 1960 and 11.8 percent in 1970, claimed a full 21.5 percent share in 1981 (see Table 12.4).[4]

Increase of Direct Investment

Parallel to the expansion and diversification in trade, other areas of the economic relationship between Latin America and Japan have also been enlarged and strengthened.

Japanese direct investment in Latin America was already significant as early as the second half of the 1950s, accounting for 30 percent of total Japanese overseas investments. After experiencing a relatively slack period, these investments have again become active since the end of the 1960s. As a result, as of the end of March 1982, the cumulative total of approved investments from Japan reached US$7.349 billion, accounting

TABLE 12.2
Japan's Trade with Latin American Countries

(Unit: millions of dollars; %)

Regions and Countries	1981 Exports			1981 Imports		
	Amount	Ratio with Previous Year	Intraregional Percentage	Amount	Ratio with Previous Year	Intraregional Percentage
Total	10,515.6	117.9	100.0	6,668.6	117.0	100.0
Central America	263.0	67.7	2.5	193.7	113.1	2.9
Guatemala	105.3	94.3	1.0	78.4	111.1	1.2
Honduras	46.4	55.7	0.4	5.2	91.5	0.1
El Salvador	30.5	101.5	0.3	40.5	111.3	0.6
Nicaragua	11.8	58.4	0.1	62.8	401.8	0.9
Costa Rica	69.1	48.1	0.7	6.8	48.8	0.1
South America	6,908.9	116.6	65.7	5,975.1	117.3	89.6
Mexico	1,705.0	139.4	16.2	1,437.4	153.9	21.6
Colombia	496.9	99.8	4.7	150.2	86.5	2.3
Venezuela	924.9	110.8	8.8	912.4	132.0	13.7
Ecuador	294.2	107.0	2.8	408.9	160.3	6.1
Peru	350.1	114.4	3.3	602.2	126.7	9.0
Bolivia	96.1	147.7	0.9	27.2	92.5	0.4
Chile	742.0	160.5	7.1	530.8	82.4	8.0
Brazil	1,367.5	122.7	13.0	1,578.5	101.1	23.7
Paraguay	77.3	108.4	0.7	32.7	95.8	0.5
Uruguay	70.3	94.1	0.7	13.7	129.1	0.2
Argentina	784.7	78.7	7.5	281.1	97.9	4.2
Other Countries						
Trinidad and Tobago	154.3	89.8	1.5	7.1	41.4	0.1
Cuba	266.8	111.8	2.5	154.3	82.3	2.3
Haiti	19.5	67.0	0.2	1.2	182.1	0.0
Dominican Republic	91.8	65.6	0.9	10.2	48.6	0.2
Puerto Rico (USA)	346.2	92.3	3.3	52.5	120.8	0.8
Netherlands Antilles	47.5	87.8	0.5	10.3	48.4	0.2
Jamaica	34.9	235.5	0.3	6.2	101.3	0.1
Panama	2,209.7	156.1	21.0	131.2	214.1	2.0
Guyana	8.8	142.7	0.1	13.4	65.5	0.2
Surinam	34.7	146.1	0.3	23.0	80.1	0.4

Source: Ministry of International Trade and Industry (MITI)
Tsusho Hakusho (White Paper on International Trade) 1982.

TABLE 12.3
Exports from Japan to Latin America

								(millions of dollars)
	1960	%	1970	%	1975	%	1981	%
Food Products	6.4	2.1	19.2	1.6	23.5	0.5	43.7	0.4
(Frozen Tuna)	(2.7)	(0.9)	(8.6)	(0.7)	(3.7)	(0.1)	(n.a.)	(n.a.)
Fuels	0.8	0.3	4.6	0.4	66.7	1.4	71.5	0.7
Textile Products	68.4	22.5	113.3	9.5	178.8	3.8	224.6	2.1
(Synthetic Textiles)	(3.4)	(1.1)	(63.9)	(5.4)	(74.3)	(1.6)	(174.0)	(1.7)
(Cotton Fabrics)	(28.7)	(9.4)	(7.9)	(0.7)	(4.1)	(0.1)	(n.a.)	(n.a.)
Chemical Products	7.7	2.5	63.1	5.3	208.2	4.4	252.1	2.4
(Plastics)	(0.8)	(0.2)	(27.5)	(2.3)	(80.5)	(1.7)	(650)	(0.6)
(Phamaceuticals)	(1.1)	(0.3)	(4.5)	(0.4)	(1.0)	(0.2)	(24.3)	(0.2)
(Chemical Fertilizer)	(2.6)	(0.8)	(2.2)	(0.2)	(6.9)	(0.1)	(5.8)	(0.1)
Non-Metal Mineral								
Products	8.4	2.8	17.2	1.4	34.0	0.7	50.2	0.5
(Ceramics)	(4.3)	(1.4)	(5.9)	(0.5)	(7.2)	(0.2)	(n.a.)	(n.a.)
(Glass Products)	(0.5)	(0.2)	(6.2)	(0.5)	(10.3)	(0.2)	(n.a.)	(n.a.)
Metal Products	31.7	17.0	309.6	26.1	1317.3	27.6	1660.7	15.8
(Iron and Steel)	(33.5)	(11.0)	(267.5)	(22.5)	(1166.3)	(24.5)	(1409.5)	(13.4)
Machinery/Instruments	133.1	43.8	587.5	49.5	2766.9	58.1	7777.5	74.0
(General Instruments)	(22.7)	(7.5)	(122.7)	(10.3)	(697.1)	(14.6)	(1637.4)	(15.6)
(Ships)	(48.0)	(19.1)	(108.9)	(9.2)	(1011.8)	(21.2)	(1738.8)	(16.5)
(Automobiles)	(5.2)	(1.7)	(106.3)	(9.0)	(304.8)	(6.4)	(1429.6)	(13.6)
(Precision								
Instruments)	(6.6)	(2.2)	(47.6)	(4.0)	(130.5)	(2.7)	(367.0)	(3.5)
(Heavy Electric								
Machinery)	(2.5)	(0.8)	(37.7)	(3.2)	(93.4)	(2.0)	(318.3)	(3.0)
(Radios)	(16.3)	(5.4)	(31.8)	(2.7)	(62.1)	(1.3)	(253.0)	(2.4)
(Television Sets)	(0.1)	(0.0)	(14.7)	(1.2)	(38.6)	(0.8)	(250.3)	(2.4)
Others	26.4	8.7	69.7	5.9	154.6	3.2	383.0	3.6
(Tire Tubes)	(2.0)	(0.7)	(16.3)	(1.4)	(41.5)	(0.9)	(93.5)	(0.9)
(Toys)	(8.4)	(2.7)	(10.7)	(0.9)	(9.9)	(0.2)	(21.6)	(0.2)
Products for Reexport								
or Special Handling	1.5	0.3	3.1	0.3	14.6	0.3	52.2	0.5
Total	304.4	100.0	1187	100.0	4764.6	100.0	10515.6	100.0

Source: MITI, Tsusho Hakusho (White Paper on International Trade) 1978, 1982.

TABLE 12.4
Imports to Japan from Latin America

	1960	%	1970	%	1975	%	1981	% (millions of dollars)
Foodstuffs and Livestock Feed	29.7	28.9	482.5	35.1	981.1	38.9	943.6	14.1
(Sugar)	(47.6)	(15.3)	(132.0)	(9.6)	(590.7)	(23.4)	(137.1)	(2.1)
(Bananas)	(0.3)	(0.1)	(89.7)	(7.3)	(7.0)	(0.3)	(1.7)	(n.a.)
(Sorghum)	( )	(n.a.)	(77.5)	(5.6)	(111.8)	(4.4)	(3.8)	(0.1)
(Maize)	(26.7)	(8.6)	(40.8)	(3.0)	(3.4)	(0.1)	(n.a.)	(n.a.)
(Coffee Beans)	(5.5)	(1.8)	(39.1)	(2.8)	(81.5)	(3.2)	(313.0)	(4.7)
(Frozen Shrimps)	(10.0)	(n.a.)	(29.1)	(2.1)	(47.5)	(1.9)	(93.4)	(1.4)
(Horse Meat)	( )	(0.7)	(22.4)	(1.6)	(44.1)	(1.8)	(73.2)	(1.1)
Raw Materials	209.3	67.5	698.2	50.8	1142.8	45.3	2148.8	32.2
(Iron Ore)	(20.7)	(6.7)	(275.0)	(20.0)	(579.7)	(23.0)	(1149.7)	(17.2)
(Raw Cotton)	(132.1)	(42.6)	(208.2)	(15.2)	(271.5)	(10.8)	(317.0)	(4.0)
(Copper Ore)	(13.0)	(4.2)	(58.1)	(4.2)	(80.0)	(3.2)	(175.5)	(2.6)
(Other Nonferrous Ores)	(12.0)	(3.8)	(93.8)	(6.8)	(121.6)	(4.8)	(203.6)	(3.1)
(Salt)	(12.0)	(n.a.)	(21.6)	(1.6)	(26.5)	(1.1)	(68.4)	(1.0)
(Wool)	(13.5)	(4.3)	(10.7)	(0.8)	(11.7)	(0.5)	(27.6)	(0.4)
Mineral Fuels	0.1	0.0	31.3	2.3	51.9	2.0	2137.8	32.1
(Petroleum)	(0.0)	(0.0)	(27.6)	(2.0)	(25.7)	(1.0)	(2006.7)	(30.1)
Chemical Products	2.2	0.9	24.0	1.8	57.8	2.3	229.4	3.4
Machinery and Equipment	2.9	0.9	1.4	0.1	77.9	3.1	216.3	3.2
Other Products	5.2	1.7	130.8	9.5	177.2	7.0	931.5	14.0
(Unwrought Copper)	(1.8)	(0.6)	(93.7)	(6.8)	(54.1)	(2.1)	(209.9)	(3.1)
(Iron and Steel)	(0.2)	(0.1)	(13.4)	(1.0)	(7.7)	(0.3)	(92.1)	(1.4)
(Precious and Semi-precious Stones)	(n.a.)	(n.a.)	(12.4)	(0.9)	(29.0)	(1.2)	(57.1)	(0.8)
(Silver and Alloys)	(1.3)	(0.4)	(6.4)	(0.5)	(60.5)	(2.4)	(131.1)	(2.0)
Products for Reexport or Special Handling	0.1	0.1	5.1	0.4	35.2	1.4	61.3	0.9
Total	311.3	100.0	1373.2	100.0	2523.9	100.0	6668.6	100.0

Source: MITI, Tsusho Hakusho (White Paper on International Trade), 1978, 1982.

for 16.2 percent of total Japanese overseas investments. This percentage represented the third-largest share in total Japanese overseas investments after those made in the Asian region (29.0 percent) and in North America (27.1 percent).

A noteworthy feature of Japan's investment in Latin America is that a larger proportion (41.3 percent) was devoted to the manufacturing sector than in other regions of the world, where the average was 31.1 percent (all percentages in terms of cumulative totals as of the end of March 1982). Another important feature is that the average amount of investment by case is much larger in Latin America than in Asian countries (see Table 12.5).

For some countries of Latin America, Japanese direct investments account for a high proportion of the total foreign direct investments: In Mexico, for example, the direct investment from Japan amounted to about US$500 million toward the end of 1980, accounting for approximately 6 percent of the total foreign investments in Mexico. Similarly, according to the official statistics of Brazil, the Japanese investments in that country reached US$1.518 billion (cumulative total reinvestment included), accounting for 9.5 percent of the total foreign investments in Brazil in 1979. According to the Japanese statistics, Japanese investments in Brazil (in terms of investment approvals of the Japanese government) amounted to the cumulative total of US$2.908 billion as of the end of March 1981, accounting for 5.6 percent of total Japanese direct investments abroad (see Table 12.6). One of the important features of Japanese investments in Latin American countries is the fact that they are highly concentrated in a small number of countries, such as Brazil and Mexico.

Expansion of Financial Cooperation

Japanese economic cooperation to Latin America in 1980 amounted to US$880 million, representing 17.0 percent of the US$5.191 billion total assistance that Japan rendered to developing countries on a bilateral basis (excluding contributions to international organizations for aid purposes).[5] It is true that Japan's official development assistance (ODA) to Latin America is relatively small, but, as will be analyzed later, this may be explained by the fact that the nations of Latin America are economically more developed than most other developing countries (see Table 12.7).

Meanwhile, some types of loans, including buyer's credit and direct loans by the Export-Import Bank of Japan (aimed primarily at the more advanced of the developing countries), have been channeled into Latin America in a concentrated manner, with the total as of the end of December 1981 coming to about US$531.4 billion or some 42 percent of all such loans to developing countries. Furthermore, bonds issued by Latin American countries in the Tokyo capital market represented 16.6 percent of total bonds issued there at the end of December 1981,

TABLE 12.5
Japanese Direct Investments in Latin America and Asia Classified by Principal Sectors
(Cumulative total as of March 1981; in millions of dollars)

	Latin America		Asia		Total (Including other areas)	
	Number of cases	Amount	Number of cases	Amount	Number of cases	Amount
Manufacturing industry	752	2,781	4,267	4,571	7,213	12,573
Food	85	134	287	148	689	587
Textile	129	351	555	920	901	1,637
Wood and pulp	37	188	224	142	353	758
Chemical products	104	501	501	721	796	2,926
Iron and non-ferrous metals	78	735	441	1,032	931	2,619
Machinery	102	249	467	273	854	894
Electric Machinery	95	212	769	544	1,159	1,579
Transport equipment	32	333	148	267	234	979
Others	90	79	875	524	1,296	894
Other industries						
Agriculture and forestry	137	133	283	216	671	609
Fishing	71	64	126	71	417	301
Mining	116	1,188	155	3,022	644	7,071
Construction	59	136	212	76	457	396
Commerce	412	437	1,368	401	6,568	5,409
Finance and insurance	78	296	158	266	510	2,426
Others	936	1,084	808	1,085	4,016	5,808
Properties and direct operations	99	23	162	37	2,539	962
Branches	45	24	424	86	913	942
Total	2,705	6,168	7,963	9,830	23,948	36,497
(percentage of the global total)	(11.3)	(16.9)	(33.3)	(26.9)	(100.0)	(100.0)

Source: MITI, Present Situation and Problems of Economic Cooperation, 1982.

TABLE 12.6
Japanese Direct Investment in Latin America Classified by Countries

(Cumulative Total as of March 1981)

(in millions of dollars)

	Number of Cases	Amount
Brazil	1,131	2,908
Mexico	179	818
Argentina	85	42
Venezuela	65	115
Colombia	38	12
Ecuador	34	8
Peru	81	490
Chile	43	124
Bolivia	44	15
Guatemala	13	31
Honduras	8	20
Nicaragua	6	4
El Salvador	13	31
Costa Rica	44	30
Uruguay	6	6
Paraguay	104	27
Dominican Republic	-	1
Haiti	-	-
Other countries	214	814
Total	2,705	6,168

Source: MITI, Present Situation and Problems of Economic Cooperation, 1982.

while approximately 30 percent of the lending abroad by Japanese private financial institutions was directed to Latin America. In fact, the cumulative amount outstanding of the medium- and long-term lending of the Japanese private institutions (banks and insurance companies) to Latin American and Caribbean countries reached 19.6 billion dollars on September 30, 1982, absorbing 33.4 percent of total amount of loans abroad of these institutions (see Table 12.8).

This amount of lending to the Latin American and Caribbean region accounted for 65 percent of the total lending of Japanese private financial institutions to developing countries. The lending to the Asian countries is much less than the lending to Latin America even though in trade the former's share is considerably higher than the latter's.

The short-term lending of the Japanese private institutions to Latin American countries has also increased considerably in recent years. The amount of short-term finance (finance for a period of less than one year)

TABLE 12.7
Economic Cooperation of Japan with Latin America, 1980 (in millions of dollars)

Region and Country	Official Development Assistance (ODA)					Other Official and Private Flow				Grand Total of Economic Cooperation
	Grants			Direct Loans	Total	Direct Investments	Security Investments, etc.	Credits	Total	
	Grant	Technical Cooperation	Sub-Total							
Central and South America	25.50	55.28	80.78	37.69	118.47	696.42	166.68	-101.38	761.72	880.19
Central America and Caribbean	6.85	12.81	19.66	8.80	28.46	588.38	0.48	-14.02	574.80	603.26
Barbados	-	0.05	0.05	-	0.05	-	-	-	-	0.05
Costa Rica	-	1.18	1.18	2.41	3.59	5.91	2.29	4.09	12.29	15.88
Cuba	-	0.06	0.06	-	0.06	-	-3.40	-1.94	-5.34	-5.28
Dominican Rep.	-	0.76	0.76	-	0.76	-	-	-2.41	-2.41	-1.65
El Salvador	-	0.05	0.05	-	0.05	11.20	-	-1.49	9.71	9.76
Guatemala	1.06	1.61	2.67	-	2.67	0.49	-	1.24	1.73	4.40
Haiti	2.21	0.03	2.24	-	2.24	-	-	-	-	2.24
Honduras	1.32	1.37	2.69	4.48	7.17	-3.84	-0.18	-1.60	-5.62	1.55
Jamaica	-	0.16	0.16	-	0.16	-	-	-2.93	-2.93	-2.77
Mexico	0.04	5.55	5.59	1.91	7.50	538.97	-80.61	27.07	485.43	492.93
Nicaragua	2.21	0.06	2.27	-	2.27	-	9.65	-	9.65	11.92
Panama	-	1.64	1.64	-	1.64	78.77	62.41	-15.44	125.74	127.38
Trinidad & Tobago	-	0.09	0.09	-	0.09	0.11	-	1.95	2.06	2.15
South America	18.65	42.00	60.65	28.89	89.54	108.04	166.24	-87.36	186.92	276.46
Argentina	-	2.55	2.55	4.98	7.53	8.61	107.53	-38.72	77.42	84.95
Bolivia	8.04	4.87	12.91	6.25	19.16	-0.61	-	-5.38	-5.99	13.17
Brazil	-	12.11	12.11	8.39	20.50	113.09	61.28	-123.50	50.87	71.37
Chile	0.18	2.74	2.92	-0.42	2.50	9.32	-2.76	-9.88	-3.32	-0.82
Colombia	2.13	2.11	4.24	0.02	4.26	0.02	0.88	9.48	10.38	14.64
Ecuador	-	0.75	0.75	3.83	4.58	0.65	4.50	10.80	15.95	20.53
Guyana	0.18	0.25	0.43	-	0.43	-0.24	-	-0.42	-0.66	-0.23
Paraguay	7.93	7.45	15.38	1.07	16.45	2.08	-	-	2.08	18.53
Peru	0.19	6.67	6.86	4.20	11.06	-33.72	-10.17	-3.24	-47.13	-36.07
Surinam	-	0.02	0.02	-0.09	-0.07	-0.40	-	-0.34	-0.40	-0.47
Uruguay	-	1.11	1.11	-	1.11	1.65	-	-0.34	1.31	2.42
Venezuela	-	1.17	1.17	0.66	1.83	7.59	4.98	73.84	86.41	88.24

Source: MITI, Keizai Kyonyoku Hakusho (White Paper on Economic Cooperation), 1981.

TABLE 12.8
Amount of Outstanding Medium- and Long-Term Loan of Japan
(as End of Sept. 1982)

	Foreign Currency Base (in millions of dollars)	Yen Base (in millions of Yen)	Total (in millions of dollars)
OECD Countries	18,322	8,058	21,313
Developing Countries	25,919	10,641	29,869
Latin America	18,248	3,880	19,653
Oil Exporting Countries	1,821	1,469	2,366
Other Asian Countries	4,250	2,432	5,153
Other African Countries	1,113	2,557	2,062
Other Developing Countries	487	403	637
Socialist Countries	3,454	946	3,805
International Organizations	336	8,386	3,449
Total	48,031	28,031	58,436
Latin America			
Brazil	5,397	1,168	5,831
Mexico	5,904	204	5,980
Argentina	1,968	318	2,087
Venezuela	1,753		1,753
Peru	254		254
Chile	692	47	709
Ecuador	393		393
Bolivia	2		2
Colombia	632	2	633
Uruguay	22		22
Paraguay	4		4
Panama	954	1,550	1,529
Bahamas	18		18
Bermuda	42	51	61
Costa Rica	81		81
Cuba		288	107
Dominican Republic	22		22
Honduras	7	5	9
Jamaica	9		9
Nicaragua	18		18
Trinidad and Tobago	32	147	87
Guatemala	7		7
Cayman	29		29
Barbados	4		4
El Salvador	1		1
Other Countries	3		3
Total	18,248	3,880	19,653

Source: Ministry of Finance data quoted in Nihon Keizai Shimbun, Jan. 13, 1983.

to principal countries of the region (Brazil, Mexico, Argentina, Venezuela, Chile, Ecuador, and Cuba) was estimated to be US$11.500 billion as of the end of September 1982. Latin American countries absorbed the greatest part of the total short-term finance of Japanese private financial institutions to developing countries and East European countries.

The scale of Japanese private institutions' lending to Latin America and Caribbean countries is appreciated better if we compare the amount of finance to an individual country and its total outstanding external debt. In the case of Mexico, for example, the loan of Japanese private financial institutions (without including the finance of, for example, the Export-Import Bank of Japan) accounts for approximately 12 percent of the cumulative external debt of Mexico. In the case of Brazil, the corresponding figure is estimated to be 10.5 percent. Similarly the figures for Venezuela and Argentina are 23.5 percent and 10.5 percent respectively.

Finally, the yen-denominated bonds issued by Latin American governments and other public agencies amounted to some 15 percent of all such foreign public bond issues in Tokyo, and similar yen bonds issued by Latin American private enterprises were greater in value than those issued by enterprises in any other region except Europe. Considering the fact that the first issue of yen-denominated bonds offered by a Latin American issuer only appeared on the Tokyo market as recently as 1973, one cannot but marvel at the rapid growth in this type of fund procurement. These statistics represent the rapid increase in the size and importance of Japanese financial cooperation to the region.

Significant progress has also been seen in specific economic cooperation projects. Commitments were made to Brazil in 1976 for funding cooperation totaling US$2.9 billion for such projects as the Tubarao iron and steel works, Amazon aluminum refinery, and Cerrado development project. Another agreement was reached in 1982 for accelerating the Cerrado project, and cooperation has been developed for the Carajas undertaking. In Mexico, commitments were made in 1978 for funding cooperation worth about US$1.1 billion for oil and power-generation development. Agreement was also reached in 1980 for Japanese cooperation in a steel project to be implemented in the industrial zone of Lazaro Cardenas Port. Cooperation with other Latin American countries is also underway in a series of projects: for example, developing the Peruvian fishing industry.

Recognizing the important role that the Inter-American Development Bank plays in the economic and social development of the Latin American region, Japan joined the banking organization as a nonregional member in 1975. Even prior to this, Japan had rendered funding cooperation to the bank to augment its capital assets. As of the end of 1981, the Japanese capital contribution to the bank was US$139.3 million, its contribution to the Fund for Special Operations US$108.8 million, and its total loans US$520.3 million. In addition, Japan has made fund contributions to two regional financial organs for development, the Central American Bank for Economic Integration (Banco Centroamericano de Integración Económica) and the Andean Development Corporation (Corporación Andina de Fomento).

Technical Cooperation

Although the amount of Japanese technical cooperation with developing countries is still small in comparison with main advanced countries, it has increased rapidly in recent years. In effect, the amount of Japanese technical cooperation reached US$278 million in 1980, which was 2.6 times the figure of five years before. At the same time the number of persons involved in technical cooperation projects, the number of foreign students and trainees received in Japan, and the number of Japanese experts sent overseas increased from about 12,000 to 17,500 in the same period. Approximately 11 percent of the total number of students and trainees in Japan came from Latin American countries in 1981. This percentage is the third largest after East Asia and South Asia (see Table 12.9).

Factors Behind the Expansion and Diversification of Economic Relations

A number of factors contribute to the expansion of economic relations discussed in the preceding section.

Timing of Development. It is well known that Latin American countries sought to develop heavy and chemical industries at the start of the 1960s by promoting economic integration. Subsequently, in the second half of the 1960s and over the next decade, they made further efforts to develop their heavy and chemical industries by adopting increasingly liberal trade policies. Consequently, the demand for imported intermediate products and capital goods expanded rapidly at the same time that Japan improved its international competitiveness in these product categories, so that Japanese exports of these products to Latin America thus increased significantly. Sizable growth was recorded in Japanese machinery and iron and steel exports, as revealed by the examination in the preceding section of the growing share of total exports that machinery and related products came to represent in the 1970s.

Categories of Export. Among Latin American exports to Japan, large increases were registered in feed grains, iron ore, and nonferrous metals. More recently, petroleum exports started to flow into Japan from Mexico, Ecuador, and Peru, contributing to the expansion of the export trade. As stated earlier, Latin American exports to Japan are noteworthy for the steady increase in manufactured products and processed goods with high added values. Nontraditional primary-product exports are also on the rise.

Diversification. It is significant that both the Latin American countries and Japan have been trying to diversify their overseas economic relations.

TABLE 12.9
Students and Trainees Sent from Latin America to Japan

	Public Agencies Programs		Private Institutions Programs		Total	
	Fiscal Year 1980	Cumulative Total as of March '81	Fiscal Year 1980	Cumulative Total as of March '81	Fiscal Year 1980	Cumulative Total as of March '81
East Asia	1,658	22,522	1,384	14,328	3,042	36,850
South Asia	643	7,448	151	2,611	794	10,059
Middle East	201	2,428	119	1,183	320	3,611
Africa	439	3,457	156	1,207	595	4,664
Latin America	701	5,395	159	1,752	860	7,147
Oceania	59	234	28	187	87	421
Europe	54	608	10	100	64	708
Other areas	-	152	17	544	17	696
Total	3,755	42,244	2,024	21,912	5,779	64,156
Brazil	169	1,067	58	660	227	1,727
Mexico	147	1,202	14	201	161	1,403
Argentina	29	300	8	54	37	354
Venezuela	23	136	1	53	24	189
Colombia	39	286	6	60	45	346
Peru	70	597	10	128	80	725
Chile	43	299	12	38	55	337
Bolivia	13	270	1	68	14	338
Ecuador	15	147	4	33	19	180
Central American countries	40	465	19	160	59	625

Source: Ministry of International Trade and Industry, Present Situation and Problems of Economic Corporation, 1981, 1982.

Attempts have been made on the part of some Latin American countries to diversify their trade structures, historically oriented toward a relatively small number of advanced countries. In the meantime, Japan has also acted to diversify its sources of supply for some resources. For example, it has tried for some time to expand iron-ore imports from Brazil and more recently, as already noted, has increased oil imports from Latin American countries. In general, the economies of Japan and the Latin American countries are mutually complementary to a considerable extent, which has contributed to the diversification of trading relations.

Japanese Direct Investment. The expansion in Japanese direct investment and technical cooperation was effected mainly through Japanese participation in the buildup of heavy and chemical industries and of natural-resources development in Latin America. Mention was made earlier of the higher share of Japanese direct investment being devoted to the manufacturing sector in Latin America than in other regions. This is a reflection of the principal mode of Japanese investments and cooperation in Latin America.

Latin American Borrowing Capacity. Important factors behind the expansion of funding cooperation are that major Latin American countries have been gradually joining the ranks of the newly industrializing countries and that their newly industrializing economies and their endowments of valuable natural resources have improved their credit standings in financial markets, enabling them to actively borrow from foreign countries. Correspondingly, as discussed earlier, Japan has provided various types of official and private funding cooperation to Latin American countries on an increasing scale.

Economic Relations Between Latin America and Japan

Economic Development of Latin America

The phase of development that the countries concerned arrived at and their resource endowments, including basic factors of production, seem to be crucial for the study of the mutual economic relations and cooperation. In this respect, at least two characteristics of the economy of Latin American countries should be stressed: their semiindustrialized phase of development (or their status of being newly industrializing countries) and their rich natural-resource endowments, especially of hydrocarbon energy. As for Japan, its capacity and priority of cooperation should be carefully identified in relation to its experience in development and its need to count on diversified and assured supplies of natural resources.

In this section I will analyze relevant aspects of the economy of Latin American countries, as well as development strategy from the above-mentioned standpoint.

Many Latin American countries have been able to enhance their standing in the international economic community by attaining the status of newly industrializing countries (NICs) or conditions closely approaching this state. Their success in doing so has been the result of many years of economic development and industrialization and/or of the possession of important natural resources. They have also improved their potential for further development in terms of industrial capacity, technological capability, and access to world capital markets. At the same time, they are faced with challenges for the future, such as problems in their external relations (symbolized by the accumulation of foreign debts) and domestic difficulties (typified by structural problems in the social and economic spheres, including unemployment).

Regarding these aspects, I find highly relevant the joint study made by the United Nations Economic Commission for Latin America (ECLA) and the International Development Center of Japan (IDCJ), *Towards New Forms of Economic Cooperation Between Latin America and Japan*, especially part I, chapter 1, "Aspects of the Newly Industrializing Process in Latin American Countries: An Overall View." This study tried to clarify the characteristics of socioeconomic development in Latin American countries on the basis of the results of theoretical and empirical analysis of their development process and of a comparison with the experience of Japan and East Asian newly industrializing countries.

I conclude from this joint study and other related studies that in the process of socioeconomic development of the semiindustrialized phase, the most important differences between Latin American NICs and East Asian contemporary NICs (Japan up to the 1960s can be included here) are observed in the pattern of industrialization and external trade and in the relation between growth and equity.

As to the first point, there has been a successive sequence in import substitution of manufactured products from nondurable consumer products to durable consumer products and finally to intermediate and capital goods in both Latin American and East Asian NICs. In the former countries, however, the fully simultaneous process of the import substitution and the so-called export substitution between traditional primary products and manufactured products has not taken place.

As to the second point, whereas Asian countries improved the distribution of income through increases in the real wage of unskilled workers and in the income of farmers, Latin American countries failed to achieve substantial improvement. Even Mexico, the country with a long history of successful efforts for social welfare and justice through agrarian reforms and labor legislation, has been far from achieving a level of equity comparable to that of Korea and Japan during the period of their high growth and industrialization in the 1960s and 1970s.

Here it seems important to distinguish two kinds of causes that explain the two particular phenomena found in Latin American NICs in comparison with East Asian NICs. One concerns those characteristics integral to the semiindustrialized phase of development and the other those characteristics particular to Latin American societies and institutions, or certain policy orientation of the governments.

First, regarding the external balance, as the possibility of accelerating development increases with the higher industrial and technological capacity of the semiindustrialized phase, it normally happens that domestic savings lag behind the financial requirements for investment. Furthermore, this savings gap generally occurs simultaneously with a trade gap, because such investment as well as high economic growth require a larger amount of imports than the capacity permitted by the export earnings.

Second, regarding the socioeconomic structure, some empirical studies have revealed a tendency for social equilibrium to deteriorate in the semiindustrialized phase. This tendency is explained by the fact that, as the modern sector (such as large and medium manufacturing industries) increases its productivity much more rapidly than the traditional sectors because of its accelerated introduction of technology, the productivity differentials among the sectors enlarge.

In Latin American countries, in addition to these causes that are quite common in semiindustrailized countries, other important unfavorable factors are observable. Among others, I should emphasize the effects of the "prolonged" import-substitution industrialization policy and of the so-called structural heterogeneity. They complicate the differential structure of productivity and income. This means that considerable differences of productivity by size of units of production in manufacturing industry, agriculture, and so on are also being intensified, in addition to the above-mentioned intersectoral differences between agriculture and industry. The importance of the high growth rate of population, especially that of the economically active population, should also be stressed.

The facts and issues analyzed in the foregoing paragraphs take on crucial importance in a consideration of the way in which Japan's economic relations and cooperation with Latin America should be pursued in the future.

Importance of Latin America to Japan

The profound changes experienced in the international economy during the 1970s have affected Japan quite deeply. This is the main reason why in Japan the need for a more active foreign policy that emphasizes "comprehensive security" is widely recognized and why there is growing awareness that Japan's economy is highly linked with peace and prosperity of the world. This explains such an initiative as the Pacific Basin Cooperation Concept or the increase in real terms of ODA in the midst of severe budgetary restrictions. The Japanese relationship with Latin America could be considered in this context. In fact, in the wake of the oil crises, the Japanese economy underwent a critical transition from the period of rapid economic growth that had lasted up until the start of the 1970s to another of more moderate economic performance, in spite of Japan's having been more successful than other OECD countries in overcoming the difficulties brought on by the two oil crises. A new pattern of stable and balanced growth seems to be gradually taking root in the Japanese economy.

Shifts are also taking place in the Japanese industrial structure in response to the changing position of Japan's economy in a new international division of labor. Various industrial readjustment measures are being taken, including those for assisting the so-called structurally depressed industries to readapt to new economic environments.

Under these circumstances, as the Ministry of International Trade and Industry (MITI) *White Paper on International Trade* points out, "the role to be played by foreign trade and particularly by exports is important for the economic growth of our nation. It is important for us to encourage the international division of labor in the years to come." The paper continues, "It is also necessary for us to strive for further sophistication in our trading and industrial structures supported by the enhancement of technological independence, in the interest of national economic growth in harmony with the world economy and of the betterment of our nation's welfare."[6]

The Latin American countries are important to this new policy orientation for two reasons. First, Latin America is a newly industrialized region that is endowed with extensive agricultural lands, large market, and abundant natural resources; it possesses vast potential for development in a world economy shorn of the hope of high growth rates in advanced countries. The Latin American region, aided by further economic development and industrialization, is expected to serve as an indispensable nucleus for demand generation in the world economy. Japan, which will rely heavily on the expansion of global trade and economic activity in the future, finds special significance in the Latin American countries' successful social and economic development.

Second, the Latin American region has already grown into an important market for many products that advanced countries are interested in exporting, such as capital and durable goods and chemicals. It is expected to provide through its economic development an ample opportunity for Japan, eager to initiate a more dynamic international division of labor through greater sophistication of its trade and industrial structures.

Today NICs are catching up with the industrialized countries by improving their competitive capabilities not only in labor-intensive light-industry products (shoes, leather goods, textiles, and the like) but also in heavy and chemical-industry fields (iron and steel, machinery, chemicals, and so on). Principal Latin American countries are thus becoming more competitive in the world and are likely to increase their shares of world exports in the course of the dynamic expansion of the international division of labor.

The *White Paper on International Trade* stated in this context that Japan will be required "to contribute to the reactivation of the world economy through our efforts in the responsible conduct of export trade, the sophistication of our export structure, the production of higher value-added products and services, the diversification of export markets, the expansion of manufactured imports, technological development, and economic cooperation."[7]

The same logic seems to apply to the trading of natural resources, energy, and foodstuffs. Stable supplies of these resources are crucial for Japan's future development, and it is obvious that Latin American countries possess large supply capabilities for many of these resources. Meanwhile, Japan is now required to readjust and reform some of its energy- and resource-intensive industries. Latin American countries are steadily improving their processing capabilities for primary products for export and are seeking to expand and diversify their nontraditional exports, including timber, wood products, marine products, and marine-product derivatives. These new trends in both Japan and Latin America will enable the countries to expand and diversify the dynamic and mutually complementary relations in the trading of primary commodities and resources and of manufactured products.

Desirable Directions in Expanding Mutual Economic Relations and Economic Cooperation

Importance of an Expanded Economic Relationship

The five factors analyzed in the earlier section, which contributed to the past expansion and diversification of economic relations between Latin America and Japan, are expected to strengthen in the future. In trade, for example, the strong, dynamic, complementary nature of the relationship and the desire on both sides to diversify trading partners will continue to be dominant factors promoting expanded relations between Latin America and Japan.

More importantly, the pattern of the international division of labor between the two is likely to undergo dynamic changes with reference to both manufactured products and primary commodities and resources. Such changes will undoubtedly contribute to the prosperity of both Latin America and Japan. In these circumstances, it will be a matter of crucial importance to Japan whether or not the changes in its import growth rate and import structure anticipated in the future pattern of Japanese economic growth can adequately respond to the needs of the Latin American economies. Equally important is the question of whether or not Japan can render necessary funding and other types of cooperation to some countries in the region over given periods of time in the event that such changes fail to meet Latin America's needs.

The success of the Latin American countries in achieving development is, as indicated earlier, vitally important to the expansion and sophistication of Japan's foreign trade. The maintenance and further improvement of Latin American supply capabilities in natural resources, energy, and foodstuffs will likewise be essential for the stable world supply of these materials and commodities and thus for the continued prosperity of the world economy.

For Japan, the importance of foreign trade to growth is keenly recognized, and a series of policy measures has recently been taken for its expansion. Specifically, the Japanese government in December 1981 implemented tariff reductions agreed upon in the Tokyo Round of Trade Negotiations two years ahead of schedule and further decided in January 1982 to simplify some inspection procedures for imported products, all in the interest of liberalized trade with other countries. Japan also maintains the generalized system of preferences for developing countries, and manufactured imports from countries taking advantage of this system have increased.

For Latin America, the role to be played by foreign trade in attaining high rates of economic growth is indeed substantial. Export promotion is now an important ingredient in national policies in the region. Nevertheless, policies on both sides of the Pacific aimed at the mutual expansion of trading relations will be better able to contribute to trade expansion and diversification when they are supported by suitable measures for economic cooperation.

In the final analysis, the likely emergence of a dynamic and mutually complementary division of labor between Latin America and Japan signifies the enhancement of interdependence between the two regions. Obviously it will become increasingly necessary for Latin America and Japan to recognize accurately the roles to be played by each in trading and economic relations, to hold adequate and timely consultations, and to expand their interdependent relations in desirable directions. Economic cooperation that is long term in perspective and comprehensive in scope will assume the utmost importance in this regard.

In the following sections I present some ideas that could be useful for the discussion on the possible lines of action toward a desirable economic relationship and cooperation between Latin America and Japan.

Basic Thoughts on Cooperation

In order for Latin American countries and Japan to attain their further economic and social development, they will have to cope with their specific requirements, which basically derive from their respective phases of development as well as from their different resource endowments. As a semiindustrialized region, Latin America will need technology, financial resources, access to markets for its manufactures and primary products, and so forth. Diversification of external relations, in terms of products and markets, is also important to both Japan and Latin American countries.

In this context, I believe that mutual cooperation is necessary in order to create, expand, diversify, and sometimes orient reciprocal economic relations that satisfy as much as possible the requirements of both sides. Here the economic relations include not only trade relations but also all kinds of transfer of goods, services, and factors of production, especially technology transfer, direct investment, and other forms of movement of financial resources and technology. In other words, mutual benefits from economic relations can be optimized through effective cooperation. In this sense, prospective mutual benefits should be evaluated in terms of the requirements for both sides as well as in terms of their respective development strategies. The diversification of economic relations, rather than simple complementarity, also constitutes one of the basic principles for cooperation.

There are different sets of forms and priorities in which the countries can cooperate, and it will be necessary to adopt the most appropriate set in order to maximize mutual benefits. Therefore, *cooperation* should mean that both sides make policy adjustments, institutional adaptations, and other efforts within a given framework (or set of forms and priorities) adopted as the most appropriate. When some contradiction emerges in the process of cooperation, it should be solved by joint efforts through careful coordination and adjustment.

Introduction of technological and institutional innovations to certain sectors of agriculture and manufacturing constitutes one of the specific areas where joint efforts for cooperation will be most fruitful. Technology itself is rather flexible, and Japan can cooperate in adapting it to the local conditions. However, such adaptation of technology frequently requires institutional adjustment, because organization is one of the key factors for a successful transfer of technology, and institutions differ substantially from one country to another. In particular, the buildup of an appropriate institutional setup by means of creating new institutions or adapting existing ones is in many cases closely related with the social structure and sociocultural factors of a recipient country. Hence the efforts to adapt technology do not necessarily produce the expected results unless they are coordinated with corresponding efforts by the recipient country. The forms of cooperation should expect effective coordination and adjustment of the respective efforts by the two parties to ensure positive results.

In order that *cooperation* in this sense be realized, efforts should not be made in an isolated manner, as has sometimes happened in the past. Different forms of cooperative efforts should be coordinated and integrated and a certain balance must be maintained between one form, or area, of cooperation and the others. The future cooperation should be increasingly diversified to cover different forms and areas, while at the same time it should be carried out in a systematic, and to some extent planned, way in the sense that it is coordinated from a long-term perspective.

Areas and Forms for Economic Cooperation

As I have just stated, cooperation should be based on mutual benefits. However, the nature of mutual benefits may differ according to sectors or areas of cooperation. The trade and transport sectors are important for the expansion and diversification of trade and economic relations in general of the countries. Improvement in some other sectors of production that are directly connected with the reciprocal trade, such as energy, certain mining sectors (nonferrous metals) and perhaps fisheries, and the construction of infrastructure, such as ports, can immediately produce favorable effects on mutual economic relations. On the other hand, there are sectors such as agriculture and industry in which development is considered of highest priority from the standpoint of the basic requirements for the economy of Latin American countries: to achieve a self-sustained economic structure, to attain the goal of employment creation, and to solve other socioeconomic problems. The possibilities of cooperation in the two types of sectors are therefore discussed separately.

Principal features of the trade, transport, and related sectors from the point of view of cooperation are as follows:

1. Cooperation in these sectors is expected to contribute substantially to the growth of output and foreign-exchange earnings as well as to the expansion and diversification of economic relations between Japan and Latin American countries. Cooperative efforts will not necessarily be very effective in realizing the development strategy of Latin American countries, however.

2. It is perfectly possible to make the cooperation in these sectors highly effective vis-à-vis the basic objectives of development by coordinating or adjusting the policy measures for cooperation, including institutional arrangements. For example, the construction of a new efficient port by itself will not produce favorable effects on employment if containerization causes some unemployment among unskilled laborers. However, complementary cooperation for the regional development in the hinterland of the port should generate positive impact on employment and other socioeconomic conditions. This type of cooperation could be carried out as an integral part of infrastructure development and/or natural-resources development, especially in remote areas.

3. Nevertheless, in order that the cooperation in these sectors be beneficial to both sides, projects must be found in those sectors where an increased output will compete well in the international market. A proposed transportation system should be efficient according to the international standard. In this sense, new cooperation projects in these sectors should be identified primarily in terms of efficiency in production and services. Although this principle of efficiency does not necessarily appear compatible with the ideas put forth in the preceding paragraph, this could be solved by combining different types of cooperation such as loans of different lending conditions, various forms of technical cooperation, and so forth. In this connection, the possibility of increasing export of processed materials with higher value added should be studied, bearing clearly in mind the competitive capacity of such products in

the international market, the effects on employment and foreign-exchange earnings, and so on.

4. As for the development and trade of natural resources (both renewable and nonrenewable resources), the environment and natural-resources conservation program as well as the overall development policy should be duly taken into account.

5. Furthermore, it should be emphasized in this connection that because a straightforward increase of trade in resources such as oil and nonferrous metals is not expected to occur, given a series of new factors and uncertainties in the world economy, closer cooperation and coordination will be needed in order to avoid unexpected conflicts concerning volumes, prices, and other related conditions that pertain to natural-resources development and trade. Under such new circumstances, it is increasingly important to incorporate a wider perspective of economic cooperation in natural-resources development and trade. Given the large volume of traded output, mutual cooperation is necessary to construct infrastructural facilities for transportation and shipment or to introduce any other convenient means to improve the existing system of trade and transport.

6. It should be added that if cooperative efforts in resources development are to be successful, it will be important to formulate a comprehensive system of cooperation comprising both government and private enterprise in the country involved. The reasons are that in many Latin American countries resources development is now undertaken directly by the government or by government-affiliated enterprises; that resources development requires a great deal of time and capital; and that sizable fluctuations can occur in prices and demand for oil, iron and steel, and nonferrous metals. Cooperation in this field should not be limited to direct development activities but should include also the preparation of infrastructure, technology, finance, and trade. The efficacy of this comprehensive systems approach has already been demonstrated on several occasions in economic cooperation rendered for so-called national projects.

In this regard, it should be noted that the government of Japan, given the importance of securing a stable supply of natural resources, has given increasingly active support to projects that concern overseas natural resources and trade.

7. The potential for expanded trade between Latin America and Japan is certainly very substantial, but the problems of geographical distance and rising fuel costs must be alleviated if this potential is to be realized. It is thus important from the long-term perspective to improve the efficiencies of ocean and other modes of transport and to expand port facilities to deal with increased trade volume. The plans for a second Panama canal, the Asia-port, the Export Corridor Project of Brazil, and the Mexican program for expanding Pacific coast port facilities all seem to be the type of projects in which Japanese cooperation will be highly meaningful.

8. Cooperation for the introduction of technological and institutional innovations in these sectors should be promoted where they are necessary and convenient. Technological progress in transportation has been considerably rapid, for example, and some institutional adjustments will be necessary in order to take full advantage of such progress.

Characteristics and possibilities of cooperation in other sectors can be defined as follows:

1. First and foremost, economic cooperation in the nontrade category must be so designed as to contribute to the future economic development of the Latin American countries. The challenges and strategies of economic development in these countries must be fully recognized, and the modes and content of cooperation rendered compatible with the needs of the recipients.

2. Brazil, Mexico, and some other nations in the region have recently been stressing employment opportunities, agricultural development, and small-business promotion. Until very recently, Japan also was a semiindustrial or newly industrializing state retaining an agricultural sector and small businesses, both with low levels of productivity. There may be many instances where Japan's experiences, techniques, and institutions that were effective in its catch-up effort in the past can be utilized in economic cooperation programs with Latin America.

It should be emphasized in this context that changes in the productive structure, technological capacity, specialization in the world economy, comparative advantages, and so forth of both Latin America and Japan that take place as a result of their development and industrialization will open up new possibilities and forms of cooperation, such as joint ventures, different types of arrangement between enterprises including international subcontracting, or other types of complementary development. These forms of cooperation can be promoted with special attention to the possibilities of exports to Japan and other markets, including such nontraditional markets as Asian countries.

3. Those Latin American countries that have attained, or are close to attaining, the status of semiindustrialized economies naturally possess the ability to absorb and adapt foreign technologies. Nonetheless, this ability still seems to be unevenly distributed among industrial sectors and business organizations of different sizes. Technical improvement is particularly urgent for subsistence farmers, small farm operators, and small businesses; the efficacy of technological transfers and technical cooperation for these entities will be greatly enhanced once the conditions and institutions around them are improved and streamlined so as to permit speedy technological progress. It is desirable that economic cooperation in this second category be fully comprehensive in scope.

As discussed in the section on economic relations between Latin America and Japan, one of the important features of agricultural and industrial sectors in Latin America is their structural heterogeneity, where the differences in such factors as productivity, technology, and access to finance and product market are very pronounced according to the size of units of production.

With respect to the manufacturing sector, it is confirmed by a recent study that its employment structure is characterized by the relatively large weight of larger enterprises on the one hand and the extremely high percentage of cottage industries (*micro-industrias*) on the other. The industrial contribution of typical small and medium enterprises is considerably smaller in Brazil and Mexico than in Japan and some East Asian NICs. Furthermore, small and medium enterprises in Latin American countries are mostly concentrated in the so-called traditional industries like textiles. In nontraditional industries, particularly in machinery industries, which have developed recently in these countries largely by the participation of transnational enterprises, the expansion of large enterprises has not been accompanied by the simultaneous development of small and medium enterprises. This is very different from the Japanese experience.

The relative lack of dynamism among small and medium industries in Latin America has been caused mainly by the following factors: the different intensity and speed at which advanced technology was introduced; the lack of institutional ties between large, small, and medium enterprises; and the relative weakness of financial and technological support to smaller enterprises from governmental and other institutions.

The promotion of small and medium firms is an example of one of the excellent ways in which the efforts of Latin American countries can be bolstered and supplemented by some new forms of cooperation between these countries and Japan. These new institutional setups will undoubtedly facilitate the introduction of technology to small and medium industries. Some specific forms and fields of cooperation are suggested in the recent study, *A Study on the Development of Manufacturing Industries in the United Mexican States: Mainly Focusing on the Casting, Forging, and Metal Machining Industries*, prepared by the International Development Center of Japan in 1981.

Regarding the agricultural sector, a similar approach can be adopted in order to identify the forms and possibilities of cooperation. There appears to be a high possibility that with the introduction of appropriate technological and institutional innovations, smaller farmers may be able to play a major role in supplying food to the domestic market while simultaneously increasing their labor productivity and income. As Japan has a long experience of intensive farming and organization of smallholders such as agricultural cooperatives, it will be able to give adequate assistance for the development of smaller farms in Latin America.

Furthermore, Japan could cooperate in specific agricultural sectors that particularly benefit small and medium farmers through intensification of their farming, such as cultivation of rice, vegetables, and fruits and the processing of agricultural products. Appropriate technology for smallholders, including the use of small tractors and other agricultural machines developed in Japan, can be introduced in the process of intensive farming, accompanied by some institutional arrangements or innovations.

Cooperation in this category of aid is not designed to directly serve expanded trade and economic relations between Latin America and Japan. Nonetheless, indirect effects to this end may be hoped for over the long term. Agricultural development can be expected to create some surplus in farm production that can be exported, and prospering small businesses can contribute to enhanced international competitiveness of manufactured exports.

Final Remarks

It must be emphasized by way of concluding that the expansion of economic relations and the execution of economic cooperation must be founded not only on the full mutual recognition of the socioeconomic structures and economic policies of the countries involved but also on a broad mutual understanding of the social and cultural background of such structures and policies. Truly effective efforts can only be made after success on this account.

We must realize, however, that compared with progress in economic relations and cooperation, cultural and academic interchange between Latin America and Japan remains in a backward state. This kind of interchange has been actively promoted between Japan and the Association of Southeast Asian Nations (ASEAN) countries, for example, and in fact, the trading volume between Japan and the ASEAN countries is not that much greater than with Latin American countries. Although it is true that there are important factors in favor of Japan-ASEAN relations, including geographical proximity, the presence of a large number of Latin American nationals of Japanese origin is an important bond between the countries. I hope that the friendly economic relations between Latin America and Japan may be further expanded on the bedrock of mutual understanding and broad interchange in cultural and academic fields involving people from all walks of life.

Notes

1. Among others, I have referred to the following studies and reports: the Economic Commission for Latin America and the International Development Center of Japan, *Towards New Forms of Cooperation Between Latin America and Japan,* 1980, Tokyo and Santiago; Interamerican Development Bank and the Export-Import Bank of Japan, *Latin America/Japan Business Cooperation Symposium,* 1979, Tokyo and Washington, D.C.; Mexico-Japan Joint Study Team, *Long Term Economic Cooperation Between Mexico and Japan: A Preliminary Approach to Some Main Opportunities,* Tokyo and Mexico City, 1982; and International

Development Center of Japan, *A Study on the Development of Manufacturing Industries in the United Mexican States*, 1981, Tokyo.

In addition to studies carried out in the Latin America Special Research Project of the University of Tsukuba, I participated in all of the above-mentioned studies and forums. Accordingly some parts of this paper are, in a sense, the summary of the information, findings, and conclusions obtained in such studies and forums.

2. Japanese statistics (e.g., the *White Paper on International Trade* and the *Present Situation and Problems of Economic Cooperation*, both published annually by the Ministry of International Trade and Industry) include the Caribbean countries and the dependencies in the region of Latin America. The export price indices of Japan in 1960 and 1981 were 72.8 and 117.9 respectively (1975 = 100).

3. The import price indices of Japan in 1960 and 1981 were 44.3 and 150.2 respectively (1975 = 100).

4. These figures are based on the *White Paper on International Trade*. Manufactured products in this instance include metal ingots such as those of refined copper alloys, which are also imported by Japan in lieu of the copper-ore imports of the past. They thus also represent higher value added in Latin American exports to Japan.

5. As is seen in Table 12.5, direct investments are included in the statistics of economic cooperation.

6. *White Paper on International Trade* (MITI), 1982.

7. Ibid.

Abbreviations and Acronyms

ACP	African, Caribbean and Pacific
ANZUS	Australia–New Zealand–United States
ASEAN	Association of Southeast Asian Nations
Benelux	Belgium-Netherlands-Luxembourg
bpd	barrels per day
CCF	Canadian Commonwealth Confederation
CCP	Chinese Communist party
CETDC	China External Trade Development Council
CHINCOM	China Coordinating Committee
CIA	Central Intelligence Agency
COMECON	Council for Mutual Economic Assistance
COREPER	Committee of the permanent representatives of the EC member states
CPSU	Communist Party of the Soviet Union
DPRK	Democratic People's Republic of Korea
EAC	European Atomic Community
EARA	East Asian Relations Association
EC	European Community
ECLA	United Nations Economic Commission for Latin America
EEC	European Economic Community
EFTA	European Free Trade Area
EPC	European Political Cooperation

GATT	General Agreement on Tariffs and Trade
GNP	gross national product
GSP	generalized system of preferences
IDA	International Development Agency
IDCJ	International Development Center of Japan
IMF	International Monetary Fund
JAL	Japan Airlines
JAPCO	Japan Atomic Power Company
JNDC	Japan Nuclear Development Corporation
JODCO	Japan Oil Development Company
JVC	joint venture corporation
LDC	less developed country
LDP	Liberal-Democratic party
LNG	liquefied natural gas
MITI	Ministry of International Trade and Industry
MTN	Multilateral Trade Negotiations
MW	megawatts
NATO	North Atlantic Treaty Organization
NIC	newly industrializing country
NIEO	new international economic order
NTB	nontariff barrier
NTT	Nippon Telephone and Telegraph Company
OAPEC	Organization of Arab Petroleum Exporting Countries
OAU	Organization of African Unity
ODA	official development assistance
OECD	Organization for Economic Cooperation and Development
OMA	orderly marketing agreement
OPEC	Organization of Petroleum Exporting Countries
OTO	Office of the Trade Ombudsman

PLO	Palestinian Liberation Organization
PRC	People's Republic of China
ROK	Republic of Korea
RONIPROT	Romanian State Corporation
STABEX	stabilization of export earnings
TEPCO	Tokyo Electric Power Company
UAE	United Arab Emirates
UN	United Nations
UNCTAD	United Nations Conference on Trade and Development
VER	voluntary export restraint

About the Contributors

Kazuyoshi Aoki: Associate Professor of African Politics and International Relations, Nihon University, Tokyo.

Walter Arnold: Assistant Professor of Political Science, Miami University, Oxford, Ohio.

William R. Campbell: Assistant Professor of Political Science, Miami University, Oxford, Ohio.

Willard H. Elsbree: Professor-Emeritus of Political Science, Ohio University.

Joseph Richard Goldman: Assistant Professor of Political Science, University of Minnesota.

Khong Kim Hoong: Lecturer, Faculty of Economics and Administration, University of Malaya.

Akio Hosono: Associate Professor, Institute of Socio-Economic Planning, University of Tsukuba, Japan.

Frank Langdon: Professor of Political Science, University of British Columbia.

Hideo Oda: Professor of African Politics, Keio University, Tokyo.

Edward A. Olsen: Associate Professor of National Security Affairs and Coordinator of Asian Studies, Naval Postgraduate School, Monterey, California.

Robert S. Ozaki: Professor of Economics, California State University, Hayward.

Alan Rix: Senior Lecturer and Director, Centre for the Study of Australian-Asian Relations, Griffith University, Brisbane, Australia.

Marlis G. Steinert: Professor of Contemporary History and International Relations, Graduate Institute of International Studies, Geneva.

J.A.A. Stockwin: Director, Nissan Institute of Japanese Studies, University of Oxford.

Index